FISH BANANAS

A COOK'S NOTEBOOK

Ian Dowding

By the same author

The Secrets of the Hungry Monk

Cooking with the Hungry Monk

Quincy's Cookery Book

FISH BANANAS

A cook’s notebook

Ian Dowding

First Published in Great Britain in 2020 by Fish Bananas Publishing

A catalogue record for this book is available from the British Library

ISBN 978-1-5272-6893-7

Set in Source Serif Pro and Source Sans Pro

Design & Layout by Kate & Martin McCully | draftdesign.co.uk
Front cover illustration by Vicky Mappin | vickymappin.co.uk
Spot Illustrations by Robert Williams

To Sue and Nigel Mackenzie
who gave me my first break.

About the Author

Ian Dowding was the original head chef of The Hungry Monk Restaurant in Jevington, East Sussex and was responsible, along with the proprietor Nigel Mackenzie, for the development of the dessert Banoffi Pie which has become a worldwide favourite.

He went on to open his own restaurant (Quincy's in Seaford) with his wife in 1988. In 2000 he became a freelance chef and consultant and was involved in a variety of projects. As well as teaching cookery evening classes at Sussex Downs College he worked on several TV programmes including Regency House Party (Channel 4), The Diets that Time Forgot (Channel 4), Turn back Time (BBC 1), and Blizzard (BBC 2), a recreation of the Scott, Amundsen race to the South Pole when he was asked to make 750 kilos of Pemmican, the iron ration that was used by both teams.

The recipe for Fish Bananas is on page 68

The recipe for Banoffi Pie is on page 288

The recipe for Pemmican is on page 419

About the recipes

The recipes in this book are a record of my fifty years of cooking professionally. It is admittedly an odd selection reflecting the different areas I have worked in from the restaurant trade to teaching adults at college and in private cookery schools.

There is a mixture of traditional, old fashioned, modern, historical and international with home cooking and comfort food in there for good measure. Food in restaurants is about fashion and therefore some of the dishes I cooked in the sixties and seventies would look out of place on modern restaurant menus which does not mean they are not valid today.

The recipes do not conform to any particular trend and they are not for any specific dietary problem, and although browsing this book it may seem that a lot of the recipes are laden with butter and cream most of these are the sort of dishes you would serve for special occasions and the last thing you think of then is the diet.

Some recipes are extremely simple others can be a bit more complex and I have had to assume a certain amount of pre-knowledge on your part. A quick read through first should tell you if it is something you wish to tackle.

Acknowledgements

Thanks are in order to too many people to count: the people I have worked for and with over the years, the customers who came to both the Hungry Monk and Quincy's and the many people who came to my courses at Sussex Downs College for their feedback, comments, suggestions, recipes, and encouragement.

Particular thanks are due to my daughter Kate and her husband Martin (McCully) for the design and layout of this book and, of course, my wife, Dawn, for her exhaustive checking, encouragement and role as guinea pig for recipe testing.

Also thanks to;
Vicky Mappin, Robert Williams, Philippa & Mike Vine, Alex Everett, John Kittle, Ivan Day and Alex Dowding.

Introduction

At the interview for my first job in a restaurant in 1966, the owner was delayed and I was asked if I would like to have lunch while I waited. I was seventeen and had never eaten anywhere this posh before but two years of college training had taught me the etiquette of dining out and how to translate menu terminology.

One dish that stood out on the menu was 'Salmon Caprice'. I knew that 'Caprice' was a garnish that contained bananas and I was intrigued enough by this combination to order it. It did indeed have bananas with it but also tomatoes, butter, lemon juice and mango chutney. It was like nothing I had ever eaten before, a taste sensation that blew me away and made me want that job so I could learn to cook food like this. Luckily I was hired and in my time there I learnt how to cook Salmon Caprice as well as a lot of other interesting and wonderful dishes.

A year later I met a couple who were opening a restaurant in Sussex and they invited me to join the team. The menu became a copy of what I had been learning over the past year. The Hungry Monk was a success and over the years the menu developed and my repertoire expanded. I continued in the restaurant business eventually opening my own restaurant Quincy's in 1988.

Salmon Caprice has been part of my repertoire for many years now and has become a family favourite. Some years later I was amused when Monty Python created a song for a court room sketch that included the words 'fish bananas' amongst other randomly unconnected items such as pyjamas and mutton and since then I have always used this as a jokey shorthand for this dish - hence the title of this book.

Most chefs have a notebook to hand in their place of work – to jot down ideas, recipes, variations and light bulb moments of inspiration (not that there are that many of those). The contents of these would probably be unintelligible to any casual browser as they rarely contain methods, only ingredients and quantities but this is how recipes evolve; every chef gives a tweak or a twist to a dish that makes it his or her own.

Over the years I have filled several of these notebooks and for the purposes of teaching I eventually turned them into proper recipes and when I found I had several hundred on my computer I corralled them into some sort of format to create this book. One thing you can be sure of is that these recipes have been cooked and tested, sometimes repeatedly, over many years.

This is not a 'lifestyle' book for the coffee table or a book for promoting a new fad, foodstuff, fashion or diet; it is a book of down to earth recipes, real food, recipes that I hope will make you salivate and want to get into your kitchen and start chopping onions and rattling pans.

Happy cooking.

CONTENTS

SOUPS

TUSCAN BEAN SOUP

INGREDIENTS (SERVES 4)

1 onion

2 medium carrots

1 stick of celery

1 leek

1 medium potato

4 tablespoons of olive oil

2 cloves of garlic

2 sprigs fresh thyme

2 tomatoes

Salt and ground black pepper

2 teaspoons of sun-dried tomato paste

A pinch of dried chillies

110g cavolo nero (or dark spring greens)

400g can of cannellini beans

Cracking croutons (see page 25)

METHOD

1. Chop the onion, carrot, celery, potato and leeks into small cubes.
2. Sweat the vegetables in the olive oil until they start to turn transparent.
3. Crush the garlic and add this along with the thyme.
4. Skin and chop the tomatoes then add to the pan.
5. Season with salt and pepper.
6. Cover with water and add the chilli, tomatoes and tomato paste.
7. Simmer until the vegetables are cooked.
8. Remove the stalk from the cavolo nero and shred it.
9. Add the cavolo nero and the beans and continue cooking until the cavolo is tender.
10. Serve with plenty of crusty bread or croutons.

THAI HOT SOUR SOUP

INGREDIENTS (SERVES 4)

8 shiitake mushrooms

12 raw king prawns

1-2 red chillies

1 stick of lemon grass

A small bunch of coriander

2 teaspoons brown sugar

1 lime

2 tablespoons Thai fish sauce (Nam Pla)

1.2 litres chicken stock

Soy sauce

METHOD

1. Slice the mushrooms.
2. Split and clean the king prawns.
3. Finely chop the chillies, lemon grass and coriander and combine these with the sugar, lime and fish sauce.
4. Bring the chicken stock to the boil and add the prawns and mushrooms and enough of the flavour mixture (i.e. the lime and Nam Pla etc.) to suit your taste.
5. Simmer until the prawns are just cooked. Season with the soy sauce and serve.

PARSNIP & APPLE SOUP

INGREDIENTS (SERVES 4)

1 large onion

350g peeled parsnips

250g peeled potatoes

1 medium Bramley apple

2 cloves of garlic

1 tablespoon sunflower oil

750ml water

Salt and ground black pepper

100ml single cream

METHOD

1. Chop the onion. Dice the parsnip and potato. Peel, quarter and core the apple. Crush the garlic.
2. Heat the oil in a saucepan large enough to take all the ingredients and sweat the vegetables, garlic and the apple until they begin to soften.
3. Add the water. Place a lid on the pan and cook until the vegetables are very soft.
4. Liquidize until smooth.
5. Stir in the cream and check the seasoning and consistency. Serve in hot bowls with a swirl of cream on top.

SPICED PUMPKIN SOUP WITH ROASTED PUMPKIN SEEDS

INGREDIENTS (SERVES 6)

2 onions

2 carrots

3cm cube of root ginger

50g butter

2 bay leaves

1 large pumpkin 3–4kg

110g red lentils

1 teaspoon ground coriander

Grated nutmeg

½ teaspoon ground cardamom

2.4 litres water

Salt and ground black pepper

150ml single cream (optional)

METHOD

1. Peel and chop the onions, carrots and ginger.
2. Melt the butter in a saucepan large enough to take all the ingredients. Add the onion, carrot and ginger and sweat together with the bay leaves.
3. Peel and de-seed the pumpkin and cut the flesh into chunks.
4. Place the seeds into a bowl with some clean water to soak.
5. Put the pumpkin into the saucepan with the lentils, spices and the water.
6. Season well, bring to the boil, cover with a lid and cook until the vegetables are soft and the lentils have broken up.
7. Wash the pumpkin seeds, dry them on kitchen paper and place them on a tray. Put them in the oven on a low heat to dry out.
8. When the soup is cooked, remove the bay leaves and purée the soup in a liquidizer or food processor.
9. Correct the seasoning, if necessary, and add the cream if you are using it.
10. Brush the pumpkin seeds with olive oil, season them well and place back in the oven on a higher heat to roast. This part can also be done in a heavy-based frying pan.
11. To serve the soup, bring it back to the boil and pour into deep bowls scattered with the roasted seeds.

PISTOU SOUP

INGREDIENTS (SERVES 4)

1 small onion

1 small carrot

1 stick celery

¼ fennel bulb

2 tablespoons olive oil

500ml water

Salt and ground black pepper

1 small courgette

25g peas

110g canned haricot beans (drained)

1 ripe tomato

FOR THE PISTOU DRESSING:

1 large bunch basil

1 clove of garlic

1 tablespoon grated Parmesan

Ground black pepper

2-3 tablespoons extra virgin olive oil

METHOD

1. To make the pistou, place the basil, garlic, Parmesan and pepper into the bowl of a food processor and whizz until finely chopped. Add the olive oil with the processor still running. Set aside.
2. Finely dice the onion, carrot, celery and fennel.
3. Sweat in the olive oil for 4-5 minutes. Add the water and season and simmer for 10 minutes until the vegetables are cooked.
4. Finely dice the courgettes and add these along with the peas and beans.
5. Peel and chop the tomato and add this also.
6. Cook for 2-3 minutes, serve in hot bowls and stir a little of the pistou into each serving.

CHILLED CUCUMBER & WATERCRESS SOUP

INGREDIENTS (SERVES 4)

1 onion

1 clove of garlic

25g butter

250g potatoes (peeled weight)

900ml water

Salt and ground black pepper

150ml single cream

1 cucumber

1 bunch watercress

METHOD

1. Chop the onion and crush the garlic. Sweat them in the butter until the onion goes translucent.
2. Chop the potatoes and add them with the salt, pepper and water.
3. Bring to the boil and simmer until the potatoes are cooked.
4. Whizz with a stick blender or in a food processor then sieve the resulting liquid.
5. Add the cream and chill.
6. Remove any coarse stalks from the watercress and chop the cucumber.
7. Process the watercress and cucumber in a blender again with the soup.
8. Serve garnished with watercress leaves.

LENTIL, SWEET POTATO & APRICOT SOUP

INGREDIENTS (SERVES 4)

1 large onion

2 cloves of garlic

450g sweet potato

1 tablespoon cooking oil

75g dried apricots

3cm cube root ginger

Salt and ground black pepper

25g tomato purée

75g red lentils

900ml water

1 teaspoon each of ground coriander and cumin

Grated nutmeg

A little chilli – if you like it hot

METHOD

1. Peel and chop the onion, garlic and sweet potato. Fry in the oil until it is beginning to colour.
2. Chop the apricots and add to pan along with the rest of the ingredients.
3. Bring to the boil, cover with a lid and simmer until all the ingredients are soft.
4. Blitz in a liquidizer or with a stick blender.

CURRIED CAULIFLOWER & APPLE SOUP

INGREDIENTS (SERVES 6)

1 medium Bramley apple

200g peeled potatoes

700g cauliflower

2 cloves of garlic

50g butter

1 tablespoon mild curry powder

700ml water

1 teaspoon cumin seeds

2 teaspoons mango chutney

Salt

50ml double cream

Cracking croutons (see page 25)

METHOD

1. Peel, quarter and core the apple and cut it into cubes. Cut the potatoes into cubes also.
2. Cut the cauliflower into florets. Keep back twelve miniature florets for garnish.
3. Crush the garlic.
4. Melt half the butter in a saucepan large enough to take all the ingredients and sweat the apple, potato and garlic in the butter.
5. Add the curry powder so it coats everything and continue cooking for a moment.
6. Put in the cauliflower and the water. Season with the salt and add the chutney.
7. Bring to the boil and simmer until the cauliflower and potato are soft.
8. Blanch the mini florets in boiling salted water and drain.
9. Toast the cumin seeds lightly in a dry pan.
10. Liquidize the soup, return it to the pan with the cream and heat through.
11. Fry the mini florets in the other half of the butter until lightly golden.
12. Serve in deep bowls and scatter the top with the florets, cumin seeds and croutons.

MUSHROOM SOUP WITH A PASTRY LID

EQUIPMENT

4 deep soup bowls

INGREDIENTS (SERVES 4)

1 onion

2 cloves of garlic

25g butter

225g wild mushroom selection (if not available use a mixture of fresh chestnut mushrooms and dried ceps)

1 large potato

1 teaspoon thyme leaves

Salt and ground black pepper

150g Puy lentils

250g ready-made puff pastry

Egg wash (see page 426)

METHOD

1. Heat the oven to 180°C/gas mark 4.
2. Peel and chop the onions and garlic and stew gently in the butter.
3. Chop the mushrooms. Peel and dice the potato. Add these to the onions along with the thyme, seasoning and lentils.
4. Continue cooking gently with a lid on the pan.
5. When the potato and lentils are cooked, liquidize briefly, still keeping the soup chunky, then correct the seasoning and consistency.
6. When the soup has cooled, cut the pastry into four pieces and roll each piece out bigger than the size of the soup bowl rim.
7. Cut the pastry into a neat circle 2cm wider than the soup bowl rim.
8. Divide the soup into the 4 bowls and wet the edge of the bowls.
9. Place the pastry over the top of the bowls making sure it sticks well to the rim.
10. Brush the pastry lightly with egg wash and place in the oven.
11. Serve as soon as the pastry is golden brown.

ROAST TOMATO & RED PEPPER SOUP

INGREDIENTS (SERVES 6)

1 onion

2 cloves of garlic

1350g fresh, ripe tomatoes

2 sweet red peppers

1 tablespoon olive oil

A small bunch of thyme

1 tablespoon sun-dried tomato paste

275ml vegetable stock or water

Salt and ground black pepper

2 teaspoons of smoked paprika
(not the hot one)

A small bunch of basil

Branch of cherry tomatoes (optional)

METHOD

1. Heat the oven to 220°C/gas mark 7.
2. Peel and chop the onion and crush the garlic.
3. Roughly chop the tomatoes, remove the core from the pepper and chop also.
4. Heat the olive oil in a roasting tray and add these ingredients along with the thyme and seasoning.
5. Turn the ingredients so they are well mixed and coated in the oil.
6. Roast in the oven for 35-45 minutes until the peppers are soft, stirring once or twice.
7. Transfer the ingredients to a saucepan (remove the thyme stalks) and add the stock/water, the paprika, basil and the tomato paste.
8. Bring to the boil and simmer for 15 minutes.
9. Liquidise the soup and pass through a sieve to remove the tomato skin and pips.
10. Serve hot with crusty bread or, in summer, chilled with a swirl of cream.
11. For really stylish presentation serve with a branch of roasted cherry tomatoes.

POTATO & LEEK SOUP

INGREDIENTS (SERVES 4)

4 medium leeks

450g potatoes

50g butter

Salt and ground black pepper

150ml double cream

Cracking croutons (see page 25)

METHOD

1. Trim the leeks but leave as much green on as possible. Split them down the centre and shred them finely. Wash well and drain. Put 100g of the leeks to one side.
2. Peel and cut the potatoes into chunks.
3. Sweat the leeks (except the 100g) in the butter but do not colour them.
4. Add the potatoes and seasoning then cover the vegetables with water.
5. Bring to the boil and allow to simmer until the vegetables are soft.
6. Purée the soup with a stick blender or liquidizer and return to the heat.
7. Check the seasoning and put in the cream.
8. Stir fry the leeks you set aside and spoon some into the centre of each bowl of soup.
9. Serve croutons separately.

CHESTNUT & CHORIZO SOUP

INGREDIENTS (SERVES 4)

1 onion

1 carrot

2 sticks of celery

2 cloves of garlic

2 tablespoons olive oil

110g chorizo

6 sage leaves

400g can of tomatoes

1 teaspoon smoked paprika (not the hot one)

450g fresh peeled chestnuts (or the vacuum-packed ones)

1 fresh red chilli

750ml water

Salt and ground black pepper

METHOD

1. Chop the onion, carrot, celery and garlic and fry in the oil until golden brown.
2. Chop the chorizo into small squares and shred the sage leaves. Add these to the pan and continue frying until the oil starts to run from the chorizo.
3. Chop the chilli up small and add this with the tomatoes, paprika, chestnuts and water.
4. Bring to the boil and season with the salt and black pepper.
5. Reduce to a simmer and cook with a lid on until everything is soft.
6. Use a hand blender or food processor to purée the soup ensuring it retains a bit of texture.

CHILLED TOMATO & BASIL SOUP WITH CRISP PANCETTA

INGREDIENTS (SERVES 2)

50g thinly sliced pancetta, Parma ham or any similar air-dried ham

350g ripe and good flavoured tomatoes

12 basil leaves

A small clove of garlic

Salt and ground black pepper

A pinch of sugar

A few drops of white wine vinegar

1 tablespoon of good quality olive oil

Cracking croutons (see page 25)

METHOD

1. Lay the pancetta or ham on a tray and place in the oven on a low heat until it is crisp.
2. Take 2 of the tomatoes, skin and de-seed them and cut the flesh into small cubes. Set this aside with 4 of the basil leaves.
3. In a food processor or liquidizer purée the rest of the tomatoes along with the debris from the first 2, the rest of the basil, the garlic, seasoning, oil, vinegar and sugar. Sieve the resulting mixture discarding the pips etc.
4. Taste the sieved mixture and correct seasoning/flavour balance then stir in the diced tomatoes.
5. Serve in chilled soup bowls scattered with croutons and crumbled pancetta.
6. Garnish with basil leaves.

PROVENÇAL FISH SOUP

With extra fish and a few small new potatoes this can become a main course.

INGREDIENTS (SERVES 2)
FOR THE SOUP

200g fresh live mussels

1 small glass of white wine

450g small fish – choose from red mullet, grey mullet, gurnard or sea bass

1 medium sized onion

½ fennel bulb

2 cloves of garlic

1 tablespoon olive oil

2 ripe tomatoes

3-4 strands of saffron

2 tablespoons of pastis or Pernod

Salt and a pinch of Cayenne pepper

450ml fish stock

Rouille croutons (see opposite)

METHOD

1. First clean the mussels discarding any that don't close when tapped. Place them in a saucepan with the white wine and steam with a lid on until they open.
2. Drain the mussels reserving the liquid then remove them from the shells keeping the mussels in the liquid. Set aside.
3. Clean and fillet the fish and cut them into bite size pieces. Leave the skin on.
4. Chop the onion and the fennel, crush the garlic and sweat in the oil for 5 minutes.
5. Skin and chop the tomatoes and add these followed by the saffron and pastis/Pernod.
6. Add fish stock and season with salt and Cayenne pepper. Cover and simmer for 15 minutes.
7. Put the fish in the soup and cook for a further 5 minutes and then add the mussels and mussel stock.
8. Serve the soup hot and in deep bowls. Float a couple of croutons on the top and serve extra separately.

ROUILLE CROUTONS

INGREDIENTS

¼ of a baguette

Olive oil

25g Emmental cheese - grated

FOR THE ROUILLE

½ teaspoon Dijon mustard

1 clove of garlic

1 tablespoon mayonnaise

METHOD

1. To make the rouille, crush the garlic to a purée and mix it into the mayonnaise with the mustard.
2. Cut the baguette into slices brush with olive oil, lay them on an oven tray and bake in a hot oven until brown and crisp.
3. Spread with a little rouille and top with some of the cheese.
4. Return to the oven briefly to melt the cheese.

MORE CRACKING CROUTONS

Soup is really just an excuse to eat lots of croutons. Croutons can be dire - deep fried, stale, dry, tasteless. Try these.

INGREDIENTS

Stale white bread (French bread or Italian ciabatta or sourdough are good).

Olive oil

Salt and ground black pepper

Finely grated Parmesan (optional)

METHOD

1. Cut the bread into cubes and don't worry about being too neat.
2. Place them in a bowl and drizzle over some olive oil whilst shaking the bowl.
3. Sprinkle over lots of black pepper and a little salt. Also toss in some finely grated Parmesan if using.
4. Scatter them onto a baking sheet and place in a very hot oven (230°C/gas mark 8).
5. 10-15 minutes should get them brown, crispy and sizzling.
6. Try to get them on to the soup before you eat them all!!

STARTERS

OLD-FASHIONED PORK TERRINE

EQUIPMENT

600ml terrine dish

INGREDIENTS (SERVES 8)

220g smoked streaky bacon

1 chicken breast

1 medium onion

25g butter

350g coarsely-minced lean pork

110g chicken livers

50ml dry white wine (or sherry)

2 cloves garlic

A small bunch of mixed herbs - sage/basil/thyme/marjoram - chopped

Salt and ground black pepper

A level teaspoon Aromatic Spice Mix (see page 411)

25g fresh white breadcrumbs

1 egg

1 tablespoon shelled pistachios, (optional)

METHOD

1. Heat the oven to 150°C/gas mark 2.
2. Line the dish with the bacon leaving some hanging over the edge to cover the top.
3. Cut the chicken breast into strips.
4. Chop the onion and fry in the butter to a golden brown. Allow to cool.
5. Remove any sinew from the chicken livers and chop them.
6. In a bowl, combine all the ingredients (except the chicken breast) and season it well.
7. Spoon a layer of meat into the dish. Lay some strips of chicken from end-to-end followed by some more mix until it is all used up. Cover with the bacon.
8. If your dish doesn't have a lid, cover the top with tin foil.
9. Stand the dish in a pan of hot water about 1 inch deep and cook for 1½ hours.
10. To test, put a skewer in the centre count to 5 then hold it against your inner wrist – if it is hot to the touch it is done.
11. Allow to cool to room temperature then cover with cling film and press with a suitable weight.
12. Can be eaten the next day but it is better after 3. It will keep for 8 days in a cold refrigerator.

MUSHROOM, HAM & GRUYÈRE GALETTE

INGREDIENTS (SERVES 4)
FOR THE PANCAKES

75g plain flour

2 eggs

150-200 ml milk

Sunflower oil

Salt

FOR THE FILLING

225g chestnut button mushrooms

1 small clove of garlic

25g butter

Ground black pepper

4 slices of Gruyère cheese (about 8cm square)

4 slices of cooked ham

1 egg

METHOD

1. Make a well in the flour, put the egg and a little of the milk in it and beat to a smooth paste, then add more milk until you have the consistency of single cream.
2. Add salt and a little oil and allow the mixture to rest.
3. Make 4 pancakes, about 25cm in diameter, and set aside.
4. Slice the mushrooms and crush the garlic.
5. Fry the mushrooms in the butter with crushed garlic and black pepper. Allow to cool.
6. Place a slice of cheese in the centre of each pancake.
7. Divide the mushrooms between the 4 pancakes and spread them out over the cheese. Arrange a slice of ham on top.
8. Fold the outer edges of the pancake over the filling, brushing with beaten egg where any pancake overlaps until you have 4 square parcels.
9. Fry slowly in oil, putting the joined side down first to seal it.
10. Take care not to tear the pancake as you manipulate it.
11. Serve straight away. The parcel should be crisp on the outside with hot filling and melted cheese on the inside.

ROQUEFORT TART WITH APPLE SALAD

INGREDIENTS (MAKES 4)

75g Roquefort (or Danish blue)

75g Philadelphia cream cheese

225g puff pastry

1 bag mixed leaves

Salad dressing (see page 400)

2 Cox's apples

Sunflower oil for frying

METHOD

1. Heat the oven to 220°C/gas mark 7.
2. Mash together the Roquefort and the Philadelphia.
3. Form into a cylinder about 8cm in diameter, wrap in cling film and refrigerate.
4. Roll out the pastry leaving it about the thickness of a £1 coin and cut 4 circles about 12cm in diameter. Cut with a knife not a pastry cutter!
5. Cut slices from the cylinder of cheese about 1cm thick and place them in the centre of each pastry round.
6. Bake in the oven for about 15 minutes. (The pastry rising around the edges traps the melting cheese).
7. Arrange the salad on the plates and dress it. Peel, quarter and core the apples and cut each quarter into 3 thick slices.
8. Fry in hot oil until golden. Arrange amongst the salad leaves. As soon as the tarts are cooked place them on the salad and serve.

RILLETTE OF DUCK WITH PICKLED APRICOTS

INGREDIENTS (SERVES 4)

4 duck legs

A glass of red wine

2 cloves garlic

4 sprigs thyme

2 bay leaves

1 piece star anise

Salt and ground black pepper

2 strips of orange zest

1 tablespoon duck or goose fat

FOR THE PICKLED APRICOTS

150ml white wine or cider vinegar

110g granulated sugar

½ cinnamon stick

2 drops of almond essence

2 teaspoons English mustard powder

250g dried apricots

METHOD

1. Heat the oven to 220°C/gas mark 7.
2. Rub some salt into the skin of the duck and roast in the oven for 15 minutes.
3. Allow the duck legs to cool enough to pull the skin off them. Set the skin aside.
4. De-glaze the roasting pan with the red wine.
5. Place all the ingredients except the skin into a casserole dish with a tight fitting lid.
6. Reduce the oven temperature to 150°C/gas mark 2.
7. Cook in the oven until the meat is very soft - about 1-1½ hours.
8. After 30 minutes check it is cooking slowly. Add more wine if it starts to look dry at any point.
9. Remove the star anise and any thyme twigs and strip the meat from the bones (it should fall away).
10. Shred the meat with a fork and mix it with the fat and juices.
11. Pack the mixture into a terrine or individual ramekins. Press down so a little fat rises to the top.
12. Place in the refrigerator to cool.
13. To crisp up the skin, cut it into strips and fry slowly until it goes crisp.
14. Serve with the crispy duck skin and pickled apricots (see below).

FOR THE PICKLED APRICOTS

15. Place the vinegar, sugar, almond essence and cinnamon into a saucepan and bring to the boil.
16. Whisk in the mustard powder. Add the dried apricots and simmer until the syrup is thick.
17. Place in a container ready for use.
18. You can heat treat these in jars so that they can be kept for longer.

PAN-COOKED CHICKEN LIVER PÂTÉ

A nice, easy and quick to cook pâté

INGREDIENTS (SERVES 4)

225g fresh chicken livers

2-3 cloves of garlic

2 leaves of gelatine

75g butter

25g pancetta or smoked streaky bacon

2 bay leaves and 3 sprigs of thyme

Salt and ground black pepper

½ teaspoon Aromatic Spice Mix (see page 411)

1 tablespoon brandy

2 tablespoons dry sherry

110g Philadelphia cream cheese

Clarified butter for sealing the pots (see page 426)

METHOD

1. Remove any dark patches or threads from the livers and cut them into small pieces.
2. Chop the garlic and soften the gelatine in cold water.
3. Melt the butter in a shallow pan and start cooking the chicken livers, bacon, bay leaves, thyme and garlic together – do not fry at a high heat the idea is that the chicken livers etc. stew gently in the butter.
4. Season with the salt, pepper and spices.
5. Test to see whether the liver is cooked by cutting open a larger piece to see.
6. When the liver is cooked add the brandy and set light to it.
7. Add the sherry and remove from the heat.
8. Remove the bay leaves and any thyme stalks.
9. Stir in the gelatine and allow the mixture to cool.
10. Before it is completely cold, purée the mixture in a food processor with the cream cheese. Taste the mixture and correct the seasoning.
11. Pass the pâté through a fine sieve and spoon into your chosen containers, which can be a dish or individual ramekins.
12. Seal the top(s) with clarified butter.
13. Refrigerate overnight. Serve with hot toast, brioche, crusty bread or oatcakes.

CHICKEN LIVER PARFAIT

EQUIPMENT

500ml terrine or loaf tin

INGREDIENTS (SERVES 6)

1 small onion

Olive oil

A small bunch each of fresh thyme and basil

1 clove of garlic

1 tablespoon brandy

2 tablespoons port

225g fresh chicken livers

225g butter

Salt and ground black pepper

Nutmeg

Ground coriander

3 eggs

METHOD

1. Heat the oven to 150°C/gas mark 2.
2. Chop the onion and fry it in a little olive oil until it browns nicely.
3. Chop the herbs and add these with the garlic and continue frying for a minute or two.
4. Remove from the heat and flambé with the brandy before adding the port. Allow to cool.
5. Check the chicken livers for gall bladders and remove them.
6. Place the livers in a food processor with the onion, garlic and herb mixture and process to a smooth purée.
7. Add the salt, pepper, spices and eggs and continue processing.
8. Melt the butter gently without getting it too hot.
9. Pour the butter onto the chicken livers with the machine on.
10. Pass the mixture through a fine sieve.
11. Lightly oil the terrine, line it with parchment paper and pour in the mixture.
12. Stand it in a pan in an inch of simmering water, cover the whole thing with several layers of tin foil and cook in the oven for 1 hour.
13. Careful cooking is crucial, the mixture should be just set – firm but wobbly.
14. When cool, this pâté can be served with hot toast and a fruity relish. It can also be successfully grilled and served hot on toasted brioche.

QUAIL EGG & MUSHROOM TART

This became a favourite at the Hungry Monk – a dish we honourably nicked from Langan's Brasserie after a staff outing there. But its lineage goes back much further and it featured on the menu of a massive bash given by the Shah of Iran in the desert in 1971 and probably further back than that as well. The original recipe was probably for gull's eggs.

EQUIPMENT

4 x 10cm diameter tart tins

INGREDIENTS (SERVES 4)

Short pastry (see page 424)

1 small onion

12g butter

110g chestnut button mushrooms

Salt and ground black pepper

1 teaspoon grain mustard

24 quail's eggs – you only need 20 (5 per tart) but I am allowing for imperfect ones

FOR THE HOLLANDAISE SAUCE

1 tablespoon white wine vinegar

1 tablespoon water

1 egg yolk

½ teaspoon Dijon mustard

110g butter

METHOD

1. Heat the oven to 180°C/gas mark 4.
2. Line 4 small tart tins with the pastry and bake them blind (see page 424).
3. To make the mushroom base, chop the onion very finely and sweat in the butter until it softens.
4. Chop the mushrooms quite small and fry these with the onion until they cook.
5. Season and continue cooking until any liquid from the mushrooms has evaporated.
6. Remove from the heat and mix in the grain mustard. Set aside.
7. Boil the quail's eggs for 5 minutes for hard boiled (3-4 if you like them softer) and cool under running cold water prior to peeling.

FOR THE HOLLANDAISE SAUCE

1. Place the vinegar in a pan and reduce it to almost nil.
2. Place the tablespoon of water in the pan and transfer it to a bowl set over simmering water.
3. Whisk in the egg yolk and keep stirring with the whisk until the mixture thickens. Do not overcook. Remove the bowl from the heat and add the mustard.
4. Melt the butter and whisk it onto the egg yolk in a thin stream. When it is incorporated the sauce is ready.
5. Use immediately or keep at this temperature.

ASSEMBLY

Spoon the mushroom filling into the tart cases, place 5 eggs in each tart and then spoon some hollandaise onto each one – serve immediately.

MINI MUSHROOM TARTS WITH QUAIL'S EGGS

INGREDIENTS (SERVES 24)

This is a canapé version of the previous recipe. For this you will need a mini muffin tin and a small wooden plunger for lining the tin with pastry. You can buy these kits in good cook shops, online and in the Lakeland chain of shops. Line the muffin tins, place in the mushroom filling and bake. When they are cooked and cooled place half a teaspoon of mayonnaise on the top and half a hard-boiled quail's egg. Decorate with a pinch of smoked paprika.

ONION TART

A dish from Alsace. Using crème fraiche nicely balances the sweetness of the onion.

EQUIPMENT

25cm diameter x 4cm deep tart tin

INGREDIENTS (SERVES 8-10)

Short pastry (see page 424)

FOR THE FILLING

3 large onions

50g butter

110g smoked bacon (or pancetta)

1 egg

200ml crème fraiche

Salt and ground black pepper

Nutmeg

METHOD

1. Heat the oven to 180°C/gas mark 4.
2. Line the tart tin with the pastry and bake blind for 10-15 minutes.
3. Slice the onions and sweat in the butter until soft and translucent (do not brown).
4. Cut the bacon into small pieces and fry with the onions until cooked.
5. Allow to cool and stir in the egg, crème fraiche, nutmeg, black pepper and a little salt if necessary.
6. Spoon the mixture into the pastry case and bake for a further 25-30 minutes until golden and set.
7. Serve warm.

POTTED PORK PÂTÉ

INGREDIENTS (SERVES 6)

900g belly pork without the skin cut into cubes

A small glass of dry white wine or cider

2 strips of orange zest

4-5 cloves of garlic, chopped

2 sprigs each of thyme and rosemary

2 bay leaves

Salt, pepper, nutmeg, juniper and allspice

Clarified butter (see page 426)

METHOD

1. Heat the oven to 150°C/gas mark 2.
2. Place all the ingredients in a deep covered casserole and cook for 2 hours.
3. Check each half hour to make sure that it is only cooking very gently and turn the oven down a notch if it isn't.
4. Add more wine/cider if it starts to look dry at any point.
5. When the meat is tender remove the bay leaves and any woody bits from the herbs.
6. Tip off some of the fat if it is excessive and set aside. Shred the meat using 2 forks and mix well with the other ingredients. Put into a dish or ramekins and seal with pork fat or clarified butter.
7. This keeps well in the refrigerator for a week to ten days.

TERRINE OF DUCK

EQUIPMENT

850ml terrine dish

INGREDIENTS (SERVES 8-10)

220g smoked streaky bacon

1 whole duck with giblets

50ml Madeira

110g lean minced pork

1 medium onion

25g butter

½ a red pepper

Chopped herbs: sage, basil, marjoram

2 cloves of garlic

Salt and ground black pepper

A pinch of ground juniper and allspice

25g fresh white breadcrumbs

1 egg

1 tablespoon shelled pistachios (optional)

METHOD

1. Heat the oven to 150°C/gas mark 2.
2. Line the dish with the bacon leaving some hanging over the sides to wrap around later.
3. Cut the legs from the duck and strip all the meat from the bones.
4. Remove the 2 breast fillets from the carcass, cut 1 of them into strips and marinate in the Madeira. (The other breast can be kept for another dish).
5. Mince the leg meat twice and combine it with the pork.
6. Chop the duck liver from the giblets and combine with the rest of the meat.
7. Chop the onion and fry in the butter until the onion begins to colour.
8. Chop the red pepper very fine and add to the frying onions for the last 5 minutes.
9. Chop the herbs and the garlic.
10. Combine all the ingredients except the breast strips and season well. Spoon a layer of meat into the terrine dish and lay some strips of duck from end-to-end. Spoon in another layer, some more strips of duck and continue until all the mix is used up. Cover with the bacon.
11. Cover with tin foil, if your dish does not have a lid. Stand the dish in a pan of hot water about an inch deep and cook for 1½ hours.
12. To test put a skewer in the centre count to 5 then hold it against your inner wrist - if it is hot to the touch it is done.
13. Allow to cool to room temperature then cover with cling film and press with a suitable weight. Can be eaten the next day but it is better after 3. It will keep for 10 days in a cold refrigerator.

CAESAR SALAD

This American favourite has nothing to do with Julius – Caesar salad was invented in 1924 by Caesar Cardini who ran a restaurant in Tijuana. There are many variations and one can usually find it on pub menus done with strips of chicken which, if not exactly authentic, at least makes it more of a meal than a snack or starter.

INGREDIENTS (SERVES 4)

1 large Cos lettuce

2 cloves garlic

2 tablespoons mayonnaise

1 tablespoon plain yoghurt

Juice of ½ a lemon

Ground black pepper

50g freshly grated Parmesan

Half a medium-sized (day-old) baguette

25ml olive oil

50g anchovy fillets

METHOD

1. Heat the oven to 230°C/gas mark 8.
2. Wash the lettuce and dry it. Tear the outer leaves into manageable pieces and place in a bowl with the heart leaves.
3. Crush the garlic then place in a bowl with the mayonnaise, yoghurt, lemon juice and black pepper. Stir in the Parmesan cheese.
4. Cut the bread into cubes and toss it in a little olive oil to get them evenly coated.
5. Place them on a tray and bake in the oven until crisp.
6. Drizzle the dressing over the lettuce leaves and toss gently to coat the leaves. Divide them into 4 bowls and dress with the torn anchovy fillets and the croutons.

FISH STARTERS

SALT & PEPPER SQUID

This is really so simple it hardly needs a recipe but here goes. Try and buy fresh, unprepared squid to ensure you are getting the real thing and not some machine prepared frozen stuff. A good fishmonger will prepare it for you if you can't face doing it.

INGREDIENTS (SERVES 4)

900g fresh squid – once prepared this amount will give you roughly half the original weight in usable squid

1 tablespoon olive oil

Sea salt, ground black pepper and nutmeg

50g butter

Juice of 1 lemon

A few rocket leaves or chopped parsley

METHOD

1. Cut the tentacles from the head, set aside.
2. Remove the head, the internal parts, the skin and discard.
3. Wash the remaining tube under cold running water.
4. Separate the tentacles and cut the 2 long ones in half. Cut the body into rings and the tentacles into reasonable lengths.
5. For this amount it is probably best to use 2 pans. Heat the oil until it is smoking.
6. Put in the squid and season it. Stir fry it until it begins to colour then take the pan away from the heat. (It is important not to overcook it otherwise it is similar to eating so many rubber bands).
7. Put the butter and lemon into the pan and swirl it around until the butter melts. Serve immediately with chopped parsley or on a few rocket leaves.

SPICED CRAB SPRING ROLL

INGREDIENTS (MAKES 8-10 ROLLS)

50g celery

½ red pepper

1 bulb of lemon grass

1 clove of garlic

1½cm cube of root ginger

Small bunch coriander

Half a hot chilli (more or less according to taste)

225g fresh white crab meat

Salt

1 packet filo pastry

Sunflower oil for frying

METHOD

1. Chop the celery and the red pepper finely.
2. Remove the tough outer leaves of the lemon grass and chop up very fine with the garlic, ginger, coriander and chilli.
3. Combine all these with the crab meat and season well.
4. Unroll the filo pastry and cut into squares roughly 18–20cm.
5. Brush each sheet with a little oil.
6. Place a dessert spoon of mixture in one corner in a cylinder shape and then roll towards the opposing corner, folding in the sides as you roll, ending up with a neat cylindrical parcel.
7. Fry in hot oil until golden all over (or alternatively brush with oil and bake in a hot oven).
8. Drain onto kitchen paper and serve immediately with sweet chilli dipping sauce.

SIMPLE SUSHI

This is a good beginner's sushi - quite easy to do and using ingredients we are reasonably familiar with.

INGREDIENTS (MAKES ABOUT 12 SUSHI)
FOR THE RICE

150g sushi or jasmine rice

300ml water

Salt

2 tablespoons sushi vinegar

FOR THE FILLING

1-2 sheets of 'nori' seaweed

2-3 small pak choi

1 sachet of 'wasabi' horseradish

Half a cucumber

50g pickled ginger

4 cooked king prawns (split lengthways) or seafood sticks

2-3 slices of smoked salmon

Light soy sauce for dipping

METHOD

1. Rinse the rice in cold water and place in a pan with the 300ml of water and some salt.
2. Bring to the boil and simmer gently until all the water is absorbed.
3. Remove from the heat, place a lid on the pan and allow it to stand for 5 minutes.
4. Stir in the sushi vinegar and add more salt if necessary.
5. Toast the nori to make it pliable.
6. Boil or steam the pak choi and cut into strips lengthways.
7. Make up the 'wasabi' to a paste with a little water.
8. Peel the cucumber, halve, remove the seeds and cut into strips.
9. If you have a sushi mat, lay a sheet of the nori onto this, if not lay out a sheet of baking parchment and use that instead.
10. Next take some of the cooked sushi rice and create a layer on the nori taking it right to the edges either side but leaving a 2cm strip top and bottom.
11. Now, using the seafood, ginger, cucumber and pak choi make a line of filling in the centre of the rice going from right to left. Dab it with the wasabi but take care with this as it is very hot.
12. Roll the sushi, using the mat or paper to encase the filling with the rice and the nori around the exterior. Compress gently to create a tight roll.
13. Refrigerate for an hour before cutting into thick (2cm) slices.

SMOKED TROUT MOUSSE

EQUIPMENT

6 small ramekins or similar moulds

INGREDIENTS (SERVES 6)

4-5g gelatine in 'leaf' form

2 smoked trout to yield about 110g of meat

A squeeze of lemon juice

Ground black pepper

Nutmeg

150ml double cream

225g of sliced smoked salmon (good quality, large slices)

METHOD

1. Soften the gelatine in cold water.
2. Purée the trout meat in a food processor with the lemon, pepper and nutmeg.
3. Drain the gelatine, warm gently in a small saucepan over a low heat to melt and add this to the meat while its going round in the processor.
4. Finally add the cream and process until smooth and creamy - do not over process.
5. Press a slice of smoked salmon into each ramekin. Spoon the trout mousse into it and fold the edges of the salmon over the top.
6. Chill. Turn out to serve.
7. You can serve it with a dressing made from half mayonnaise and half plain yoghurt flavoured with horseradish and chopped chives.

TARAMASALATA

INGREDIENTS (SERVES 4)

50g white bread, without crusts (fairly stale)

50ml water

1-2 cloves of garlic

75g smoked cod's roe – minus the skin

Ground black pepper

Juice of 1 lemon

50ml olive oil

Black olives to garnish

METHOD

1. Soak the bread in the water.
2. Skin and crush the garlic.
3. Skin the cod's roe.
4. Squeeze the excess water out of the bread and place in the food processor with the garlic, pepper, roe and lemon juice.
5. Process until smooth and then add the olive oil in a thin stream.
6. Chill. Serve in pots with good quality black olives, pita bread, toast or crusty French bread.

HOT SUSSEX SMOKIE

I 'borrowed' this recipe from a pub called the Suffolk Arms many moons ago.

INGREDIENTS (SERVES 4)

450g un-dyed smoked haddock fillet

400ml milk

2 bay leaves

50g butter

25g plain flour

2 tablespoons double cream

25g strong Cheddar – grated

Ground black pepper

25g grated Parmesan

METHOD

1. Skin the haddock if necessary and place in a shallow pan with the milk and bay leaves. Bring to the boil then remove the pan from the heat. Leave for 10 minutes and the fish will finish cooking in the residual heat. When cooked, set aside and remove bay leaves.
2. In another pan melt the butter and then stir in the flour. When sizzling, slowly add the poaching milk.
3. As it boils it will thicken, then add the cream, Cheddar cheese and the black pepper.
4. Flake the fish and combine with the sauce. Spoon the mixture into ramekins.
5. Sprinkle with the Parmesan and grill until brown and crunchy on the top.

SMOKED HADDOCK & LEEK TART

EQUIPMENT

20cm diameter x 3.5cm deep tart tin

INGREDIENTS (SERVES 4)

Short pastry (see page 424)

2 medium leeks

350g–450g un-dyed smoked haddock fillet

300ml milk

300ml single cream

1 egg and 1 egg yolk

A squeeze of lemon juice

Ground black pepper

METHOD

1. Heat the oven to 190°C/gas mark 5.
2. Line the tart tin with the pastry and bake it blind (see page 424).
3. Reduce the oven heat to 170°C/gas mark 3.
4. Trim and slice the leeks finely, wash well and steam briefly. Spread them out on a tray to cool.
5. Skin the haddock and place it in a pan with the milk. Bring it to the boil then remove the pan from the heat. Leave for 10 minutes and the fish will finish cooking in the residual heat.
6. Drain the haddock reserving the milk then flake it into a bowl removing any bones that are left.
7. Add the leeks to the bowl.
8. Whisk the egg into the cream with 2 tablespoons of the poaching milk a squeeze of lemon and the pepper.
9. Combine with the fish and leeks and spoon the mixture into the pastry case.
10. Bake in the oven for 20-25 minutes until the filling is set.

SMOKED FISH TERRINE

EQUIPMENT

A 1 litre terrine dish

INGREDIENTS (SERVES 8-10)

200g un-dyed smoked haddock

300ml milk

200g smoked salmon slices

8g gelatine in 'leaf' form

250g smoked trout fillet

Nutmeg and ground black pepper

300ml double cream

A small bunch of fresh dill

150g hot-smoked salmon

150g smoked mackerel fillet

FOR THE SAUCE

Milk (from poaching the haddock)

150ml double cream

1 teaspoon Dijon mustard

1 teaspoon horseradish sauce

METHOD

1. Skin the haddock, cut it into strips and poach gently in the milk.
2. Lightly oil the terrine dish and line it with a single sheet of parchment paper.
3. Now line the terrine with the smoked salmon slices leaving some hanging over the sides to fold over the completed terrine. Set aside.
4. Soften the gelatine in cold water.
5. Place the smoked trout in the food processor with the nutmeg and pepper and run it until the trout turns to a purée.
6. Drain the gelatine and melt it gently. Pour the gelatine onto the trout mixture with the machine running so it incorporates it evenly.
7. Put all the cream into the trout mix and process in short bursts until the mixture thickens.
8. Chop the dill and stir it into the trout mix.
9. Spread a layer of the purée into the terrine and then arrange strips of haddock, hot smoked salmon and mackerel along the length of the terrine. Spread another layer of the trout mix over the fish pressing it well into the gaps. Create another layer of fish strips and trout purée and repeat until the terrine is full. (Be sure to alternate the different fish in the layers so they are evenly distributed.)
10. Fold the smoked salmon lining over the top to encase the whole terrine. Compress lightly and refrigerate overnight.
11. To make a sauce for serving with the terrine, reduce the milk that the haddock was poached in by half and add the cream. Bring to the boil and whisk in the Dijon mustard and horseradish and allow to cool.
12. To serve the terrine, turn it out of the dish, remove the lining paper and cut it in slices with a very sharp knife. Decorate with the sauce and sprigs of dill or chervil.

GAZPACHO WITH STIR FRIED TIGER PRAWNS

INGREDIENTS (SERVES 2)

350g ripe tomatoes

½ red pepper

½ cucumber

1 clove of garlic

Salt and ground black pepper

2 teaspoons white wine vinegar

150ml tomato juice

1 tablespoon olive oil

2 tablespoons fresh white breadcrumbs

2 slices white bread

4 large, raw tiger prawns

Basil to garnish

METHOD

1. Peel, quarter and de-seed the tomatoes. Sieve the seeds and reserve the juice. Discard the seeds.
2. Peel, quarter and de-seed the pepper. Peel the cucumber. Peel and crush the garlic.
3. Reserve 4 quarters of the tomato and place the rest in a food processor with the red pepper, cucumber, salt, pepper, vinegar, tomato juice and garlic.
4. Whizz to a purée, add the olive oil and bread crumbs. Whiz again briefly and then correct the consistency with either a little more water or bread crumbs if necessary.
5. Correct the seasoning. Refrigerate while you prepare the rest of the ingredients.
6. Chop the remaining tomato into small dice. Cut the bread into cubes and fry in a little oil to make croutons, drain on kitchen towel.
7. To prepare the tiger prawns, pull off the head and tail and peel off the shell. Cut the prawns in ½ lengthways and remove the intestine.
8. To serve, fry the prawns in hot oil and season them. Stir the gazpacho and transfer to individual plates or bowls. Arrange the prawns on top and scatter with the croutons and chopped tomato. Garnish with sprigs of basil.

CRAB QUICHE

EQUIPMENT

20cm diameter x 4cm deep tart tin

INGREDIENTS (SERVES 8)

Short pastry (see page 424)

1 cooked crab weighing 650-750g

A small clove of garlic

3 eggs

300ml double cream

Salt and ground black pepper

Nutmeg

1 teaspoon Dijon mustard

A squeeze of lemon juice

2 tablespoons of good mayonnaise

Chopped parsley

METHOD

1. Pre heat the oven to 190°C/gas mark 5.
2. Roll out the pastry, line the tart tin and bake blind (see page 424).
3. Reduce the oven heat to 170°C/gas mark 3.
4. Prepare the crab (see page 78 for instructions), keeping the brown and white meat separate.
5. Crush the garlic and combine with the brown crab meat, eggs, cream, seasoning, mustard and lemon juice.
6. Spoon the filling into the tart case and bake for 25-35 minutes until the filling is just set.
7. Mix together the white crab meat, mayonnaise and chopped parsley.
8. Allow the quiche to cool a little but serve warm with a spoonful of the white meat/mayonnaise on the side.

EASY PRAWN TOASTS

INGREDIENTS (MAKES 16)

110g raw peeled prawns

110g raw salmon fillet

A sliver of garlic

Salt and ground black pepper

Nutmeg

1 egg white

150ml double cream

2 tablespoons of sesame seeds

4 slices white bread (crusts removed)

1-2 tablespoons sunflower oil

METHOD

1. Heat the oven to 220°C/gas mark 7.
2. Place the prawns, salmon, garlic and seasonings into the food processor and process to a purée.
3. Add the egg white and run the machine again until it is incorporated.
4. Add the cream and process just long enough for the mixture to thicken.
5. Allow the mixture to rest and chill down.
6. Spread the mixture thickly and evenly over the slices of bread.
7. Sprinkle generously with sesame seeds.
8. Oil a baking sheet liberally and put the slices of bread on it.
9. Bake for 10–15 minutes until the tops are golden. Check the underside of the bread to ensure it has toasted and is also golden brown.
10. These are delicious cut into 4 and served piping-hot onto a dressed salad as a starter or lunch dish. Alternatively, they can be served as a canapé. For this each slice should be cut into 8.

FRAGRANT THAI MUSSELS

INGREDIENTS (SERVES 2)

1 kilo mussels

1 small red chilli

1 clove of garlic

1½cm cube root ginger

1 bulb of lemon grass

1 tablespoon sunflower oil

200ml full fat coconut milk (canned)

Small bunch of coriander and basil

METHOD

1. Wash the mussels really well discarding any that remain open or are broken.
2. Chop the chilli, garlic, ginger and lemon grass very fine.
3. Take a large saucepan, heat the oil in it and fry the chilli etc. to release the flavours.
4. Pour in the coconut milk. Bring it to the boil and put in the mussels.
5. Place a lid on the pan and keep it over a high heat, shaking the pan occasionally.
6. When all the mussels have steamed open tip them into a colander with a bowl underneath to catch the juices.
7. Chop the coriander and basil and add to the drained juices.
8. There are two ways to serve this - either pile the mussels, still in their shells, into deep soup plates and pour over the juice or, remove the mussels from their shells, put them back into the liquid and serve in soup bowls.

THAI FISH CAKES

You can use other fish for this recipe but it works well with an oily and a non-oily fish.

INGREDIENTS (SERVES 2)

1½ cm cube root ginger

1 clove of garlic

1 bulb of lemon grass

¼ red pepper

A small bunch coriander

110g fresh haddock or cheaper white fish

110g salmon

1 teaspoon red Thai curry paste

1 tablespoon Thai fish sauce

METHOD

1. Chop the ginger, garlic and lemon grass very fine.
2. Finely dice the red pepper. Chop the coriander.
3. Make sure the haddock and salmon are free of skin and bone and grind to a paste in a food processor.
4. Remove from the processor and combine it with the other ingredients.
5. Form into small cakes and shallow fry in oil.
6. Serve with sweet-chilli dip.
7. Make small ones for starters or canapés or larger ones to serve with salad as a main course.

SMOKED TROUT WITH ASPARAGUS & HORSERADISH CREAM

INGREDIENTS (SERVES 4)

24 asparagus spears

Olive oil

Salt and ground black pepper

110g full fat crème fraiche

2 teaspoons of good quality horseradish sauce

Milk

225g smoked trout fillet

METHOD

1. Heat the oven to 220°C/gas mark 7.
2. Trim the woody stem from the asparagus and peel the lower end of the stalk if you wish but I think it is unnecessary.
3. Place them on a baking sheet allowing gaps between each spear and drizzle with olive oil. Season them with the salt and pepper and roast in the oven for 10 minutes.
4. Meanwhile mix the horseradish into the crème fraiche and thin with a little milk to get a drizzling consistency.
5. To serve, lay 6 asparagus spears on each plate, flake the trout over the asparagus and then drizzle with the sauce.

SMOKED MACKEREL & WHISKY PÂTÉ

INGREDIENTS (SERVES 4)

225g smoked mackerel fillet

50g butter

1 teaspoon soft green peppercorns

Juice of half a lemon

2 tablespoons of whisky

METHOD

1. Skin the mackerel and remove any bones. Place the fish in a bowl and mash with a fork.
2. Melt the butter and chop the peppercorns. Mix these into the fish with the lemon juice and whisky.
3. Press the mixture into a loaf-shaped dish (avoid metal), lined with some parchment paper to facilitate easy removal.
4. Refrigerate until firm, remove from the dish and cut into thickish slices.
5. Serve with warm crusty bread or wholemeal toast.

SALT COD CROQUETTES

Traditional salt cod can be obtained from good fishmongers, specialist shops or online. It looks like a large crusty finnan haddock and will take a lot of soaking and water changes to render it usable. An easier way is to make your own. This way you can control the amount of salt and the finished result tastes authentic. To do it, buy some fresh cod fillet and skin it. Next, get a glass or china dish, put the cod in it and sprinkle over a thick layer of coarse sea salt. Turn the fillets over so they are well coated. Leave overnight in the refrigerator. Next morning your cod will have shrunk and there will be no visible salt just a lot of salty water surrounding your fish. This is because the salt will have drawn water from the cod which will feel quite leathery. Tip away the water and rinse the fish well under cold running water. The fish is now ready to use.

INGREDIENTS (MAKES 12)

400g potatoes (King Edwards are best as they have a high dry matter content)

225g salt cod – the weight after salting

300ml of milk

2 bay leaves

1 small onion

Small bunch of parsley

1 teaspoon plain flour

Ground black pepper

Garlic mayonnaise

Oil for deep frying

METHOD

1. Peel the potatoes. Boil and drain them well.
2. Poach the cod very gently in the milk with the bay leaves until it is cooked.
3. Lift the fish out of the milk, remove any bones and mash with a fork.
4. Mash the potatoes with a fork and combine with the fish.
5. Chop the onion very finely or grate it.
6. Chop the parsley.
7. Combine all the ingredients including the flour and shape into croquettes.
8. Deep fry at 190°C until golden and drain on kitchen paper.
9. Serve hot with garlic mayonnaise.

GRAVADLAX & POTATO PANCAKES WITH DILL & MUSTARD SAUCE

This is one of the most popular starters we served at Quincy's. Unlike its cousin, smoked salmon, you can make this easily at home. Unfortunately, it is not worth making in small quantities. It also requires the pungent mustard and dill sauce to bring it alive. It is worth making if you are entertaining a lot of people and it will freeze well.

INGREDIENTS (SERVES 20)

1 whole salmon 3kg or larger

225g coarse sea salt

225g granulated sugar

2 teaspoons ground black pepper

2 tablespoons dried dill

Small bunch of fresh dill - chopped

METHOD

1. Fillet the salmon removing all the pin bones.
2. Trim the tail end back about 8-10cm and use the ends for something else.
3. Mix together the salt, sugar, pepper and dried dill.
4. Lay out a long sheet of cling film and spoon a layer of the dry mixture on it roughly the shape of 1 fish fillet and about a centimetre deep.
5. Lay one of the fillets on this skin-side down.
6. Spoon a thick layer of the mix onto the fish and then cover with the second fillet skin-side up.
7. Finish with a layer of mix then wrap the cling film tightly around the fish making sure there are no gaps. Wrap in a further 2 layers of cling film.
8. Place in a tray and refrigerate. Turn after 24 hours. After another 24 hours unwrap the fish discarding all the liquid that has resulted.
9. Scrape or rinse off the remaining cure mix and pat dry with kitchen paper. Sprinkle the upper surfaces with the fresh dill and wrap each fillet individually. Refrigerate for a further 24 hours.
10. Carve the gravadlax into slices diagonally as you would smoked salmon but slightly thicker.

INGREDIENTS

FOR THE POTATO PANCAKES (MAKES 6)

110g cooked potato

35g self-raising flour

1 egg

75ml milk

Salt and ground black pepper

Olive oil for frying

FOR THE DILL AND MUSTARD SAUCE

1 egg yolk

3 teaspoons Dijon mustard

2 teaspoons grain mustard

1 teaspoon white wine vinegar

Salt and ground black pepper

1 teaspoon runny honey

Small bunch fresh dill

Lemon juice

300ml sunflower oil

METHOD

FOR THE POTATO PANCAKES

1. Place the potato in a bowl and mash it with the back of a fork.
2. Add the flour, egg and a little of the milk. Beat the mixture with a whisk to a cohesive mix then add the rest of the milk.
3. Season with the salt and pepper.
4. Heat a nonstick pan and then add a little oil.
5. Fry spoonfuls of the batter to make thick pancakes about 7cm in diameter.
6. Turn them over when they are cooked on one side.
7. Remove from the pan when cooked through and store ready for use.

FOR THE DILL AND MUSTARD SAUCE

1. Make sure all ingredients are at room temperature. Place all the ingredients, except the oil, into a food processor with 1 tablespoon of warm water. Process until the dill is well chopped.
2. Pour the oil into this mixture in a thin stream. Finally add more water to get it to a pouring consistency. Correct the seasoning and acidity (with lemon juice).

TO SERVE

Place a pancake in the middle of each plate and spoon the sauce around the pancake.

Take a good slice of the gravadlax and coil it onto the pancake so it stands up a bit.

Garnish with some dill or chives or even a dollop of caviar and serve.

SALMON MOUSSELINE STUFFED WITH MUSSELS

EQUIPMENT

6 x 150ml aluminium pudding basins

INGREDIENTS (SERVES 6)
FOR THE MOUSSELINE

225g fresh skinless salmon fillet

Salt and ground black pepper

Nutmeg

2 egg whites

300ml double cream

FOR THE FILLING

1 kilo live mussels

100ml white wine

1 small onion

25g butter

1 teaspoon plain flour

1 tablespoon double cream

Ground black pepper

METHOD
FOR THE MOUSE

1. To make the mousseline, place the salmon fillet in the food processor and process until it becomes a paste.
2. Add the seasoning and the egg whites and process again to a smooth purée.
3. Finally add the double cream and process until mixed and firm (do not over process at this stage as the cream may separate).
4. Remove from the food processor and refrigerate to become firmer.

FOR THE FILLING

5. Wash the mussels discarding any damaged or open ones. Place them in a large saucepan and put in the white wine.
6. Cover with a lid, place the pan over a high heat and allow the mussels to steam open, shaking the pan from time to time.
7. When they are all fully open tip the mussels into a colander with a bowl underneath. Once the liquid has drained into the bowl, allow it to settle then pour it carefully into another receptacle taking care to leave behind any debris at the bottom.
8. Now remove the mussels from the shells and steep them in this liquor. Also remove any beards that are still attached.
9. Chop the onion very finely and fry it gently in the butter until it is soft.
10. Sprinkle in the flour and let it sizzle in the butter before adding enough of the mussel stock to make a light sauce.
11. Add the cream and then add a little black pepper (it should not need any salt).

12. Drain the mussels and add them to the sauce. (Keep a little of the sauce back to decorate the plate).
13. Put the salmon mousse into a piping bag with a plain 8mm nozzle. Line the pudding basins with the mousse piping in a coil fashion right up to the rim.
14. Fill the centres with the mussel mixture and then seal the top with more mousse.
15. Stand the mousses in a shallow pan with 2cm of water in it. Cover the pan with a lid and steam the mousses gently for 10-15 minutes until the top is firm.
16. To serve gently unmould the mousses onto plates, (you may have to run a knife very carefully around the outside).
17. Drizzle a little of the saved sauce around the mousses.

CRAB & BRIOCHE SANDWICH

INGREDIENTS (SERVES 4)

A small clove of garlic

A few sprigs of parsley

150g fresh crab meat
(see page 78 on how to prepare a crab unless you are buying it ready prepared).

Salt and ground black pepper, nutmeg and Cajun spice

50g cream cheese

8 thin slices brioche loaf

METHOD

1. Heat the oven to 220°C/gas mark 7.
2. Crush the garlic and chop the parsley.
3. Combine with the fresh crab meat, seasoning and cream cheese.
4. Make four sandwiches with the brioche and cut each sandwich into 4 triangles.
5. Place them on an oven tray spaced slightly apart.
6. Bake in the oven for 10 minutes or until they are browning well and piping-hot.
7. Serve immediately.

GRILLED MUSSELS WITH GARLIC & HERB BUTTER

Do not attempt to serve mussels this way unless they are a decent size and that the mussels inside the shells are a good size also.

EQUIPMENT

4 heat proof platters

INGREDIENTS (SERVES 4)

2 kilos fresh mussels

2 tablespoons white wine

2 tablespoons of fresh herbs: parsley, basil, tarragon

2 cloves of garlic

Ground black pepper

110g butter

50g fresh white bread crumbs

METHOD

1. Make sure all your mussels are tightly shut and unbroken. Wash them well and remove any beards and barnacles.
2. Place them in a large pan with the white wine. Cover with a lid and place over a high heat. Shake the pan a couple of times as they steam open. Drain through a colander into a bowl to reserve the stock.
3. Remove the mussels from the shells and steep them in the stock to prevent them from drying out.
4. Keep back 80 of the nicest looking half shells and discard the rest.
5. Chop the herbs and crush the garlic. Knead them into the butter with the pepper. If you are using unsalted butter put in a little salt.
6. Have ready 4 heat-proof platters and put your grill on to heat up.
7. Arrange 20 shells per person onto each platter.
8. Drain the mussels again but keep the stock for another fish dish (it is too good to waste - freeze it if you have to).
9. Place a mussel into each half shell, or 2 if there is room and you have enough mussels.
10. Dot the mussels with the butter and scatter with the bread crumbs.
11. Grill until the whole platter is sizzling and the bread crumbs have browned. Serve immediately.

CRAB MOUSSE WITH APPLE, CREAM & CURRY SAUCE

EQUIPMENT

6 x 150ml aluminium pudding basins

INGREDIENTS (SERVES 6)

110g raw prawn meat

110g raw salmon fillet

Salt and ground black pepper

Nutmeg

2 egg whites

300ml double cream

225g fresh crab meat
(see page 78 on how to prepare a crab unless you are buying it ready prepared).

FOR THE SAUCE

1 Cox's apple

110ml fish stock

1 teaspoon mild curry powder

½ teaspoon Dijon mustard

150ml double cream

25g butter

Lemon juice

METHOD

1. Place the prawn meat and salmon in the food processor with the seasoning and purée briefly.
2. Add the egg whites and process again until smooth.
3. Add the cream and process until the cream thickens (do not take it too far as the cream will separate).
4. Remove from the processor and fold in the crab meat. Spoon into individual basins and stand in a pan of simmering water about 2cm deep and cover with tin foil. Steam until just set.

FOR THE SAUCE

5. Peel, quarter and core the apple.
6. Cut it into neat dice and fry gently in the butter.
7. Add the curry powder and allow it to cook a little in the butter.
8. Add the fish stock and reduce by half.
9. Stir in the mustard followed by the cream. Cook until it thickens.
10. Add a little lemon juice.
11. Turn the crab mousses out onto warm plates and serve the sauce around.

DEVILLED SQUID & MUSSEL STEW

INGREDIENTS (SERVES 6-8)

450g fresh squid

1kg live mussels

90ml white wine

1 onion

1 red pepper

110g button mushrooms

110g celery

2 cloves garlic

400g can tomatoes

2 tablespoons olive oil

1 teaspoon Aromatic Spice Mix (see page 411)

Several sprigs each of tarragon, marjoram and parsley

Salt

1 teaspoon flour

150ml single cream

Tabasco sauce

Up to 600ml mussel stock (the amount of liquid in the mussels will vary so don't worry if it is a bit less than this).

Croutons (see page 25)

METHOD

1. Clean the squid removing all the innards and the head. Cut the tentacles into 5cm lengths and the body into rings. Set aside.
2. Clean the mussels, discarding any open or damaged ones and steam in the white wine until all are open and cooked. Drain them reserving the liquid.
3. Take the mussels out of the shells and put them into the liquid to keep moist.
4. Chop the onion, red pepper, mushrooms and celery quite small and crush the garlic.
5. Chop the tinned tomatoes. Chop the herbs.
6. Heat a pan large enough to take all the ingredients and put in the oil.
7. Fry all the vegetables with the garlic until they begin to turn opaque.
8. Put in the squid and continue to cook. At this point, add the spices, herbs and a little salt.
9. Sprinkle over the flour and stir until it disperses then put in the tomatoes and 300ml of the mussel stock. Simmer gently for 10 minutes.
10. Now add the mussels, any remaining liquid and the cream.
11. Use your judgement to assess whether there is enough liquid if not add a little water, wine or fish stock if you have it.
12. Bring back to the boil and taste. Add salt if it is required and as much Tabasco as suits your taste. Serve in deep bowls with croutons or crusty bread.

PRAWN & CRAB ROULADE

EQUIPMENT

24 x 34cm (1cm deep) aluminium baking tray

Baking parchment.

INGREDIENTS (SERVES 8)

175g cooked spinach

Salt and ground black pepper

Nutmeg

3 eggs

FOR THE FILLING

150g peeled prawns – drained well

110g fresh crab meat
(see page 78 on how to prepare a crab unless you are buying it ready prepared).

A small bunch of parsley

½ long red pepper

1 stick of celery

110g mayonnaise

110g smoked salmon slices

METHOD
FOR THE ROULADE

1. Heat the oven to 200°C/gas mark 6.
2. Oil the tray lightly, line it with baking parchment then turn it over so it is oiled both sides.
3. Make sure the spinach is quite dry and grease free. Place it in the bowl of a food processor and season it with the salt, pepper and nutmeg.
4. Separate the eggs and put the yolks in with the spinach. Switch the food processor on and process to a purée.
5. Whisk the egg whites to a stiff foam.
6. Lightly fold the spinach mix into the egg white then tip it out onto the tray.
7. Spread it evenly over the tray and then bake it for 8 minutes in the oven. Allow to cool.

FOR THE FILLING

8. Place the crab and prawns into a bowl.
9. Finely chop the pepper, celery and parsley and add them to the bowl with the crab and prawns.
10. Use just enough mayonnaise to bind everything together.
11. Turn the roulade base out onto a piece of clean parchment paper and carefully peel away the paper it was baked on.
12. Spread a thin layer of mayonnaise onto the base and then arrange a layer of smoked salmon on top of it.
13. Spoon the filling onto the salmon and spread it out to reach the sides but leaving a gap top and bottom.
14. Roll up the roulade like a Swiss roll using the paper to facilitate the process. Serve in thick slices.

CANAPÉS – A SELECTION OF THINGS YOU CAN SERVE AS CANAPÉS OR APPETIZERS

A lot of the recipes in the starter section can be used to make canapés. Some may need adapting by making them smaller, such as sushi, crab spring roll, prawn toasts, Thai fish cakes and salt-cod croquettes.

PRAWN COCKTAIL PROFITEROLES

INGREDIENTS (MAKES 18)
FOR THE CHOUX PASTRY

125ml water

125ml milk

100g butter

150g plain flour

3 eggs

FOR THE FILLING

110g peeled prawns - de-frosted and drained

50g ricotta cheese

1 tablespoon chopped chives

Ground black pepper

FOR THE TOPPING

2 heaped tablespoons mayonnaise

1 teaspoon tomato ketchup

Cream

METHOD

1. Oven temp: 220°C/gas mark 7.
2. Bring the water, milk and butter to the boil then beat in the flour in one go and keep over the heat for 2 minutes until the mixture ceases to be sticky.
3. Cool slightly and beat in the eggs a bit at a time.
4. Pipe out small amounts about the size of your first finger joint onto a baking sheet.
5. Bake for 20 minutes or until puffed-up and evenly golden brown.
6. Pierce the base with the point of a knife to allow the steam to escape. Put back in the oven to dry out for a few minutes. Allow to cool.
7. Mix together the prawns, ricotta and chives and season with the black pepper.
8. Split the profiteroles and stuff with the prawn mixture.
9. Flavour the mayonnaise with the ketchup and create a smooth consistency with the cream.
10. Spoon a little of the sauce onto each profiterole.

HERB PANCAKES STUFFED WITH SMOKED SALMON & CREAM CHEESE

INGREDIENTS (MAKES 24)

50g plain flour

1 egg

150-200ml milk

Olive oil for the pancakes

Several sprigs of some or all the following herbs - parsley, dill, tarragon and chives

200g good quality smoked salmon

200g cream cheese

Ground black pepper

METHOD

1. Beat the egg into the flour with a little of the milk to form a smooth batter.
2. Dilute to the consistency of single cream with the milk. (You are aiming for thin 'crepe' so the thinner the batter the thinner the pancake).
3. Chop the herbs and add them along with the seasoning.
4. Whisk a little oil into the batter and then make four pancakes in the normal way.
5. Lay the pancakes out and spread with a thin layer of the cream cheese.
6. Lay slices of smoked salmon over this and then spread a very scant layer of cream cheese onto the smoked salmon.
7. Scatter with some black pepper and roll them up tightly. Trim off the ends and store ready for slicing. Chill well.
8. To serve cut into pieces about 2cm thick and serve with the cross-section uppermost.

A GRAVADLAX ALTERNATIVE

Use gravadlax in place of smoked salmon. Make a strong mustard and dill mayonnaise by mixing chopped dill, grain and Dijon mustard into ready-made mayonnaise and use in place of the cream cheese.

A SWEET PEPPER & GOAT'S CHEESE ALTERNATIVE

You can also make a red pepper and goat's cheese vegetarian version using the long Romano peppers. Split them down the middle and grill under a hot grill until the skin blisters. Peel off the skin and allow them to cool. Pat them dry with kitchen paper, season well and use in place of smoked salmon. Use a creamy goat's cheese in place of the cream cheese.

FISH MAIN COURSES

FISH BANANAS

INGREDIENTS (SERVES 2)

2 fillets of fish weighing about 150g each (you can do this with any meaty fish such as halibut or salmon).

Olive oil

2 bananas

2 medium tomatoes

Juice of half a lemon

2 teaspoons of mango chutney – chopped (you can also use Sweet Chilli Sauce)

Salt and ground black pepper

50g butter

METHOD

1. Heat the oven to 150°C/gas mark 2.
2. Fry the pieces of fish in the oil to give them a bit of colour and then transfer them to an oven-proof dish. It doesn't matter if the fish is not fully cooked.
3. Peel the bananas, split them lengthways and fry these also to a golden colour.
4. Carefully lay two lengths of banana on each piece of fish.
5. Skin and de-seed the tomato. Place the pips in a sieve and squeeze the juice from them. Chop the flesh of the tomato and place it in a pan with the tomato juice, lemon and chutney.
6. Season with the salt and pepper.
7. Heat the mixture and when it starts to bubble put in the butter a little at a time swirling the pan around to incorporate it.
8. Spoon this sauce over the fish and bananas.
9. Place it in the oven for 10-15 minutes to finish cooking the fish and to allow the flavours to mingle.
10. Serve immediately.

TANDOORI BAKED MULLET WITH MINT RELISH

Use grey mullet for this dish – it is similar to sea bass and half the price - or use any other firm white fish. You can also use the marinade for making tandoori monk fish kebabs - great for barbecuing.

INGREDIENTS (SERVES 2)

2 x 175g pieces of mullet fillet – skinned

FOR THE MARINADE

2 cloves of garlic

2cm cube of ginger

1 heaped tablespoon thick yoghurt

½ teaspoon of chilli powder – or more or less according to taste

1 teaspoon ground cumin

1 teaspoon chick pea flour (gram flour)

½ a bunch of fresh coriander – chopped

½ a tablespoon of sunflower oil

Salt and ground black pepper

Wedges of lemon

FOR THE MINT RELISH

Large bunch of fresh mint

1 teaspoon Dijon mustard

1 green chilli

Juice of a lemon

50ml sunflower oil

METHOD

1. Grate or crush the garlic and ginger then mix with the rest of the marinade ingredients.
2. Steep the fish in the marinade for 30-40 minutes.
3. To cook the fish, heat the oven 220°C/gas mark 7.
4. Lift the fish out of the marinade but leave any mix that sticks to the fish. Place on a tray and bake for 20 minutes.
5. You can also grill the fish under a hot grill. Serve on flat bread or with rice.

FOR THE MINT RELISH

1. Place all the ingredients except the oil in a blender and whizz until smooth.
2. Keep whizzing whilst adding the oil in a thin stream.
3. Refrigerate and use within 2 days.

BARBECUE ALTERNATIVE

For the monk-fish kebabs, soak some wooden skewers in water, cut the monk fish into chunks and marinate for 30-40 minutes. Thread them onto the skewers and grill under a very hot grill or cook on the barbecue.

BAKED BREAM 'EN PAPILLOTE'

A foolproof way of cooking fish with no smelly pan to wash up afterwards! This is just one fish and one set of flavourings. You can use this method for other fish and different ingredients.

EQUIPMENT

2 sheets of tin foil 30x40cm

INGREDIENTS (SERVES 2)

2 sea bream – head and guts removed, de-scaled and spines trimmed

1 small red onion

½ a long red pepper

2 cloves garlic

8 cherry tomatoes

A small bunch of basil

Olive oil

12 Kalamata olives

1 tablespoon capers

Salt and ground black pepper

2 slices of lemon

White wine or vermouth

METHOD

1. Heat the oven to 200°C/gas mark 6.
2. Peel and thinly slice the onion, slice the pepper, crush the garlic and tear up the basil. Halve the tomatoes. Place them all in a bowl with the olives and capers.
3. Drizzle it all with a little olive oil and season.
4. Rub a little oil on the centre of each piece of foil.
5. Divide the mixture placing it on the lower half of the sheets of foil.
6. Place a fish on each pile, place a lemon slice on top and then arrange the rest of the ingredients on and around the fish.
7. Splash a little white wine or vermouth over each fish.
8. Fold the other half of the foil over the fish to encase it. Crimp the foil round in a semi-circle, like you were making a turnover, taking care not to pierce the foil and try to get an air-tight seal.
9. Place the parcels on a tray and bake in the oven. It will take about 15-20 minutes but you can tell the exact moment it is cooked as the bag will 'balloon' if you have a tight seal.
10. To serve, snip the foil just above the crimped semi-circle and fold it back.

RED THAI PRAWN CURRY WITH PAPAYA SALAD

INGREDIENTS (SERVES 4)
FOR THE PASTE

2 lemon grass stalks

1 red chilli

2 cloves garlic

2cm cube of root ginger

4 kaffir lime leaves

2 red peppers from a tin or a jar

1 teaspoon sun-dried tomato purée

1 teaspoon fish sauce (Nam Pla)

1 tablespoon soy sauce

Juice and zest of a lime

1 teaspoon smoked paprika

1 teaspoon ground cumin

1 teaspoon ground coriander

TO FINISH

150g sugar snap peas

400g can of full-fat coconut milk

450g large raw peeled king prawns

FOR THE PAPAYA SALAD

1 ripe papaya

Assorted baby green leaves

4 spring onions

1-2 red chillies

Juice of a lime

1 teaspoon soft brown sugar

1 teaspoon Thai fish sauce

1 tablespoon sunflower oil

METHOD

1. Finely chop the lemon grass, red chilli, garlic, ginger, lime leaves and peppers.
2. Place all the ingredients for the paste in a food processor and process until it forms a paste. Take care with the soy and fish sauce as they are both quite salty.
3. Cut the sugar snap peas into diagonal slices.
4. Place the curry paste into a shallow pan and stir whilst it heats through. Cook for 5 minutes.
5. Put in the coconut milk and simmer until the sauce thickens.
6. Add the prawns and sugar snap peas and cook until the prawns are done.
7. Serve immediately with fragrant rice (see page 109) and papaya salad.

FOR THE PAPAYA SALAD

1. Peel the papaya, halve it and scoop out the seeds.
2. Cut it into slices along the length (top to tail) and lay them on a bed of the green leaves.
3. Slice the spring onions and chillies and scatter them over the papaya.
4. Mix together the lime juice, sugar, fish sauce and oil and spoon over the salad.

THAI SEAFOOD CURRY

INGREDIENTS (SERVES 2)

1 small monk fish tail (about 110g)

4–8 scallops depending on size

8 raw tiger prawns

You can use any fish that is available but try to use firm fleshed fish and ones that will give you a variety of textures.

16 sugar snap (or snow) peas

4 spring onions

250ml full fat coconut milk

Salt

½ tablespoon vegetable or sesame oil

Fragrant rice (see page 109)

FOR THE GREEN THAI CURRY PASTE (THIS WILL MAKE MORE THAN YOU NEED BUT CAN BE FROZEN)

2 green chillies

1cm cube of root ginger

2 cloves of garlic

2 bulbs of lemon grass

1 bunch of coriander

1 lime

1 teaspoon ground cumin

1 tablespoon Nam Pla (Thai fish sauce)

METHOD

1. De-seed the chillies. Peel and chop the garlic and ginger.
2. Remove the tough outer leaves of the lemon grass and chop it finely.
3. Peel a couple of strips of the lime zest. Place all these ingredients for the paste together with the juice of the lime into a food processor and grind to a purée.
4. Cut the monk fish and scallops, if they are large, into pieces.
5. Peel the prawns and remove the intestine.
6. Cut the sugar snap peas into strips and finely chop the spring onions.
7. Heat a non-stick pan and put in the oil.
8. Fry the fish until just cooked and remove from the pan onto a plate.
9. Put the coconut milk into the pan and add 2 teaspoons of the curry paste (or more if you prefer).
10. Season with the salt, bring to the boil and reduce until it thickens.
11. Put in the peas and onions and continue cooking for a further minute before putting the fish back.
12. Serve in deep bowls with fragrant rice.

SEARED SALMON WITH COUSCOUS, LIME & CORIANDER

INGREDIENTS (SERVES 2)

2 boneless slices of salmon (cut at an angle from the fillet) weighing about 110g

1 small onion

1 clove of garlic

½ a small red pepper

1 lime

A small bunch of coriander

Salt and ground black pepper

1 lemon

2 tablespoons olive oil plus extra for frying

110g couscous

110ml boiling water

METHOD

1. Chop the onion and red pepper very finely. Crush the garlic.
2. Sweat the onion, pepper and garlic in half a tablespoon of olive oil until soft then transfer to a bowl.
3. Season well and put in the couscous.
4. Add the boiling water, stir and add the juice of the lemon and the rest of the olive oil.
5. Allow the couscous to stand and absorb the liquids, turning it regularly with a fork to separate the grains.
6. Cut the lime into 4 wedges. Chop the coriander.
7. Season the salmon steaks with the salt and pepper.
8. Heat a heavy-based frying pan and put in it a little olive oil.
9. Sear the salmon steaks on both sides and continue cooking until they are just done (or a little underdone if you like them that way).
10. Stir half the chopped coriander into the couscous and place a mound on each plate. Place a piece of salmon on each plate, on top of the couscous, squeeze a wedge of lime over each portion.
11. Scatter the other half of the coriander over the salmon and place a wedge of lime on the side.

SMOKED HADDOCK PASTIES

INGREDIENTS (MAKES 6)

300g smoked haddock
(un-dyed, skinned)

200ml milk

15g butter

15g plain flour

350g cooked potato

110g peeled prawns

50g grated cheddar

Ground black pepper

A small bunch of parsley

375g ready-made puff pastry

Egg wash (see page 426)

METHOD

1. Heat the oven to 190°C/gas mark 5.
2. Poach the haddock gently in the milk until it is cooked. Reserve the milk.
3. Melt the butter in a pan and add the flour. Wait until it is sizzling then add enough of the milk to create a thick sauce (this will take just over half the quantity you have).
4. Add the grated cheese and black pepper.
5. Chop the parsley and cut the potato into cubes.
6. Flake the haddock and place it in a bowl with the potato, the drained prawns and the parsley.
7. Add a few turns of the pepper grinder and fold in enough sauce to bind the mixture together.
8. Allow to cool.
9. Cut the pastry into 6 equal-sized pieces and roll each one out to be roughly circular.
10. Place a spoonful of mixture onto each piece, wet the edges of the pastry and fold over to create a semi-circle.
11. Crimp the join to seal it well then turn the parcel upright so the join is on the top (pasty style).
12. Brush with egg wash and bake in the oven for 15-20 minutes until golden brown.

KEDGEREE WITH A LIGHT CURRY SAUCE

INGREDIENTS (SERVES 2 AS A MAIN COURSE OR 4 AS A STARTER)

350g un-dyed smoked haddock

2 bay leaves

2 eggs

1 small onion

½ a red pepper

1 tablespoon sunflower oil

150g Basmati or long grain rice

50g sultanas

175g de-frosted, drained prawns

1 tablespoon chopped parsley

Ground black pepper

FOR THE CURRY SAUCE

25g butter

20g plain flour

2 teaspoons curry powder

300ml haddock stock or water

Squeeze of lemon juice

2 teaspoons mango chutney

2 tablespoons double cream

METHOD

1. De-skin the haddock, place it in a shallow pan with the bay leaves and cover with water.
2. Simmer until the haddock is just cooked and then drain it reserving the stock and discarding the bay leaves.
3. Hard boil the eggs.
4. Cut the onion and pepper into small dice and fry in the oil without colouring.
5. Put in the rice, then measure out 300ml of the fish stock and add this to the pan with the sultanas. Bring to the boil and simmer gently until all the water is absorbed.
6. Remove from the heat and cover with a lid.
7. After about 10 minutes, fluff up the rice with a fork and transfer it to a bowl.
8. Flake the haddock and combine it along with the prawns, parsley and pepper with the rice.
9. The eggs can either be quartered and served as a garnish or chopped and stirred into the mixture.
10. The kedgeree can be microwaved to serve hot but beware of the egg as the hard-boiled white can explode if it gets too hot.

FOR THE CURRY SAUCE

1. Melt the butter and stir in the flour and the curry powder.
2. Let it sizzle for a bit, then add the stock or water to create the sauce.
3. Add the lemon and the chutney and finally the cream.
4. Serve the sauce separately.

SALMON IN PASTRY WITH PESTO

EQUIPMENT

Pastry lattice cutter

INGREDIENTS (SERVES 2)

225g fresh skinless salmon fillet

1 bunch basil (20g)

1 small clove of garlic

1 tablespoon freshly grated

Parmesan

Ground black pepper

1 tablespoon pine kernels
(or ground almonds)

110g puff pastry

Fresh tomato sauce (see page 242)

Egg wash (see page 426)

METHOD

1. Set oven at 220°C/gas mark 7.
2. Place the basil, garlic, Parmesan, pepper and nuts into the food processor and grind to a paste.
3. Cut the salmon into 4 strips and sandwich together each pair with the pesto.
4. Cut the pastry into 2 pieces and roll out each piece to about 10x15cm.
5. Cut through each piece, longways, with the lattice cutter.
6. Roll a piece of pastry around each salmon parcel and seal by moistening the edge.
7. Place seal side down onto a lightly oiled baking sheet.
8. Brush with egg wash and bake for 15-20 minutes until the pastry is golden brown.
9. Serve with the fresh tomato sauce.

SKATE WITH CAPER BERRIES & PEPPERS

INGREDIENTS (SERVES 2)

2 x 175g wings of skate

Olive oil

Plain flour for coating

Salt and ground black pepper

1 long red pepper

20 caper berries

50g butter

Juice of one lemon

A small bunch of parsley

METHOD

1. Use a frying pan or pans large enough to take the skate and heat with a little olive oil. Dust the fish with the flour, pat off the excess and place in the pan.
2. Wait until the first side is cooked to a light gold colour then turn. (Skate being rather fragile it is a good idea not to handle it too much so try to turn it only once.)
3. The pan can be placed under the grill to help cook it from both sides. The time the skate takes to cook will depend on the thickness of the pieces. Season the skate on one side just before turning and the other side when turned.
4. While the fish is cooking, heat a separate pan for cooking the garnish.
5. De-seed and cut the pepper into rings and cut the caper berries in half.
6. Fry the peppers gently in olive oil until almost soft then put in the butter.
7. When the butter is sizzling put in the caper berries and the lemon juice.
8. Chop the parsley.
9. Place the cooked skate onto warmed plates, add the chopped parsley to the garnish and spoon it over the fish.

DRESSED CRAB

Crab is easy to prepare once you know which bits to remove and, contrary to popular belief, there are no poisonous bits in it. Crabs are usually sold by a fishmonger ready cooked. Buy one that is heavy for its size. Remove the claws and the legs by twisting them off. Then separate the part the legs were attached to from the main body of the crab.

You can now get at the bits we want to remove. The lungs or 'dead men's fingers' as they are sometimes known look like grey feathers and are attached to the bit you have just removed and some are left in the other bit; discard all of these. Next, remove any membrane that looks a bit like cling film.

You will find the mouth in the flat shell part near where the eyes are at the front. Press on this with your thumb until you hear it crack then pick it up and remove it including the small stomach sac that is attached just behind it. Discard this. Now the rest, apart from the shell, is all edible – promise.

Scoop the brown meat out of the main shell and place it in a bowl. There is also a small amount of brown meat in a groove of the other bit you removed.

Crack the claws to remove the white meat and place this in another bowl. There is also some white meat in the first section of the legs and in the part the legs were attached to.

The bigger the crab the more return you will get from the fiddly awkward bits – in a small crab the return from these bits may not be worthwhile – it depends on how much time you've got or how hungry you are!

The meat from a hand-picked crab is far superior to commercially, machine-retrieved crab meat – a reward for your hard work. Crab is wonderfully versatile. The flavour is superb and you get two types of meat.

TO CONTINUE

A cooked crab of 500-650g will make a dressed crab of 1 portion.

1 hard-boiled egg per crab

PLUS

Salt and ground black pepper

1 tablespoon mayonnaise

1 tablespoon chopped parsley

Paprika

METHOD

1. Season the white meat with salt and pepper.
2. Bind the brown meat with a little mayonnaise.
3. Clean the shell well and break off the side pieces where you can see a natural line in the shell.
4. Place the prepared meat into the back shell by putting the brown meat on the sides and the white meat down the middle.
5. Separate the egg white from the yolk and finely chop both or push through a sieve. Decorate the top with the egg, parsley and paprika. For a really spectacular look you can make stripes of red, white, yellow and green.
6. Serve with hot new potatoes and salad.

HOT DRESSED CRAB 'AU GRATIN'

INGREDIENTS (SERVES 1)

1 crab (500-650g) prepared as on page 78 but not 'dressed'

1–2 tablespoons of cream sauce (see page 426)

½ teaspoon English mustard

Salt and ground black pepper

25g strong Cheddar cheese – grated

12g Parmesan cheese – grated

METHOD

1. Heat the oven to 200°C/gas mark 6.
2. Mix both the brown and white meat with the cream sauce, mustard, salt and pepper.
3. Place the meat back into the shell (sides removed as above) and sprinkle over the Cheddar cheese followed by the Parmesan.
4. Bake in the oven until piping hot – 10–15 minutes. Finish under a hot grill if the cheese is not browned enough.

CRAB CAKES WITH SWEETCORN RELISH

INGREDIENTS (SERVES 8 FOR A STARTER OR 4 FOR A MAIN COURSE)

225g peeled King Edward potatoes

4 spring onions

225g prepared brown and white crab meat (see page 78)

1 egg yolk

Salt and ground black pepper

Pinch Cayenne pepper

Squeeze of lemon juice

½ teaspoon English mustard

1 tablespoon chopped parsley

Olive oil for frying

FOR THE SWEET CORN RELISH

1 teaspoon Dijon mustard

Juice of 1 lime

1 tablespoon sweet-chilli sauce

2 tablespoons sunflower oil

1 small red onion

1 stick of celery

½ a long red pepper

1 tomato

2cm cube of root ginger

1 small bunch of coriander

195g can of sweetcorn

TO SERVE

Salad leaves or samphire

METHOD

1. Boil the potatoes in seasoned water until cooked, drain them and put them back in the dry saucepan. Leave for 10 minutes to dry out well.
2. Slice the spring onions very fine. Mash the potatoes with the back of a fork leaving them a little bit chunky.
3. Combine all the ingredients and mix well. Check the seasoning.
4. Shape into 8 cakes and fry in the olive oil on both sides until golden.

FOR THE SWEET CORN RELISH

1. Place the mustard, lime juice and sweet chilli in a bowl and stir with a whisk to amalgamate them.
2. Add the oil in a thin stream.
3. Finely chop the onion, celery and pepper. Peel and chop the tomato.
4. Finely chop the coriander.
5. Combine all the ingredients with the dressing and stir well.
6. Serve the crab cakes on plates garnished with some salad leaves or samphire and spoon the relish next to them.

POSH FISH CAKES WITH DILL SAUCE

INGREDIENTS (MAKES 6-8 FISH CAKES)

NB: All fish (apart from the prawns) should be uncooked, boneless and skinless

110g salmon

110g white fish (either cod, haddock, coley or gurnard)

110g smoked haddock (un-dyed)

450g potatoes – King Edwards, Reds or Maris Piper but King Eds preferably

50g cooked peeled prawns

25g butter

A small bunch of parsley

Squeeze of lemon juice

Salt and ground black pepper

Nutmeg

FOR THE DILL SAUCE

25g butter

20g flour

300ml pint fish stock or water

½ teaspoon Dijon mustard

1 teaspoon grain mustard

2 tablespoons double cream

Squeeze of lemon juice

Salt and ground black pepper

Small bunch of fresh dill

METHOD

1. Peel the potatoes and cut it into chunks. Boil in salted water until cooked.
2. Drain the potatoes well then mash them.
3. Poach the raw fish in seasoned water.
4. Drain the fish reserving the liquid (for the dill sauce).
5. Flake the fish into a bowl.
6. Add the potato, prawns, butter and lemon and mix lightly with a fork.
7. Chop the parsley and add it to the mix.
8. Add pepper and nutmeg and check the seasoning. If the mixture is a little dry add some of the reserved cooking liquor.
9. Form the mixture into 6-8 flat cakes.
10. Shallow fry them in oil until golden on both sides.
11. They can also be dipped in egg and breadcrumbs prior to frying.

FOR THE DILL SAUCE

1. Melt the butter and stir in the flour.
2. Let it sizzle for a bit before adding the stock or water to make the sauce.
3. When it comes to the boil, whisk in the mustard, cream and lemon juice and seasoning.
4. Finally add the chopped dill.

SALMON MOUSSELINE STUFFED WITH LOBSTER

EQUIPMENT

2 x 150ml aluminium pudding basins

INGREDIENTS (SERVES 2)
FOR THE MOUSSELINE

110g fresh salmon fillet – without skin

Salt and ground black pepper

Nutmeg

1 egg white

150ml double cream

FOR THE FILLING

1 x 500g live hen lobster

FOR THE FISH STOCK

1 onion

½ bulb fennel

Parsley stalks

1 small ripe tomato

1 glass white wine

FOR THE SAUCE

200ml of the stock

1 tablespoon double cream

12g butter

10g plain flour

Salt and ground black pepper and a sliver of garlic

The coral from the lobster – if any

METHOD

1. To make the mousseline, place the salmon fillet in the food processor and process until it becomes a paste.
2. Add the seasoning and the egg white and process again to a smooth purée.
3. Finally add the double cream and process until mixed and firm (do not over process at this stage as the cream may separate).
4. Remove from the food processor and refrigerate for the mixture to become firmer.
5. Put the lobster into boiling water (the water should be seasoned to the same density as sea water: 65g salt to 3lt water) and simmer for 15-20 minutes. Remove from the water and allow to cool.
6. Split the lobster in half and remove the meat reserving any coral.
7. To make the stock, chop the onion and fennel and fry in a splash of oil until translucent.
8. Crush the lobster shell and add to the pan along with the tomato, parsley stalks and wine.
9. Cover with water, bring to the boil and simmer for 20 minutes. Strain the stock.
10. To make the sauce, melt the butter then stir in the flour. When it is sizzling add the fish stock (200ml) stirring all the time.
11. Bring to the boil and add the cream. Bring to the boil again and season.
12. Crush the coral to a purée with the garlic and add it to the sauce.

13. Cut the lobster into chunks about the size of your first little finger joint and bind with the sauce, keeping a little of the sauce back for serving with the dish.
14. Put the salmon mousseline into a piping bag with a plain 8mm nozzle.
15. Line the pudding basins with the mousse piping it in a coil fashion right up to the rim. Fill the centres with the lobster mixture and then seal the top with more mousse.
16. Stand the mousses in a shallow pan with 2cm of water in it. Cover the pan with a lid and steam for 10-15 minutes until the top is firm.
17. To serve, gently unmould the mousses onto plates. (You may have to run a knife very carefully around the outside.)
18. Place your reserved sauce into a pan and loosen it with a little cream. Bring to the boil and swirl in a little butter. Serve the sauce drizzled around the mousse on the plate.

SQUID STUFFED WITH RICE PILAF, SQUID INK SAUCE

INGREDIENTS (SERVES 4)

4 medium size fresh squid

10g dried porcini mushrooms

1 small onion

1 clove of garlic

1 small red pepper

½ tablespoon sesame oil

175g Thai fragrant rice

300ml fish stock

A small bunch of parsley

Salt and ground black pepper

½ glass of white wine

METHOD

1. Prepare the squid (see the recipe for Salt and Pepper Squid on page 42).
2. Put the 'tubes' to one side and cut the fins and tentacles into small pieces.
3. Pour boiling water over the porcini mushrooms to reconstitute them.
4. Chop the onion, garlic and pepper very fine. Fry these in the oil until lightly coloured. Add the chopped squid and cook until it turns opaque then put in the rice.
5. Continue cooking to get the rice hot then put in the fish stock with 50ml of the mushroom stock.
6. Chop the mushrooms and add them. Season with salt and pepper.
7. Simmer gently until all the liquid is absorbed. Remove from the heat and place a lid on the saucepan. Leave for 5-10 minutes then fluff up with a fork. Chop the parsley and stir in.
8. Heat the oven to 180°C/gas mark 4.
9. Fill the squid tubes with the pilaf compacting it gently.
10. Secure the ends with cocktail sticks and lay them in a deep tray or casserole.
11. Pour in the white wine and season with salt. Cover with a lid or foil and place in the oven.
12. Cook for 20-30 minutes until the flesh of the squid has turned opaque. Take care as overcooking can result in squid splitting.
13. Allow the squid to rest while you make the sauce.

INGREDIENTS
FOR THE SQUID INK SAUCE

1 ripe tomato

Liquid from cooking the squid

½ glass red wine

1 tablespoon squid ink*

1 teaspoon Dijon mustard

50g butter

A few drops of red-wine vinegar

*If you don't have a friendly fisherman handy to supply you with this commodity it can be obtained in sachets from good fishmongers or online.

METHOD
FOR THE SAUCE

14. Chop the tomato roughly and stew in the red wine and the liquid from cooking the squid. When the tomato is soft, pass it through a sieve and discard the skin and pips.
15. Put the resulting purée into a pan with the ink and mustard. Bring to the boil and add the butter a bit at a time.
16. Check the seasoning and add a little wine vinegar if it needs acidulating.
17. Divide the sauce between 4 warmed plates then cut the squid into thick rings arranging them on the sauce.

PITHIVIER OF LOBSTER

EQUIPMENT

Pastry lattice cutter

INGREDIENTS (SERVES 4)

2x675g live lobsters

300ml fish stock (see below)

25g butter

25g plain flour

50ml double cream

Salt and ground black pepper

A sliver of garlic

1 tomato

1 small leek

500g puff pastry

Egg wash (see page 426)

FOR THE FISH STOCK

1 onion

½ bulb fennel

Parsley stalks

Skin and seeds from the tomato (see method)

1 glass white wine

METHOD

1. Put the lobsters into boiling water (the water should be seasoned to the same density as sea water 65g salt to 3lt water) and simmer for 20-25 minutes. Remove from the water and allow to cool.
2. Split the lobsters in half and remove the meat reserving any coral.
3. Chop the onion and fennel and fry in a splash of oil until translucent.
4. Crush the lobster shells and add to the pan along with the tomato skin and seeds, parsley stalks and wine.
5. Cover with water, bring to the boil and simmer for 20 minutes.
6. Strain the stock.
7. Melt the butter then stir in the flour. When it is sizzling add the fish stock (300ml) stirring all the time.
8. Bring to the boil and add the cream. Bring to the boil again and season.
9. Crush the coral to a purée with the garlic and add it to the sauce.
10. Cut the leek into fine dice and sweat in a little butter. Spread on a plate to cool quickly.
11. Skin and de-seed the tomato and cut the flesh into small dice.
12. Cut the lobster meat into chunks.

13. Place the lobster, leek and tomato into a bowl, then add enough of the sauce to bind the ingredients together.
14. Allow to get completely cold.
15. Heat the oven to 200°C/gas mark 6.
16. Cut the pastry into 8 equal pieces.
17. Take 4 pieces of the pastry and roll into rectangles about 13x10cm.
18. Cut each piece through with the lattice cutter along the 13cm length. Set aside.
19. Take the rest of the pastry and roll out 4 circles about 13cm in diameter.
20. Divide the lobster filling between the 4 pastry circles, spooning it into the centre.
21. Wet the edges of the pastry and cover with the lattice cut pastry, pulling it apart slightly to open up the lattice.
22. Press down the edges to get a good seal and then trim into neat circles.
23. Place on a baking sheet, brush with egg wash and bake for 15 minutes.
24. Serve immediately.

SEARED TUNA STEAK WITH PUY LENTILS & SALSA VERDI

INGREDIENTS (SERVES 2)

2 tuna steaks of about 150g

1 onion

2 cloves of garlic

225g Puy lentils

Salt and ground black pepper

450ml water

1 glass of red wine

2 bay leaves/a sprig of thyme

1 tablespoon tomato purée

½ teaspoon Cajun spice

A little sweet chilli sauce, soy sauce, Thai fish sauce (all optional)

FOR THE SALSA

1 small clove of garlic

30g of flat leaf parsley

30g of fresh basil

1 tablespoon capers (rinsed)

1 teaspoon Dijon mustard

50ml olive oil

TO COMPLETE THE DISH

200g baby leaf spinach

METHOD

1. Chop the onion, crush the garlic and fry in a little oil until they start to brown.
2. Put in the lentils and stir to get them hot, then put in the water, wine, herbs, tomato purée, spice, seasoning and any of the optional ingredients you choose.
3. Simmer until the lentils are soft. Add more liquid if necessary during the cooking but the finished consistency should be just moist as the liquid gets absorbed by the lentils.

FOR THE SALSA

4. Place all the ingredients except the oil into a food processor.
5. Run the machine, stopping occasionally to press the ingredients down from the sides.
6. Finally add the olive oil slowly as the machine runs. Store in a refrigerator.

TO COMPLETE

7. Make sure your lentils are cooked and the salsa is made.
8. Wilt the spinach in a hot pan with a little oil (i.e. cook until it just collapses).
9. Spoon the lentils onto plates making a well in the centre.
10. Place the wilted spinach in this well.
11. Sear the tuna in a hot pan – a minute or so each side (depending on the thickness) – it should be rare.
12. Place a tuna steak onto the spinach and spoon some salsa onto each one.

POACHED SMOKED HADDOCK WITH CREAMED LEEKS

Use 75g of fish for a starter or 150g for a main course. This recipe is for four as a starter.

INGREDIENTS (SERVES 2)

4 x 75g pieces of un-dyed smoked haddock

150ml water

2 teaspoons white wine vinegar

4 crushed white peppercorns

2 bay leaves

400g young leeks

4-5 sprigs of thyme

25g butter

50ml double cream

Salt and ground black pepper

METHOD

1. Remove any small bones from the haddock and place it in a shallow pan with the water, vinegar, peppercorns and bay leaves.
2. Bring to the boil then remove from the heat. The haddock will cook in the residual heat.
3. Trim the ends off the leeks but leave plenty of green, split them down the middle and cut into inch lengths. Wash them well and drain well.
4. Melt the butter in a shallow saucepan then put in the leeks, thyme and a little salt and pepper. Cover with a lid and cook slowly until the leeks are tender.
5. Remove the thyme stalks (the leaves stay in) and purée the leeks in a food processor or liquidizer.
6. Return the purée to the pan and add the cream. Heat through and check the seasoning and consistency.
7. If the purée is too thick add a little liquid from the haddock.
8. Place a pool of the purée in the centre of the warmed plates and carefully place a piece of haddock on top of each one.

SALMON AND SEA BASS IN PASTRY WITH LEEKS, GINGER & VERMOUTH SAUCE

EQUIPMENT

Pastry lattice cutter

INGREDIENTS (SERVES 2)

150g boneless skinless salmon fillet

150g boneless skinless sea bass fillet

1 medium leek

110g ready-made puff pastry

2cm cube root ginger

Salt and ground black pepper

Egg wash (see page 426)

METHOD

1. Cut the salmon into two even sized strips then cut the sea bass into two roughly the same size. Set aside.
2. Finely chop the leek, wash it well and drain.
3. Steam the chopped leek until just soft and spread it out to cool on a plate.
4. Heat the oven to 220°C/gas mark 7.
5. Cut the pastry into 2 and roll out each piece to a rectangle about 15x10cm. Cut each piece through with the lattice cutter along the 15cm length.
6. Lay a piece of salmon across the width of the pastry in the middle.
7. Gently squeeze any excess moisture from the leeks and place a small quantity on top of it.
8. Next cut some very fine strips of ginger (you may not need it all) and arrange them on the leeks.
9. Now place a piece of sea bass on top of the leeks.
10. Wet the ends of the pastry and roll it up. Repeat for the second parcel.
11. Place the parcels on a baking sheet with the join side down.
12. Brush the parcels with egg wash sparingly.
13. Bake for 20 minutes until they are golden brown.

INGREDIENTS
FOR THE VERMOUTH BUTTER SAUCE

150ml weak stock (fish, chicken or vegetable) made from a cube – or fresh if you have it

1 tomato

50ml dry vermouth

1 teaspoon Dijon mustard

100ml double cream

25g unsalted butter

A few chives

Salt and ground black pepper

METHOD
FOR THE SAUCE

1. Peel, quarter and de-seed the tomato. Sieve the juice from the seeds and add to the fish stock.
2. Cut the flesh into small dice. Set aside.
3. Place the stock and vermouth into a shallow pan and reduce by half.
4. Whisk in the mustard, followed by the cream then bring to the boil.
5. Add the butter a little at a time whisking it into the sauce.
6. Check the seasoning.
7. Chop the chives and add these with the chopped tomato flesh and stir into the finished sauce.
8. Spoon onto warm plates then place the fish on top.

SALMON IN PASTRY WITH GINGER, CURRANTS & A BUTTER SAUCE

This is a very old recipe and can be traced back to Tudor times. It became a signature dish of George Perry Smith the famous proprietor of The Hole in the Wall in Bath. It is an acquired taste for some, matching sweet crystallized ginger and currants to salmon.

I re-created it whilst working on the Regency House programme where we made it using a whole salmon for a banquet.

EQUIPMENT

Pastry lattice cutter

INGREDIENTS (SERVES 2)

250g skinless salmon fillet

120g ready-made puff pastry

A small bunch of chervil

2 teaspoons of currants

2 pieces of stem ginger in syrup

Salt and ground black pepper

Nutmeg

Egg wash (see page 426)

FOR THE BUTTER SAUCE

50ml fish stock

50ml white wine

1 tablespoon of the ginger syrup – from the ginger jar

1 teaspoon of Dijon mustard

2 tablespoons of cream

50g butter

A squeeze of lemon juice

METHOD

1. Heat the oven to 220°C/gas mark 7.
2. Cut the salmon into 4 even sized strips.
3. Cut the pastry into 2 and roll out each piece into a rectangle, about 15x10cm.
4. Cut each piece through with the 'lattice cutter' along the 15cm length.
5. Chop the ginger into small pieces.
6. Lay a piece of salmon across the width of each rectangle of pastry and arrange some ginger, currants and sprigs of chervil along it.
7. Season with salt, ground black pepper and nutmeg.
8. Lay the remaining strips of salmon over the top, moisten the furthest edge of the pastry and roll it firmly around the fish parcels.
9. Place them on a lightly oiled baking sheet, with the join underneath.
10. Brush the pastry with the egg wash.
11. Bake the parcels for 20 minutes or until the pastry is a golden brown.
12. Serve immediately with the butter sauce.

FOR THE SAUCE

1. Place the fish stock and wine in a shallow pan over a high heat and reduce by half.
2. Add the ginger syrup and mustard.
3. Bring back to the boil then add in the cream.
4. Whisk in the butter piece by piece to thicken the liquid and add a squeeze of lemon juice.

CHAMP WITH SCALLOPS POACHED IN BUTTER

See page 416 for more information on 'champ' and its relatives.

INGREDIENTS (SERVES 2)

250g mashed potato

Milk

Ground black pepper

A small quantity of chives and parsley

6-8 scallops (depending on size)

50g butter

Juice of ½ a lemon

METHOD

1. Make the mash very creamy with the milk and add some pepper.
2. Chop the chives and parsley and mix them into the mash.
3. Trim the scallops and wipe them. (Avoid washing them as they tend to soak up water.)
4. Divide them up if they are large, i.e. separate the coral from the muscle and if very large cut the muscle in two.
5. The idea of poaching in butter is to cook them without colouring the flesh, so don't get the butter too hot, just let it gently bubble.
   They will only take a couple of minutes – don't overcook them.
6. Place the hot champ in the centre of each plate and make a shallow well in the centre.
7. Squeeze some lemon juice onto the scallops and spoon them with the butter into the well of the champ.

PAN-FRIED GURNARD WITH POTATO WEDGES & BROAD BEAN PURÉE

A healthy alternative to fish and chips with mushy peas.

Gurnard is a spectacularly ugly fish (perhaps it got its name from the art of gurning) which belies how good it is to eat. One large fish will give you two meaty fillets of white, firm-fleshed fish. The low price of this fish is reason enough to give it a try and, perhaps, being a bit more adventurous when buying fish will take the pressure off the less-sustainable varieties.

INGREDIENTS (SERVES 2)

2 fillets of Gurnard weighing about 175g each (skin on)

Olive oil

Salt and ground black pepper

25g butter

1 lemon

FOR THE POTATO WEDGES

These potatoes are very quick to make (especially if you microwave the potato). They are healthy and tasty and save all the palaver of setting up a deep fryer.

2 medium size potatoes King Edwards, Desiree Red or Maris Piper

1 clove garlic

1-2 sprigs rosemary

1-2 tablespoons olive oil

Salt and ground black pepper

METHOD

1. My favourite way of pan-frying fish is to use a heavy-based pan which you get hot first and the grill which you also pre heat.
2. Season the fish fillets. Place the oil in the hot pan to heat up then lower the fillets into the pan skin-side down. Cook for a couple of minutes then drizzle a little oil onto the surface of the fish and place under the grill. (This way the fish cooks from both sides, and you don't have to turn it over.)
3. When the fish is done, and it doesn't take long so don't overcook it, place the pan back over the heat and put in the butter. When the butter has melted and is sizzling squeeze the lemon over it and serve immediately.

FOR THE POTATO WEDGES

1. Cook the potatoes in their skins either by baking or boiling or microwaving.
2. Cut the potato into wedges, crush the garlic, and chop the rosemary.
3. Heat the olive oil in a frying pan large enough to hold all the potatoes.
4. Fry the potatoes with the salt and pepper until golden on all sides.
5. Add the garlic and rosemary and perhaps another glug of olive oil and cook for a further 5 minutes taking care not to burn the garlic.

INGREDIENTS
FOR THE BROAD BEAN PURÉE

Use older larger broad beans so that the skinning process won't be too time consuming.

500g fresh broad beans (weight after removing from the outer pods)

Salt and ground black pepper

25g butter

METHOD
FOR THE BROAD BEAN PURÉE

1. Cook the broad beans in boiling salted water until tender.
2. Drain and refresh under running cold water.
3. Drain and slip the inner bean out of the skin.
4. Purée in a food processor with a little black pepper.
5. To serve - reheat in the microwave and stir in the butter.

GOAN FISH CURRY

INGREDIENTS (SERVES 4)

600g boneless fish (huss, gurnard, grey mullet, squid, swordfish) – try just 1 or a selection

1 clove of garlic

2½cm cube of fresh ginger

1-2 fresh green chillies

Salt

1 tablespoon sunflower or sesame oil

2 teaspoons ground cumin

1 teaspoon ground coriander

½ teaspoon ground turmeric

1 lime

400ml can full-fat coconut milk

METHOD

1. Cut the fish into largish chunks.
2. Peel the garlic and the ginger, split and de-seed the chilli then finely chop them all.
3. Season the fish.
4. Heat a frying pan and sear the fish in a little oil until nicely browned.
5. Remove from the pan and set aside.
6. Place the chopped garlic etc in the pan with the spices and fry them.
7. Add the juice of the lime and the coconut milk.
8. Cook to a thick consistency then return the fish to the pan.
9. Cook until the fish is just done.
10. Serve straight away with a little wilted spinach and some rice (see page 115).

RED MULLET WRAPPED IN PARMA HAM WITH A MUSTARD & CHIVE SAUCE

INGREDIENTS (SERVES 4)

4 fillets of red mullet weighing about 175g or 8 smaller fillets

4 slices of Parma ham

FOR THE SAUCE

2 tomatoes

150ml fish stock

50ml vermouth

1 teaspoon Dijon mustard

1 teaspoon grain mustard

300ml double cream

A bunch of chives

METHOD

1. Leave the skin on the red mullet but make sure they are de-scaled.
2. If you have small fillets and are serving two they can be sandwiched together before wrapping in the ham.
3. Wrap the ham around the fish and place on an oiled tray and brush the parcels lightly with oil.
4. The fish takes only a short time to cook so make the sauce first.
5. Peel and de-seed the tomato and cut the flesh into small dice, set aside.
6. Chop the chives and set aside also.
7. Simmer the skin and seeds of the tomato in the fish stock then sieve it.
8. Put the fish stock back into a clean pan, add the vermouth and reduce by one third.
9. Stir in the two mustards followed by the cream and bring to the boil. Remove from the heat while you prepare the fish. (The sauce will thicken as it stands).
10. Heat the oven to 220°C/gas mark 7.
11. Bake the fish in the oven for about 10-15 minutes depending on their size.
12. Finish the sauce by bringing it back to the heat and finally adding the chopped tomato and the chives.
13. Thin it with a little vermouth if it has become too thick.
14. Spoon the sauce into the centre of warmed plates and place a parcel of fish onto each one.

ROAST HUSS WITH SWEET POTATOES & CORIANDER RELISH

Huss is dogfish which in turn is a type of shark. It used to be popular as a choice in fish and chip shops where it was also called by the quaint euphemism rock salmon. It lost popularity but is slowly coming back. Worth checking out for its price.

INGREDIENTS (SERVES 4)

Allow a 175g chunk of boneless huss per person

600g sweet potatoes

1 clove of garlic

2cm cube of fresh ginger

Salt & ground black pepper

Olive oil

Cajun spices

FOR THE RELISH

75g fresh coriander (leaves and fine stems)

½ a hot green chilli

2 teaspoons ground cumin

Juice of 1-2 limes

Salt and ground black pepper

1 teaspoon Dijon mustard

2-3 tablespoons sesame oil

METHOD

1. Peel and cook the sweet potatoes in boiling salted water.
2. Drain and allow them to steam dry in the hot pan.
3. Finely chop or crush the ginger and garlic and add these to the potatoes with black pepper, a little olive oil and more salt if necessary.
4. Mash with a fork but leave chunky. Keep warm.
5. Heat the oven to 220°C/gas mark 7.
6. Season the pieces of huss with salt and Cajun spices, drizzle with oil and roast in the oven for about 15-20 minutes depending on the thickness of the pieces.
7. For the relish, put all the ingredients into the food processor, except the oil, and process until it produces a smooth purée. It may be necessary to push the ingredients down from the sides periodically. Finally, drizzle in the oil.
8. To serve, make a bed of the sweet potatoes in the middle of warmed plates, top with the fish and drizzle over the relish. It is quite strong so be sparing and serve extra separately. The only accompaniment this needs is a simple salad.

SEARED MONK FISH WITH A FRICASSEÉ OF WILD MUSHROOMS

INGREDIENTS (SERVES 2)

300g boneless monkfish tail

1 tablespoon olive oil

2 slices of Parma ham

1 onion

25g butter

250g mixed wild mushrooms

Salt and ground black pepper

1 tablespoon tarragon vinegar

50ml white vermouth

½ teaspoon Dijon mustard

100ml double cream

4-5 fronds of tarragon

METHOD

1. Heat the oven to 180°C/gas mark 4.
2. Place the slices of Parma ham in a single layer onto an oiled baking tray.
3. Cook until they have buckled and crisped, set aside.
4. Trim any skin and membrane from the fish and cut it into thick medallions. Set aside.
5. Chop the onion very fine and cook gently in the butter without colouring.
6. Chop the wild mushrooms and cook these with the onion. Season with salt and pepper. Remove the mushrooms from the pan, place in the tarragon vinegar and reduce to almost nil. Pour in the vermouth and reduce this also.
7. Stir in the mustard followed by the cream.
8. Check the seasoning, tear up the tarragon and add this then put back the mushrooms.
9. Put to one side while cooking the fish.
10. Get a pan big enough to cook all the pieces of monk fish, get it very hot then put in the oil.
11. Season the fish with salt and pepper and cook briefly on both sides until nicely browned. Put the fish onto a warm plate and keep warm.
12. De glaze the frying pan with a little extra vermouth or white wine.
13. Bring the fricassee back to heat, add the pan juices and any liquid that has come out of the monk fish.
14. Reduce the sauce if it has become too thin and then divide it between two plates. Arrange the fish on top of the fricassee and crumble the Parma ham over the top.

SEARED SCALLOPS WITH PEA PURÉE, CHORIZO & CAPERS

INGREDIENTS (SERVES 2)

350g scallops (without shell)

150g fresh or frozen peas

50g Chorizo sausage in the piece

Salt and ground black pepper

1 tablespoon capers (well rinsed)

2 tablespoons fish stock

Squeeze of lemon juice

1 tablespoon chopped parsley

50g butter

METHOD

1. Cook the peas in boiling salted water, drain, purée in a food processor and keep warm.
2. Remove any intestine or unwanted part from the scallops and wipe clean of any grit etc. Halve any that are very large by cutting through the white part horizontally (i.e. to make two discs). Do not wash the scallops.
3. Cut the chorizo into small dice.
4. Have warm plates ready and waiting.
5. This last stage has to be done fairly quickly and sent to the table immediately:
6. In a hot frying pan, sear the scallops both sides. Season lightly during this process.
7. Divide the hot pea purée between the 2 plates by putting a small mound in the centre of each plate.
8. Arrange the seared scallops around the purée.
9. Put the chorizo and capers into the pan to fry briefly, then scatter them over the scallops.
10. Put the fish stock into the pan. Swirl it around, add the lemon and parsley and finally the butter.
11. When the butter has melted, drizzle this sauce around the scallops.

PLAICE FLORENTINE

EQUIPMENT

You will need a dish large enough to hold the 2 portions.

INGREDIENTS (SERVES 2)

2 x 175g plaice fillets

2 tablespoon white wine

225g leaf spinach

225g mashed potato

Salt and ground black pepper

Nutmeg

25g butter

20g plain flour

2 tablespoons double cream

1 teaspoon Dijon mustard

50g strong Cheddar (grated)

Freshly grated Parmesan

METHOD

1. Heat oven to 180°C/gas mark 4.
2. Skin the plaice fillets if not already done so and fold them in three to make two neat parcels.
3. Place in a suitably sized oven proof dish, season with salt and pepper and pour over the wine.
4. Cover with a piece of oiled tin foil and place in the oven for 15 - 20 minutes until lightly steamed.
5. While this is cooking, heat a large saucepan and stir fry the spinach until it just collapses. Spread it out on a tray to cool as quickly as possible.
6. Pipe or arrange the mashed potato around the edge of the serving dish you are using.
7. Squeeze the excess moisture out of the spinach and then chop it with some salt, pepper and a little nutmeg. Place it in the centre of the mashed potato.
8. Drain the plaice fillets and put these on top of the spinach.
9. Put the liquid from cooking the plaice fillets into a measuring jug and increase the volume to 300ml with water or fish stock if you have it.
10. Melt the butter in a pan then add the flour.
11. Cook this roux gently for a couple of minutes before adding the fish stock.
12. Bring to the boil and when the sauce thickens add the cream, mustard and Cheddar cheese and cook until smooth.
13. Spoon the sauce over the plaice fillets, sprinkle with the Parmesan cheese and put it under a hot grill to brown. Serve immediately.

RED MULLET WITH AUBERGINE PURÉE & A TOMATO & HERB SAUCE

INGREDIENTS (SERVES 2)

2 good sized red mullet - filleted and de scaled

1 large aubergine

6-8 slivers of garlic

Salt and ground black pepper

Olive oil for brushing

FOR THE SAUCE

2 tablespoons of olive oil

1 small onion

1 clove of garlic

A small bunch of coriander, basil and tarragon

175g ripe tomatoes

Squeeze of lemon juice

Salt and ground black pepper

METHOD

1. Pre-heat the oven to 220°C/gas mark 7.
2. Split the aubergine in half lengthways and score the flesh deeply with a sharp knife. Insert garlic slivers into the slits.
3. Oil an oven tray and place the aubergine halves flat side down onto the tray.
4. Oil the skin of the aubergine and season it.
5. Roast in the oven until it is soft.
6. Allow to cool, then purée in the food processor. You can discard the skin but it is not necessary – you just get a slightly darker purée.
7. Add seasoning as required.
8. To make the sauce, chop the onion and crush the garlic and sweat them in the olive oil until they begin to soften.
9. Peel and chop the tomatoes and add to the pan. Cook until they begin to break down and thicken.
10. Chop the herbs and add these along with the seasoning and lemon juice. Set aside.
11. To cook the red mullet brush with olive oil, season and pan fry or grill.
12. Serve the fish on top of the aubergine purée with the sauce on the side.

LIGHTLY SMOKED SALMON WITH WILTED ROCKET & SPICED YOGHURT

A very simple supper or lunch dish.

A few supermarkets are now selling this lightly-smoked salmon which is cold smoked so still in its raw state.

INGREDIENTS (SERVES 2)

2 x 150g lightly-smoked salmon pieces

A small clove of garlic and a same size piece of ginger

225g thick yoghurt

½ teaspoon Cajun spices

½ teaspoon of roasted cumin seeds

Small bunch chopped coriander

Salt and ground black pepper

Olive oil/sunflower oil

100g rocket

METHOD

1. Finely chop or crush the garlic and ginger and stir it into the yoghurt with the spices and coriander. Season with salt and pepper.
2. Brush the salmon with a little olive oil and place under a hot grill.
3. Heat a teaspoon of sunflower oil in a frying pan and wilt the rocket, season.
4. Make a heap of rocket in the centre of two plates and place the salmon on top.
5. Spoon some yoghurt over the salmon.

GOUJONS OF DOVER SOLE WITH SHRIMPS & BROAD BEANS

A good way of using very large Dover soles which can usually be bought cheaper than portion sized ones. Goujons are fat strips of boneless fish. Dover sole is ideal for this dish as it is very firm and does not tend to break up during the cooking process.

INGREDIENTS (SERVES 2)

1 large Dover sole (1 kg or bigger)

25g clarified butter (see page 426)

25g thin pancetta (cut fine)

2 tubs of potted shrimps

100g baby broad beans or skinned larger beans

Salt and ground black pepper

Juice of a lemon

Chopped parsley

METHOD

1. Fillet and skin the sole and cut into large goujons.
2. Fry the goujons in the clarified butter. Remove them from the pan when they are cooked and set aside.
3. Fry the pancetta until it begins to crisp then put in the shrimps and the beans.
4. When the butter of the shrimps has melted put the sole back in the pan followed by the parsley.
5. Finally squeeze in the lemon, seasoning if necessary, and serve.
6. A few new potatoes are all that is required as accompaniment.

SALMON EN CROÛTE

This makes a nice change from the ubiquitous poached salmon, it is easy to carve and looks sensational. A great centre piece for a cold buffet.

INGREDIENTS (SERVES 12-15)

5kg whole salmon

1 small onion

1 small head of fennel

50g butter

1 lemon

A bunch of fresh herbs to include: parsley, dill, basil, and tarragon

200g cooked prawns

110g fresh white breadcrumbs

700g ready-made puff pastry

Salt and ground black pepper

Egg wash (see page 426)

METHOD

1. Heat the oven to 200°C/gas mark 6.
2. Fillet and skin your salmon and remove any pin bones so you have two fillets.
3. Dice the onion and fennel very fine and sweat in the butter without colouring.
4. Grate the zest from the lemon, chop the herbs and add these. Season with the salt and pepper and remove from the heat
5. Drain the prawns, chop them coarsely and add them with the breadcrumbs.
6. Squeeze a little juice of the lemon into it. Set aside.
7. Roll out the pastry large enough to encase the whole salmon.
8. Lay the first fillet onto the pastry, then make a layer of stuffing over the whole fillet and put the other fillet on top.
9. Wrap the pastry around the stuffed fish, wetting the edges to seal the pastry. Transfer to a baking sheet.
10. Brush the surface of the pastry with egg wash.
11. Bake for 30-40 minutes. Allow to rest for 15 minutes before cutting into slices. I know this seems like a very short cooking time for a large piece like this but it will cook in 30 minutes – give it 40 minutes if you are not confident about it. Cooking for this minimum time means your salmon will carve seamlessly and not flake and look ragged.

MACKEREL FILLETS WITH RISOTTO CAKES & A TOMATO SALSA

INGREDIENTS (SERVES 4)

8 mackerel fillets

1 small onion

1 tablespoon olive oil – plus extra for frying the fish

100g Arborio rice

Salt and ground black pepper

2 sprigs of thyme

350ml chicken or fish stock

25g butter

25g grated Parmesan cheese

2 tablespoons dry vermouth

Rocket and watercress to serve

FOR THE TOMATO SALSA

2 ripe tomatoes

1 square cm of fresh root ginger

Small bunch coriander

Pinch of sugar

Squeeze of lemon juice

Salt and ground black pepper

2 tablespoons olive oil

METHOD

1. Chop the onion and fry it in the olive oil until soft.
2. Add the rice, seasoning and thyme and cook until the rice is hot.
3. Add half the stock and simmer until it is absorbed.
4. Keep adding the rest of the stock a little at a time until it is all absorbed and the rice is cooked. Stir frequently during this process to encourage the starch out of the rice.
5. Remove from the heat and stir in the butter, Parmesan and vermouth.
6. Spoon the risotto onto a flat tray and spread out to a thickness of 15mm.
7. Allow to get cold - preferably overnight.
8. To make the salsa, peel, quarter and de-seed the tomato. Chop the flesh and place in a bowl. Press the seeds through a sieve to extract the juices and add to the tomato. Discard the seeds and skin.
9. Peel the ginger and cut it into fine shreds. Chop the coriander. Add these to the tomato along with the sugar, lemon juice and oil. Season to taste.
10. To complete the dish, cut out four rice cakes with an 8-9cm diameter cutter.
11. Fry in olive oil until crisp and golden. Set aside.
12. Fry the mackerel fillets in a hot pan for 2 minutes on each side. Arrange two mackerel fillets on top of each rice cake and serve the salsa next to it. Serve with a simple salad of rocket and watercress.

POSH FISH PIE

I always think it is a bit of a shame when you have an array of interesting fish in your fish pie to then cover it all over with mashed potato – much better to make a border of mash in a dish whether you pipe it or just arrange it with a fork, put your fish pie mix in the centre then glaze it under the grill with cheese. Lovely. You can make it even posher by adding scallops, scampi or lobster – depending on how deep your pockets are.

INGREDIENTS (SERVES 4)

175g salmon fillet

175g cod fillet

175g un-dyed smoked haddock

110g prawns cooked and defrosted

Small glass of dry white wine

½ small onion

3 bay leaves

50g butter

35g plain flour

A small bunch of parsley

Squeeze of lemon juice

Salt and ground black pepper

120ml double cream

450g mashed potato

110g finely grated Parmesan cheese or a mixture of Cheddar and Parmesan

METHOD

1. Skin the fish and remove any bones.
2. Put all the fish except the prawns into a shallow pan or dish. Pour over the wine, then add enough water to just cover the fish. (There should be enough salt in the smoked fish to season the whole dish).
3. Peel and cut the onion into four and add to the pan with the bay leaves.
4. Poach the fish until it is just cooked.
5. Drain the fish reserving the poaching stock. Discard the onion and bay leaf.
6. Flake the fish into a bowl and add the drained prawns.
7. Add any juices from the prawns to your fish stock.
8. Melt the butter, stir in the flour and cook until it starts to sizzle.
9. Slowly work in 450ml of the fish stock until you have a smooth sauce.
10. Chop the parsley and add this along with a squeeze of lemon juice.
11. Check the seasoning and finally add the cream.
12. Make sure there is no residual liquid in the drained fish and pour enough sauce over the fish to bind it together. (You may have some sauce over).
13. Fold the sauce very gently into the fish so as not to break it up too much.
14. Make some very smooth, creamy mashed potatoes (King Edwards are best, see page 264).
15. Using either one large dish or 4 individual dishes pipe or arrange the mashed potato around as a border and then spoon the fish filling into the centre and sprinkle with the cheese. Glaze under the grill before serving.

STEAMED COD WITH AIOLI & NEW POTATOES

INGREDIENTS (SERVES 2)

2 pieces of cod fillet weighing about 175g each or more

2 cloves garlic

2 tablespoons ready-made mayonnaise

1 tablespoon chopped parsley

350g Charlotte new potatoes

2 tablespoons white wine

75g butter

Salt and ground black pepper

METHOD

1. Heat the oven 180°C/gas mark 4.
2. Crush the garlic to a purée and stir it into the mayonnaise with the chopped parsley. Keep at room temperature.
3. Peel the potatoes and cook them in boiling salted water.
4. Skin the fish and remove any small bones.
5. Place the fish in a suitable deep oven dish, pour over the wine, season it and place a knob of butter on each one.
6. Cover the dish with foil or use the lid if it has one.
7. Cook in the oven for 8-10 minutes. (Cooking time can vary quite a lot depending on the thickness of the fish).
8. When the potatoes are cooked, drain them well and mash them roughly with the back of a fork. Add a little butter and season with black pepper and some more salt if necessary. Make a bed of the potato in the centre of each warmed plate.
9. Place a portion of the cod onto each potato base.
10. Stir in some or all of the poaching liquor to the aioli until it thins to a pouring consistency. Spoon the aioli over the cod. Serve with a steamed vegetable such as broccoli.

SALMON IN RED WINE WITH WILD MUSHROOMS

I know, fish with red wine, sounds wrong but it works.

INGREDIENTS (SERVES 2)

2 pieces of boneless skinless fresh salmon weighing about 150g each. (You can also use the lightly smoked variety, available in some supermarkets, for this dish).

100g Cavalo nero

Oil for shallow frying

1 shallot

5g dried porcini mushrooms

25g button chestnut mushrooms

75ml red wine

Salt & ground black pepper

½ teaspoon Dijon mustard

45g unsalted butter

A splash of dark soy sauce

METHOD

1. Trim the cavalo nero and cook in boiling salted water until tender. Drain and set aside to cool.
2. Pour 75ml of boiling water onto the porcini mushrooms.
3. Squeeze the cavalo dry, chop it with a pinch of black pepper and set it aside.
4. Chop the shallot very fine. Chop the mushrooms.
5. Sear the salmon in a hot pan in a little oil and set aside. Light the grill to finish cooking the salmon when the sauce is made.
6. Reduce the heat of the pan and place in the chopped shallot. Fry gently until it starts to colour then put in the chopped chestnut mushrooms.
7. While the mushrooms are frying lift the porcini from the water and chop them. Do not throw away the water.
8. When the mushrooms are looking cooked put in the porcini mushrooms, the mushroom stock and the red wine.
9. Increase the heat and reduce the liquid in the pan by half.
10. Stir in the Dijon mustard and make sure it disperses throughout the liquid in the pan.
11. While it is still boiling add the rest of the butter a little at a time, swirling it around to thicken the sauce.
12. Add the splash of soy and correct the seasoning if necessary. If at any time the sauce looks too reduced just add a splash more red wine.
13. To serve, finish cooking the salmon under the grill and heat the cavalo nero in the same way. Place the cavalo nero in the centre of two plates with the salmon on top. Spoon the sauce around the plate or spoon it over the salmon.

FRAGRANT RICE

INGREDIENTS (SERVES 2)

1 cup (150ml volume) of Thai fragrant rice

½ tablespoon of sunflower or sesame oil

2 cups (same size as rice) of water

1 piece of star anise

½ teaspoon turmeric

1 bay leaf

½ stick cinnamon

Salt and ground black pepper

METHOD

1. Fry the rice gently in the oil before adding the water.
2. Crush the star anise and put it in with the turmeric, bay leaf, cinnamon and seasoning.
3. Bring to the boil and then reduce the heat and simmer until all the water is absorbed.
4. Remove from the heat and cover with a lid.
5. After 10 minutes fluff up the rice with a fork and remove the bay leaf and cinnamon.

CHICKEN & DUCK

CRISP CHICKEN THIGHS WITH SATAY SAUCE

INGREDIENTS (SERVES 2)

4 chicken thighs – boned, skin on

Salt and ground black pepper

2 teaspoons ground cumin

2 teaspoons ground coriander seed

2 teaspoons turmeric

1 teaspoon chilli powder

½ teaspoon ground cardamom

2 teaspoons paprika

1 tablespoon vegetable or sesame oil

FOR THE SATAY SAUCE

1 clove of garlic

3 tablespoons of crunchy peanut butter

2 teaspoons soft brown sugar

Juice of ½ a lemon

2 tablespoons dark soy sauce

1 tablespoon Nam Pla (Thai fish sauce)

METHOD

1. Mix the spices together with the salt and pepper. Rub it well into the chicken. Fry the chicken in the oil slowly keeping it mainly skin side down to get it really crisp.

FOR THE SATAY SAUCE

2. Crush the garlic.
3. Place all the ingredients into a saucepan with a little water.
4. Stir over a low heat until all the ingredients are mixed and hot.
5. Add more water if the consistency is too thick.
6. Serve this with the chicken when it is ready.
7. Serve with rice and some wilted greens.

FIVE-SPICE ROAST CHICKEN DRUMSTICKS

INGREDIENTS (SERVES 4)

1 kg chicken drumsticks

1 tablespoon of sunflower or similar light oil

3 cloves garlic

30g root ginger

1 tablespoon rice wine or dry sherry

2 tablespoons light soy sauce

2 teaspoons of five spice powder

2 tablespoons runny honey

METHOD

1. Heat the oven to 180°C/gas mark 4.
2. Peel and chop the ginger and garlic.
3. Place all the ingredients except the drumsticks into a bowl and mix well.
4. Put the drumsticks into the marinade and make sure they are well coated.
5. Leave to marinate for as long as possible, 2 hours minimum or overnight, turning them occasionally.
6. Place the chicken in a roasting tray with the marinade and roast for 30 minutes until the skin of the chicken is golden and marinade has caramelized on the chicken.
7. Serve with rice and wilted greens.

KASHMIRI CHICKEN

INGREDIENTS (SERVES 2)

2 skinless chicken legs – jointed

6 cardamom pods

1 tablespoon coriander seeds

1 tablespoon cumin seeds

2cm piece of cinnamon stick

10 peppercorns

4 cloves

50g ground almonds

1 tablespoon vegetable oil

1 small onion

2 cloves garlic

4cm piece of fresh ginger

1 teaspoon turmeric

100ml water - minimum

125g thick, full fat yoghurt

Salt

METHOD

1. Remove the seeds from the cardamom pods.
2. Place a frying pan over a low heat and put in the cardamom seeds, coriander, cumin, cinnamon, peppercorns and cloves. Toast gently then grind in a spice grinder.
3. Heat the oil in a pan and fry the chicken on all sides until golden.
4. Meanwhile chop the onion, ginger and garlic very fine.
5. Transfer the chicken to a saucepan and place the onion, garlic and ginger into the frying pan. Continue cooking until they start to colour. Add the spices including the turmeric.
6. Transfer everything to the saucepan with the chicken.
7. Rinse the frying pan with the water and add to the chicken. You may need a bit more than 100ml to cover the chicken.
8. Check the seasoning, cover and simmer for 30 minutes.
9. Stir in the ground almonds and the yoghurt and simmer uncovered for 10 minutes. Remove from the heat and stir in the yogurt.
10. Serve with rice or spicy roast potatoes (see opposite).

SPICY ROAST POTATOES

INGREDIENTS (SERVES 2)

350g King Edward potatoes

Salt and ground black pepper

2 cloves garlic

½ teaspoon ground coriander

½ teaspoon ground cumin

½ teaspoon smoked paprika

½ teaspoon turmeric

1 tablespoon sunflower oil

METHOD

1. Heat the oven to 200°C/gas mark 6.
2. Peel the potatoes and cut into chunks.
3. Par-boil in salted water and drain well.
4. Crush the garlic and mix with the oil, spices and pepper.
5. Toss the potatoes in this mixture until they are well coated.
6. Roast in the oven for 30–40 minutes until cooked and golden.

COOKING PERFECT RICE

There are many ways of cooking rice. I find this one works well for me. It uses volume rather than weight so the cup can be any size depending on how many people you are cooking for. The amount here will serve two people.

INGREDIENTS (SERVES 2)

1 cup (150ml volume) of Basmati rice

2 cups (same size) of water

Salt

1 tablespoon of sunflower oil

METHOD

1. Place all the ingredients into a saucepan and allow the rice to soak for 30 minutes before cooking.
2. Bring to the boil then turn down to a slow simmer (without a lid).
3. Cook until all the water is absorbed. (It must cook slowly).
4. Remove from the heat and place a lid on the saucepan.
5. After 10 minutes fluff the rice up with a fork.
6. It is now ready to serve.

CHICKEN KORMA

INGREDIENTS (SERVES 4)

500g chicken thigh meat (prepared weight)

2 cloves garlic

2½cm square cube ginger

1 onion

2 tablespoons sunflower oil

1 green chilli (less if you don't want it too hot)

400g can full fat coconut milk

1 teaspoon garam masala

1 teaspoon turmeric

10 crushed black peppercorns

10 cardamom pods (split, remove black seeds and crush them)

2 teaspoons ground coriander

A pinch of sugar

A pinch of salt

2 tablespoons ground almonds

150ml plain thick yoghurt

Handful fresh coriander

METHOD

1. Remove the skin and bone from the chicken and cut into chunks.
2. Crush the garlic and ginger to a paste. Peel and chop the onion.
3. Heat the oil in a frying pan and fry the onion until it starts to colour.
4. Add the chicken along with the ginger, garlic and chilli.
5. Fry until the chicken begins to colour then transfer it to a large saucepan.
6. Add the coconut milk, garam masala, turmeric, pepper, cardamom, ground coriander and the pinch of sugar and salt.
7. Bring to the boil, then simmer over a low heat, until the chicken is cooked.
8. Stir in the almonds and cook until thick and creamy.
9. Chop the coriander.
10. Prior to serving, add the yoghurt and the fresh coriander and correct the seasoning if necessary. (Do not boil after adding the yogurt).
11. Serve with rice (see page 115).

THAI GREEN CHICKEN CURRY

Most bottled Thai curry pastes are a very dull affair, the zesty tastes of lime, coriander and lemon grass dissipate with keeping. Making your own not only overcomes this but gives a bright green colour to the finished result. It is worth making a large batch of the paste as it can be frozen and used another time – the flavour and colour also stays fresh by freezing.

INGREDIENTS (SERVES 2)

2 boneless chicken breasts

75g sugar snap peas

1 tablespoon sesame oil

200ml full fat canned coconut milk

A small bunch of Thai basil

2 tablespoons of double cream

Salt

Thai fragrant rice (see page 109)

FOR THE THAI GREEN CURRY PASTE

1 lime

A bulb of lemon grass

25g root ginger

1 clove of garlic

1 small green chilli

50g fresh coriander

1 tablespoon Nam Pla (Thai fish sauce)

1 teaspoon each of ground cumin, coriander and turmeric

METHOD

FOR THE THAI GREEN CURRY PASTE

1. Pare 2 strips off the lime with a potato peeler then finely chop it with the lemon grass, ginger, garlic, chilli and coriander, and then purée to a paste with the Nam Pla, lime juice and spices in a food processor or liquidizer.

FOR THE CURRY

2. Cut the chicken breast into strips.
3. Cut the sugar snap peas into thin strips.
4. Heat the oil in a shallow pan and fry the chicken until cooked.
5. Lift the chicken out of the pan then put in your curry paste.
6. Stir continuously until it gets hot then add the coconut milk.
7. Bring the whole thing to the boil and reduce if it is too thin. When the desired consistency has been reached put in the sugar snap peas.
8. Tear the basil leaves and add these also.
9. Finally add the cream and the chicken and check if it needs salt (the Nam Pla being salty it may only need a little).
10. Serve the chicken, when it is hot, in deep plates with Thai fragrant rice moulded in a timbale and served in the centre.

CHICKEN CASSEROLE

INGREDIENTS (SERVES 4)

1 chicken

1 tablespoon olive oil

12 baby onions or 1 medium onion

110g smoked bacon lardons

110g button chestnut mushrooms

1 clove of garlic

10g plain flour

400g tin of chopped tomatoes

1 glass of red wine

4-5 sprigs of thyme

Salt and ground black pepper

METHOD

1. Heat the oven to 180°C/gas mark 4.
2. Joint the chicken and cut each joint in half so you have 8 pieces.
3. Fry the chicken joints in the olive oil until they are evenly golden.
4. As they become cooked place them in a deep casserole.
5. Peel the baby onions or peel and chop the medium onion.
6. Fry the onions, bacon and mushrooms in the same pan until browned then put these in with the chicken leaving behind any fat.
7. Place the flour in the pan and stir it into this fat to make a roux.
8. Add the red wine and the tomatoes and continue cooking.
9. Crush the garlic to a paste and add with the thyme.
10. Season to taste and add a pinch of sugar if you find the taste a little acidic.
11. When the sauce is bubbling, add further wine (or water) if it is a little thick.
12. Pour the sauce over the chicken, cover the casserole and cook for about 1 hour.
13. Serve with mashed potatoes and a green vegetable.

CHICKEN BREASTS WITH WILD MUSHROOMS, CREAM & SHERRY

INGREDIENTS (SERVES 2)

2 chicken supremes (with the skin on and the wing bone attached)

FOR THE SAUCE

7g dried porcini mushrooms

110g of mixed wild mushrooms (if wild are not available use a mixture of cultivated mushrooms; chestnut, shitake etc.)

100ml fresh chicken stock or weak stock from a cube

Sliver of garlic

1 tablespoon of olive oil or clarified butter

A small glass of dry sherry

A teaspoon of Dijon mustard

150ml double cream

Salt and ground black pepper

2-3 drops of sherry vinegar

METHOD

1. Heat the oven to 150°C/gas mark 2.
2. Place the dried porcini mushrooms in a saucepan, cover with the stock, bring to the boil and then remove from the heat and allow to stand for one hour.
3. Check the wild mushrooms over, remove any dirt and slice them.
4. Crush the garlic and fry the wild mushrooms and garlic in half the butter or oil. If this results in any liquid coming out of the mushrooms, carry on cooking until it has evaporated. Remove from the pan and set aside.
5. Trim the chicken breasts of all bone except the little wing bone. Leave the skin on and season them.
6. Wipe the frying pan, place over the heat and add the remaining butter/oil. Cook the chicken breasts skin side down until golden. Turn them over and cook the other side. Transfer them to another pan and place in the oven to finish cooking.
7. Remove the dried mushrooms from the stock and set aside.
8. Deglaze the pan with most of the sherry and add the chicken stock. Reduce by half, whisk in the mustard then pour in the cream.
9. Season and add the chopped mushrooms and the dried porcini.
10. Taste to check the seasoning and the balance of flavour.
11. Finally add the last bit of the sherry, the sherry vinegar and any juices from the chicken.
12. Spoon the sauce onto the plate and place the chicken on it.

POULET L'ESTRAGON

INGREDIENTS (SERVES 2)

2 chicken supremes (with the skin on and the wing bone attached)

25g clarified butter (see page 426)

Salt and ground black pepper

1 tablespoon tarragon vinegar

100g of dry white wine

½ teaspoon Dijon mustard

150ml full-fat crème fraiche

6 sprigs tarragon

METHOD

1. Fry the chicken supremes gently in the butter skin-side down at first. Wait until the skin is golden then turn them to cook the other side for about 5 minutes.
2. Remove them from the pan and place them somewhere warm skin-side up. Season them with salt and black pepper. Do not be concerned if they are not quite cooked as they will be going back in the pan when the sauce is made.
3. De-glaze the pan with the tarragon vinegar and reduce to nil.
4. Pour the white wine into the pan and boil briskly until it has reduced by half.
5. Whisk in the Dijon mustard then add the crème fraiche.
6. Bring to the boil and place the chicken breasts into the sauce with any juices that have come from the chicken.
7. Simmer until the sauce has thickened and the chicken is fully cooked.
8. Chop 4 of the tarragon sprigs finely and add to the sauce just prior to serving.
9. Decorate the chicken with the remaining 2 sprigs.

SPATCHCOCK POUSSIN WITH ITALIAN STUFFING

INGREDIENTS (SERVES 2)

2 poussin (or 2 chicken breasts with the skin on)

1 small onion

1 tablespoon pine nuts

6 thin slices of Milano salami

50g sun-dried tomatoes

1 small bunch basil

100g ricotta cheese

1 tablespoon grated Parmesan

Ground black pepper

1 tablespoon olive oil

2 tablespoons white wine

1 teaspoon Dijon mustard

100ml double cream

METHOD

1. Heat the oven to 190°C/gas mark 5.
2. Spatchcock the poussin by removing the backbone and flattening them.
3. Chop the onion and fry it in oil until golden then add the pine nuts and fry until golden.
4. Chop the salami, tomatoes and basil and place in a bowl with the onion and pine nuts.
5. Add the ricotta, Parmesan and pepper and mix with a fork.
6. Carefully loosen the skin that covers the breasts of the poussin and place under it a layer of the stuffing.
7. Lightly oil a baking tin and place in the poussin making sure they do not touch.
8. Brush with oil and season.
9. Roast for 45–50 minutes until cooked and the skin is golden brown.
10. Remove the poussin from the pan and pour in the white wine.
11. Place over the heat and stir to melt all the flavours of the pan into the wine.
12. Stir in the mustard then add the cream. Bring to the boil and season.
13. Place the poussin onto plates and drizzle the sauce around.

CHICKEN PIE

INGREDIENTS (SERVES 4)

1 medium chicken

1 onion

2 bay leaves

4 sprigs of thyme

Salt and ground black pepper

1 red pepper

100g chestnut button mushrooms

50g butter

35g plain flour

600ml stock (from the poaching of the chicken)

50ml double cream

2 tablespoons dry sherry (optional)

Short pastry (see page 424)

Egg wash (see page 426)

METHOD

1. Heat the oven to 180°C/gas mark 4.
2. Joint the chicken, chop the onion and place them in a pan with the bay leaf and thyme. Season with salt and pepper, cover with water and poach until the chicken is cooked.
3. Chop the pepper and quarter the mushrooms.
4. Melt the butter in a pan and sweat the pepper and mushrooms until cooked but not coloured.
5. Stir in the flour and let it cook for a couple of minutes.
6. Slowly add the stock from the chicken (600ml) whilst stirring until you have a creamy sauce. Finally add the cream and sherry and taste to check the seasoning.
7. Take the chicken off the bone removing any skin, chop into chunks and add to the sauce.
8. Place the mixture in a deep pie dish.
9. Roll out the pastry large enough to cover the top of the pie dish.
10. Wet the edges of the dish, cover with the pastry and trim the edges.
11. Brush with milk or egg wash and bake for 30–40 minutes until the pastry is a golden brown.

CHICKEN BREASTS STUFFED WITH HERB MOUSSELINE

INGREDIENTS (SERVES 2)

2 chicken breasts

75g boneless, skinless chicken thigh meat

1 egg white

A sliver of garlic

Salt and ground black pepper

15g tender spinach leaves or rocket

A small bunch of fresh herbs – chives, basil, parsley

110ml double cream

10 rashers of streaky pancetta (thin cut)

METHOD

1. Heat the oven to 180°C/gas mark 4.
2. Remove any sinew from the chicken thigh meat and process in a food processor.
3. Add the egg white, salt and pepper, garlic, spinach and herbs and process again until the mixture thickens.
4. Add the cream and process again until firm then refrigerate.
5. Open up the chicken breast and beat out to flatten it.
6. Divide the mousseline down the centre of each breast and reshape.
7. Wrap 5 rashers of pancetta around each breast.
8. Place on an oiled baking sheet and brush the top of the breasts with oil.
9. Place in the oven and cook for 20-25 minutes.

STUFFED CHICKEN LEGS WITH CREAMED CABBAGE

INGREDIENTS (SERVES 6)

6 chicken legs, boned and skinned

18 slices of streaky pancetta (thin cut)

FOR THE STUFFING

2 medium onions

2 cloves of garlic

10 sage leaves, 6 sprigs of thyme

1 sweet red pepper

100g fresh breadcrumbs

100g minced pork

Salt and ground black pepper

50g pistachios

Oil

FOR THE CABBAGE

1 medium tenderheart (pointed) cabbage

2 carrots

1 small celeriac

25g butter

Salt and ground black pepper

Nutmeg

100ml double cream

METHOD

1. Heat the oven to 180°C/gas mark 4.
2. Chop the onion, crush the garlic and chop the herbs.
3. Fry the onions in the oil with the garlic.
4. Finely chop the pepper and add this - cook gently until the vegetables begin to soften.
5. Allow to cool then combine with the other ingredients for the stuffing.
6. Stuff the chicken legs with the stuffing, re-form them and wrap 3 rashers of pancetta around each one.
7. Place on an oiled tray, brush with a little oil and cook for 20-25 minutes.
8. Allow to rest before carving into thick slices.

FOR THE CABBAGE

1. Quarter the cabbage, remove the stalk and discard.
2. Shred the cabbage finely.
3. Peel and grate the celeriac and carrots and place them in a shallow pan with the butter, seasoning and a tablespoon of water.
4. Place a lid on the pan and place over a high heat until it is steaming.
5. Drain any excess liquid and put in the cream.
6. Return to the heat and stir.

TO SERVE

Make a bed of the cabbage in the centre of the plate and serve the chicken slices on top of it.

CHICKEN IN CIDER

INGREDIENTS (SERVES 2)

2 chicken supremes (chicken breasts with the wing bone still attached and the skin still on)

½ tablespoon olive oil

1 shallot

1 stick of celery

25g butter

1 eating apple (Cox or Braeburn)

1 tablespoon of Calvados

1 rounded teaspoon plain flour

150ml dry cider

150ml chicken stock

Salt and ground black pepper

100ml full fat crème fraiche

Chives or tarragon to serve

METHOD

1. Fry the chicken supremes in the olive oil until they are golden on both sides. Set aside.
2. Chop the shallot and the celery very fine.
3. Place the butter in the pan and fry the shallot and celery until the onion is opaque.
4. Peel, quarter and core the apple and cut it into wedges. Add to the pan and continue cooking.
5. Add the Calvados and ignite, (mind your eyebrows).
6. Sprinkle in the flour and stir to incorporate it.
7. Add the cider and stock and bring to the boil whilst stirring.
8. Check the seasoning and place the chicken breasts back in the pan.
9. Simmer the chicken in the sauce until it is cooked, this will not take long as the original cooking should have almost cooked it through.
10. Finally add the crème fraiche and the chopped herbs.

PAPRIKA CHICKEN

INGREDIENTS (SERVES 4)

8 chicken thighs

200g can of tomatoes

2 ripe fresh tomatoes

2-4 cloves of garlic

2 teaspoons of Cajun spice

1 tablespoon olive oil

1 glass of white wine

2 teaspoons of smoked paprika (the mild not the hot)

2 tablespoons sweet chilli sauce

50g chorizo sausage cut into small dice

Salt

2 sprigs of thyme

METHOD

1. Heat the oven to 170°C/gas mark 3.
2. Place the canned and fresh tomatoes into a food processor with the garlic and whizz to a purée.
3. Dust the chicken thighs with the Cajun spices.
4. Fry the chicken in a pan with the olive oil so the skin is nice and golden.
5. Remove the thighs from the pan and set aside.
6. Pour the wine into the pan with the tomato mixture, paprika, sweet chilli and chorizo.
7. Bring to the boil stirring and add salt to suit your taste. Add the thyme.
8. Spoon the sauce into a shallow dish and place the chicken thighs, skin side up on top of the sauce.
9. Place in the oven and cook for 25-35 minutes.
10. If the sauce has reduced too much add a little more white wine to the dish.

CHICKEN DAUPHINOISE

EQUIPMENT

Casserole or shallow baking dish large enough to take all the ingredients.

INGREDIENTS (SERVES 4)

1 medium size chicken

1kg waxy potatoes such as Desiree reds

300ml single cream

Salt and ground black pepper

2 cloves of garlic

50g butter

1 tablespoon olive oil

METHOD

1. Heat the oven to 180°C/gas mark 4.
2. Joint the chicken and cut each joint in half so you have 8 pieces.
3. Peel and slice the potatoes and place them in a bowl with the cream.
4. Season well with the salt and pepper. Crush the garlic and mix this in well.
5. Transfer the potatoes into the dish and press them down until they are level.
6. Melt the butter and brush it over the top of the potatoes.
7. Bake in the oven for 30 minutes.
8. Fry the chicken pieces in the olive oil until they are lightly golden.
9. Remove the dish from the oven and place the chicken pieces, skin side up, on top of the potatoes.
10. Sprinkle the chicken skin with a little salt and return to the oven for 45 minutes to 1 hour.

MOROCCAN CHICKEN PIE

EQUIPMENT

A round cake tin about 20cm in diameter.

INGREDIENTS (SERVES 4)

300g skinless chicken thigh meat

2 onions

2 tablespoons sunflower oil

2 teaspoons of Ras el Hanout spice mix

Juice of ½ a lemon

Salt and ground black pepper

Small bunch coriander

50g flaked almonds

200g filo pastry

75g melted butter

Egg wash (see page 426)

Icing sugar & ground cinnamon for dusting

METHOD

1. Cut the chicken meat into cubes.
2. Slice the onions and fry them in the oil until soft and beginning to colour.
3. Add the Ras al Hanout and the lemon juice.
4. Add the chicken and seasoning and continue cooking until the chicken is cooked and any moisture has evaporated.
5. Allow the mixture to cool. Chop the coriander and add it to the mixture.
6. Toast the almonds. Cut the filo pastry into squares 23 x 23cm.
7. Butter the cake tin and layer in it 4 sheets of the filo pastry, buttering each one.
8. Spoon the chicken into the pie and fold over the filo pastry.
9. Scatter with the almonds and finish with 2 more sheets of filo, tucking in any edges.
10. Brush the top of the parcel with egg wash.
11. Bake in the oven for 30–40 minutes.
12. Serve hot, dusted with icing sugar and cinnamon.

SINGAPORE POT-ROASTED CHICKEN

INGREDIENTS (SERVES 4)

1.5kg free range roasting chicken (without giblets)

1 medium onion

2 cloves garlic

1-2 fresh red chillies

25g butter

2 teaspoon ground coriander

2 teaspoon ground cumin

1 level teaspoon turmeric

Finely grated zest and the juice of 1 lemon

400ml can of full-fat coconut milk

Salt and ground black pepper

1 tablespoon ground almonds

12 even sized peeled potatoes

METHOD

1. Preheat the oven to 180°C/gas mark 4.
2. Place the chicken in a deep casserole.
3. Peel the onion, chop it roughly and place it in a food processor or blender with the garlic and chillies. Blend to a smooth paste.
4. Melt the butter in a frying pan and fry the onion mixture with the coriander, cumin and turmeric.
5. Add the lemon, coconut milk and almonds and season well.
6. Stir the mixture then spoon it over the chicken in the casserole.
7. Place the casserole in the oven without a lid.
8. Cook the chicken for 1½-1¾ hours basting the chicken with the sauce every 20 minutes. 30-40 minutes before the end of the cooking time place the potatoes around the chicken and make sure they are well coated in the sauce.
9. When the cooking time is reached and the potatoes are soft remove the casserole from the oven and allow the dish to 'rest' for 20 minutes.
10. Cut the chicken into portions and serve with the sauce, potatoes and perhaps some stir fried pak choi as a vegetable.

CRISP DUCK WRAPS

INGREDIENTS (SERVES 2)

2 duck legs

¼ cucumber

2/4 spring onions

A jar of oriental plum sauce

FOR THE WRAPS

225g plain flour

50g lard

1 level teaspoon salt

150ml warm water

METHOD

1. Heat the oven to 200°C/gas mark 6.
2. Rub salt into the duck legs and roast them for 1 hour. Allow to cool.
3. Peel and quarter the cucumber and remove the seeds. Cut it into strips.
4. Trim the spring onions and cut them into similar lengths to the cucumber.
5. To make the wraps, rub the lard into the flour and salt.
6. Make a dough by adding the water. Knead until it ceases to be sticky.
7. Take 45-50g pieces and roll each one into a circle about 24cm in diameter.
8. Get a clean, dry frying pan moderately hot and dry fry each one for 30-40 seconds per side.
9. Cut the duck off the bone and into small bite sized pieces.
10. Fry until thoroughly crisp.
11. Lay out the wraps and spread a little sauce over the centre of each one.
12. Arrange some duck, cucumber and onion onto the sauce.
13. Fold the edges in, then roll up the wrap.
14. Cut in half diagonally and arrange on a dish – eat whilst still warm.

SINGAPORE NOODLES

Normally this dish would be made from start to finish in a large wok over a high heat. This recipe is adapted to work well in a domestic kitchen.

INGREDIENTS (SERVES 2)

110g vermicelli noodles

8 shiitake mushrooms

1 long red pepper

1 head of pak choi

75g smoked streaky bacon

1 red chilli

2½cm cube root ginger

2 cloves garlic

2 tablespoons sunflower oil

175g shelled raw tiger prawns

110g cooked chicken breast, cut into strips

1 tablespoon light soy sauce

1 tablespoon oyster sauce

1 tablespoon sweet chilli sauce

A few drops of rice or cider vinegar

1 tablespoon toasted sesame oil

1 heaped teaspoon turmeric

1 small bunch fresh coriander

METHOD

1. Pour boiling water over the noodles and make sure they are immersed. Leave for 15 minutes and drain.
2. Slice the mushrooms, pepper and pak choi. Chop the bacon and chilli. Finely chop the ginger and garlic. Cut the cooked chicken into strips.
3. Fry the mushrooms in one tablespoon of the sunflower oil.
4. Add the bacon, pepper, pak choi and when they are nearly cooked add the chilli, ginger, and garlic.
5. Do it in stages if the pan gets a bit crowded using the rest of the sunflower oil.
6. Transfer them to a bowl then fry the prawns until they turn pink – place them in the bowl with the vegetables.
7. Place the noodles in with the other ingredients including the cooked chicken.
8. Spoon over the soy, oyster and chilli sauces, the vinegar and the sesame oil.
9. Chop the coriander and stir this in along with the turmeric. Mix well.
10. This can now be microwaved to serve or heated quickly in a hot wok depending on the number of portions you are making.

MEAT FEAST CALZONE PIZZA

INGREDIENTS (SERVES 2)

½ quantity of the white bread dough (see page 354)

110g chestnut button mushrooms

½ red pepper

2 tablespoons olive oil

110g baby leaf spinach

Salt and ground black pepper

2 skinless chicken thighs

2 good quality sausages

1 tablespoon of sun dried tomato purée

110g Cheddar cheese - grated

½ tablespoon of fresh thyme leaves

Egg wash (see page 426)

METHOD

1. Heat the oven to 230°/gas mark 8.
2. Slice the mushrooms and pepper and fry in a little of the olive oil until soft. Put the spinach in the same pan until wilted. Season and set aside to cool.
3. Cut the chicken into bite sized pieces and fry until lightly browned and cooked through.
4. Remove the skins from the sausages and divide into 4 pieces, again fry until lightly browned.
5. Divide the dough in half and roll each half into a circle.
6. Spread the tomato purée onto the pizza taking care not to get any on the edges.
7. Divide the cooked ingredients between the two pizzas again taking care not to get any on the edges of the dough.
8. Sprinkle over the cheese and the thyme leaves.
9. Wet the edges of the dough then fold in half encasing the ingredients. Pinch the edges to seal well and place on the baking sheet.
10. Brush the top of the dough with egg wash.
11. Bake for 10-12 minutes until well browned and serve immediately.

PAELLA

EQUIPMENT

33.5cm diameter paella pan

INGREDIENTS (SERVES 16)

500g live mussels

½ small glass white wine

75ml olive oil

500g raw, skinless chicken meat

16 large raw prawns

2 large onions

2 red peppers

8 cloves garlic

Salt and ground black pepper

100g Chorizo sausage

500g Calasparra rice

1.75 litres chicken stock (with mussel stock added)

2 teaspoons of smoked paprika (or 3g of saffron strands)

400g can red kidney beans

75g cherry tomatoes

225g baby spinach

METHOD

1. Wash the mussels discarding any open or broken shells. Steam them in a little white wine and drain reserving the stock.
2. Remove the mussels from their shells and put them in the stock to keep moist. Retain a few nice shells for garnish.
3. Cut the chicken into small pieces.
4. Chop the onions and peppers and crush the garlic.
5. In a pan large enough to take all the ingredients heat 2 tablespoons of the oil and fry the chicken. (It may be necessary to do this in batches in case the pan loses heat). Brown the chicken and remove from the pan. Set aside.
6. Fry the prawns and set these aside also.
7. Put more oil in the pan and fry the onions, peppers and garlic until they start to colour. Add some seasoning and the Chorizo and add more oil if it starts to look dry at any stage. Put the rice in the pan and keep stirring to get it hot and mixed with the peppers etc.
8. Put the chicken back in the pan, followed by the hot stock and the paprika and saffron.
9. Bring the whole thing to the boil and then reduce the heat to a simmer. Taste the stock at this point to assess the seasoning, adding more if necessary. Cook for about 15 minutes until the rice has absorbed most of the stock. The rice should be soft but moist.
10. Drain the beans and cut the tomatoes in half.
11. Stir fry the spinach in a separate pan until it wilts.
12. Add the beans, tomatoes, spinach, mussels and prawns and press them down into the mixture. Turn off the heat and allow to stand for 5–6 minutes. Garnish with the saved mussel shells and take the dish to the table.

JAMBALAYA

INGREDIENTS (SERVES 4)

2 chicken breasts (boneless and skinless)

2 onions

2 sticks celery

1 red pepper

4 cloves garlic

50g Chorizo sausage

2 tablespoons olive oil

175g long grain rice

2 ripe tomatoes

350ml chicken stock

1 red chilli

Salt and ground black pepper

Cajun spice

2 bay leaves

3-4 spring onions

8 raw tiger prawns

METHOD

1. Cut the chicken breasts into strips. Chop the onions, celery and red pepper into small dice. Crush the garlic. Cut the chorizo into chunks.
2. Heat a frying pan and using 1 tablespoon of the oil fry off the strips of chicken until they are cooked through and golden on the outside. Fry the chorizo with the chicken for the last few moments. Remove from the pan and set aside.
3. Next fry the onions, celery, pepper and half the garlic over a lower heat until the vegetables start to look translucent.
4. Put the rice in the pan with the vegetables and fry to get it hot.
5. Chop the tomatoes and add to the pan with the chicken stock.
6. Chop the chilli up fine and add less or more depending on how hot you like it.
7. Season with the salt, pepper and Cajun spice.
8. Crumble in the bay leaves. Bring to the boil and then reduce the heat to a simmer.
9. When all the liquid has been absorbed and the rice is cooked, put the chicken back into the pan and cover with a lid. Remove from the heat.
10. Slice the spring onions. In another pan heat the other tablespoon of oil and fry the rest of the garlic, the spring onions and the prawns.
11. To serve, spoon the Jambalaya into deep bowls and spoon the prawns etc. on the top.
12. Have some Tabasco or chilli sauce for those who like it extra hot!

HUSH PUPPIES

This is a term used for the corn bread or snacks traditionally served with Cajun food. There are many versions and many names, corn dodgers, spoon bread, Johnny cakes but try this deep-fried version that are like little savoury dumplings. The name is said to originate from the practice of giving them to dogs to stop them whining when they could smell food being cooked.

INGREDIENTS
(MAKES APPROXIMATELY 30)

350g polenta flour or corn meal

150g plain white flour

1 teaspoon bicarbonate of soda

1 teaspoon baking powder

Salt and ground black pepper

1 small onion

1 egg

450ml buttermilk

500ml sunflower oil

METHOD

1. Place the dry ingredients into a bowl. Chop the onion up small and add to mix.
2. Make a well in the centre and put in the egg.
3. Start to mix adding the buttermilk as you go.
4. Hold back some of the buttermilk and judge the final consistency. What you want is a soft dough of dropping consistency. Season the mixture.
5. Heat the oil in a pan to 190°C.
6. Drop in spoon size dollops of the mixture and fry for about 5 minutes until golden brown and crisp.
7. Serve hot with the Jambalaya.

CONFIT OF DUCK WITH SWEET POTATO, GINGER & APPLE

INGREDIENTS (SERVES 4 OR 2 VERY HUNGRY PEOPLE)

4 duck legs

Salt and ground black pepper

450g duck or goose dripping*

3 cloves of garlic

Some sprigs of thyme and rosemary

1 piece of star anise - crushed

1 small glass of red wine

1 tablespoon soy sauce

1 teaspoon of cornflour

2 sweet potatoes

2cm cube root ginger

2 Cox apples

*Supermarkets now sell duck/goose dripping in jars which you can purchase for this dish. It can be used repeatedly and for other things such as roast potatoes.

METHOD

1. Heat the oven to 150°C/gas mark 2.
2. Melt the dripping. Rub the duck legs with salt and pepper and place them in a deep casserole with the dripping.
3. Break 2 garlic cloves with the flat of a knife and add to the casserole with the herbs and star anise. Cook in the oven for 2 hours after which the meat should be very tender.
4. Allow the dish to cool. Lift the legs out of the dripping and allow them to drain. Put the dripping into a Pyrex jug or container. When it settles remove the dripping from the layer of meat juices.
5. Put the meat juices into a pan with the wine and the soy sauce and bring to the boil.
6. Mix the cornflour with a little water and pour enough into the mixture to thicken it.
7. Increase the oven temperature to 190°C/gas mark 5.
8. Peel the sweet potatoes and cut them into wedges. Place in a roasting tin and brush with a little of the duck fat. Bake in the oven until cooked and nicely browned.
9. Peel and finely chop the ginger and remaining garlic clove. Peel, quarter and core the apples. Towards the end of the cooking time of the sweet potatoes place the ginger garlic and apple into the pan and turn the mixture several times to ensure that everything is distributed evenly and the apples are coated in the fat. Return the tray to the oven for a further 10-15 minutes.
10. Remove the tray from the oven and keep warm. Increase the oven temperature to 220°C/gas mark 7.

11. Place the duck legs on another tray and roast in the oven until they are really crisp.

12. Serve the duck legs sitting on the sweet potato / apple mix and serve the sauce around.

PAN-FRIED BREAST OF CHICKEN WITH LEMON, TARRAGON & CAPERS

INGREDIENTS (SERVES 2)

2 breasts of free range chicken with the skin still on

1 bunch of tarragon

1 tablespoon olive oil

Salt and ground black pepper

50g butter

Juice of a lemon

1 tablespoon of small capers (well rinsed)

METHOD

1. Take 2 nice tips from the tarragon and slide them under the skin of the chicken. Chop the rest.
2. Heat the oil in a frying pan.
3. Season the chicken breasts and place them in the pan.
4. After the initial browning, turn down the heat so they can cook through slowly.
5. Pay particular attention to the skin to ensure it is crisp and golden.
6. When the breasts are done, pour off any excess fat but not the juices. Melt the butter in the pan and when it is bubbling add the juice of the lemon, capers and the chopped tarragon. Serve straight away.

BONED STUFFED DUCK

Great served cold as part of a cold buffet.

INGREDIENTS (SERVES 6-8)

1 whole duck

1 large onion

110g celery

50g smoked streaky bacon

25g duck dripping or olive oil

20 fresh sage leaves

110g good quality black pudding

110g soft prunes

110g fresh wholemeal bread crumbs

Salt and ground black pepper

1 egg

2 chicken breasts – skinless and boneless

METHOD

1. First bone the duck, starting along the back bone and working round until the whole carcass bone structure can be removed. Leave the bone in the legs and wings, set aside.
2. Chop the onion, celery and bacon and fry in the dripping or oil. Cut the sage leaves into strips and add these.
3. When the onion, celery etc. are cooked place them in a bowl.
4. Cut the black pudding into cubes and fry until cooked then place these in the bowl also.
5. Add to the other ingredients along with the quartered prunes and the bread crumbs. Season, add the egg and mix to the consistency of stuffing. If it is a little dry add some water.
6. Heat the oven to 180°C/gas mark 4.
7. Lay the boned duck, skin-side down on your work top and season it with salt and pepper. Arrange half the stuffing onto the centre part of the boned duck then place the chicken breasts on top of this.
8. Place the rest of the stuffing over the chicken breasts.
9. Reform the duck by folding the body around the stuffing.
10. Secure with cocktail sticks (or sew it closed) and turn the duck over.
11. Truss it with string to keep its shape and prick lightly all over with a carving fork.
12. Place in a roasting tray and rub the skin with oil and salt.
13. Roast in the oven for 1½-2 hours.
14. Allow to cool and serve in slices as part of a cold buffet.

PERFECT CRISP DUCK WITH PARSNIPS, APPLES & RED WINE GRAVY

INGREDIENTS (SERVES 4)

2 duck 'crowns' (Remove the legs and cut off the parson's nose end of the carcass) Freeze the legs and use for another dish

2 large parsnips

2 flavoursome eating apples such as Cox

Salt and ground black pepper

150ml red wine

1 teaspoon plain flour

300ml beef or chicken stock

1 teaspoon tomato purée

1 tablespoon soy sauce

METHOD

1. Heat the oven to 180°C/gas mark 4.
2. Prick the skin of the ducks lightly and place in a roasting tray large enough so they don't touch.
3. Sprinkle with salt and roast for 90 minutes. Set aside to cool.
4. Peel the parsnips and cut them into chunks (not too small).
5. Par-boil the parsnip pieces in salted water and drain.
6. Peel, quarter and core the apples. Place the apples and parsnips in a clean roasting tray with some of the fat from the ducks. Season with salt and pepper. Roast until cooked through and nicely coloured.
7. Remove the ducks from the tray and remove the breast joints from the carcass.
8. Tip out any excess fat from the tray and de-glaze it with some of the red wine to dissolve all the deposits in the tray. Transfer this to a jug.
9. Scrunch up some tin foil, place it in the duck tray and position the duck breasts on it skin-side up.
10. Increase the oven temperature to 220°C/gas mark 7 and cook the duck breasts a second time until they are really crisp.
11. To make the gravy, put a little duck dripping in a pan over the heat and add the flour. Cook until the mixture begins to sizzle then add the wine and stock. Bring to the boil then add the tomato purée and soy sauce. Check the seasoning then strain.
12. Serve the duck breast on the parsnips and apples and pour a little gravy around the plate.

FRAGRANT DUCK SALAD

INGREDIENTS (SERVES 2)

2 duck legs

2 teaspoons of five spice powder

Salt

FOR THE SWEET AND SOUR RADISH SALAD

½ cucumber

110g radish (mooli radish if available) – finely sliced

1 medium red chilli

The zest of 1 lime

A small bunch of fresh coriander

¼ of an iceberg lettuce (shredded)

FOR THE DRESSING

Juice of the lime

1 tablespoon sweet chilli sauce

1 small garlic clove

1 tablespoon light soy sauce

2 tablespoons toasted sesame oil

METHOD

1. Heat the oven to 180°C/gas mark 4.
2. Dry the duck legs if they are damp and dust with the spice and salt.
3. Place in a roasting tray and cook for 1 hour. Allow to cool.
4. Peel, halve and de-seed the cucumber and cut it into chunks. Split and deseed the chilli and cut up very fine. Chop the coriander. Grate the zest from the lime.
5. Mix all the ingredients for the salad together and set aside.
6. Crush the garlic and squeeze the lime.
7. Mix all the ingredients for the dressing together.
8. Cut the meat from the duck legs and cut it into chunks.
9. Place some of the duck fat from the roasting into a frying pan or wok.
10. Fry the pieces of duck until they are really crisp.
11. Place the salad into two bowls.
12. Spoon over the dressing and top with the duck pieces.

PORK

STICKY CAJUN PORK RIBS

INGREDIENTS (SERVES 2)

Allow 4-5 pork ribs per person

1 red chilli

2cm cube root ginger

2 cloves garlic

110ml red wine

2 teaspoons Cajun spice mix

50ml soy sauce

35g soft brown sugar

1 tablespoon of wine or cider vinegar

Salt and ground black pepper

METHOD

1. Make a paste of the chilli, ginger and garlic using a food processor then combine it with all the other ingredients except the pork.
2. Rub this marinade well into the pork ribs and leave for as long as possible to marinate, 2 hours minimum or overnight. Turn the ribs occasionally to get them well coated.
3. Heat the oven to 150°C/gas mark 2.
4. Place the ribs in a deep tray or casserole with the marinade, cover with a lid or foil and cook slowly in the oven until the pork is tender (1-1½ hours).
5. Check regularly to make sure the marinade does not reduce by too much. Add a splash of water if necessary.
6. When the pork is tender, remove the ribs from the marinade and place them in a clean roasting tin. Increase the oven heat to 220°C/gas mark 7.
7. Brush the ribs with sunflower oil and put them back into the oven until caramelized and crisp.
8. Transfer the marinade to a saucepan and thicken with a little cornflour.
9. Serve with plain rice and some wilted greens or pak choi.

PORK & PRAWN DUMPLINGS

EQUIPMENT

Steamer - any will do but a Chinese bamboo steamer is ideal.

INGREDIENTS (MAKES 10)

10 wonton wrappers (available from Asian food shops)

Oil to grease

1 tablespoon hot chilli sauce

2 tablespoons light soy sauce

FOR THE FILLING

110g raw tiger prawns

2 spring onion

2cm cube root ginger

150g minced pork

1 tablespoon light soy sauce

1 tablespoon rice wine (or dry sherry)

1 teaspoon toasted sesame oil

2 teaspoons cornflour

Salt and ground black pepper

METHOD

1. Shell the tiger prawns removing the intestine and chop them roughly.
2. Chop the spring onions very fine and grate the ginger.
3. Mix all the ingredients for the filling in a bowl.
4. Take 2 teaspoons of the filling and place it in the centre of the wonton wrapper.
5. Crimp the wrapper around the filling so it sticks but leave the top exposed and the filling visible. (Like a slightly open money purse.)
6. Line a steamer with parchment paper lightly oiled on either side.
7. Place the steamer over a pan of boiling water making sure the bottom doesn't touch the water.
8. Steam for 8-10 minutes.
9. Mix the chilli and soy sauces and place in a dish ready for dipping.
10. Eat the dumplings as soon as they are cooked.

FRICASEÉ DE PORC À L'ANCIENNE

INGREDIENTS (SERVES 2)

1 small tenderloin of pork (about 350g)

1 onion

110g button chestnut mushrooms

½ tablespoon olive oil

110ml dry white wine

15g butter

10g plain flour

150ml light chicken stock (from a cube)

2 tablespoons double cream

1 clove of garlic

2 sprigs of thyme

Salt and ground black pepper

METHOD

1. Trim the pork removing any of the silver membrane and cut it into medallions about 1cm thick.
2. Chop the onion very fine, slice the mushrooms and crush the garlic.
3. Fry the medallions in the olive oil until they are evenly golden. Set aside.
4. Fry the onion and mushrooms in the same pan with the garlic then put these with the pork.
5. De-glaze the pan with the white wine, bring to the boil and reduce by half.
6. Pour into a container and set aside.
7. Wipe the pan then put it back over the heat. Put in the butter and allow it to melt.
8. Place the flour in the pan and stir it into the butter.
9. Add the wine and the stock and stir until the sauce thickens.
10. Add the cream and the thyme and check the seasoning.
11. Place the pork and mushrooms etc. into the sauce and simmer for 5 minutes.

SWEET & SOUR PORK CURRY

INGREDIENTS (SERVES 2)

350g pork shoulder – cut into cubes

1 large onion

3cm cube root ginger

3 cloves garlic

1 tablespoon sunflower oil

1 small pineapple (about 250g flesh) or a small tin

½ teaspoon salt

1 teaspoon each of ground black pepper, cumin, coriander and turmeric

Juice and zest of a lime

110g crunchy peanut butter

1 tablespoon honey

1 tablespoon sweet chilli sauce

300ml of water

METHOD

1. Cut the pork into bite size cubes. Chop the onion, grate the ginger and crush the garlic.
2. Fry the onion in the oil until it starts to colour then add the pork and continue frying.
3. When the pork is sealed transfer the contents of the frying pan to a saucepan.
4. Add the rest of the ingredients and bring to the boil.
5. Simmer slowly for 30-45 minutes without a lid until the pork is tender and the sauce thick.
6. This is not a hot curry so you can serve some finely chopped chilli to sprinkle over for those who like it hot. Serve with rice (see page 115).
7. Best eaten the next day.

LOIN OF PORK WITH A PARMESAN CRUST & BARBECUE SAUCE

INGREDIENTS (SERVES 2)

2 boneless pork loin chops (about 1cm thick)

6 sage leaves

50g grated Parmesan

50g fresh white breadcrumbs

Ground black pepper

25g plain flour

1 egg (beaten)

Oil for frying

FOR THE BARBECUE SAUCE

1 onion

2 cloves garlic

1 tablespoon of sunflower oil

400g can of tomatoes

2cm cube root ginger

1 teaspoon English mustard

1 tablespoon mango chutney (chopped)

1 tablespoon soy sauce

1 tablespoon Worcester sauce

Salt and ground black pepper

1 teaspoon of soft brown sugar

METHOD

1. Chop the sage leaves and combine with the Parmesan, breadcrumbs and pepper in a food processor.
2. Dust the pork with flour and pat off the excess.
3. Dip in the beaten egg and then coat with the breadcrumb mix. (Press down firmly to get a good adhesion.)
4. Heat the oil in a non-stick frying pan and fry the chops until a golden brown and cooked through. (Avoid handling or turning too often to retain the crust.)
5. Serve immediately with the barbecue sauce to the side.

FOR THE BARBECUE SAUCE

1. Chop the onion finely and crush the garlic and grate the ginger.
2. Fry them in the oil until soft and add all the other ingredients.
3. Bring to the boil and simmer gently for 10 minutes.
4. Taste to check the flavour then whizz in a food processor or with a stick blender.
5. Serve separately with the pork.

SPINACH & BACON QUICHE

EQUIPMENT

25cm diameter x 4cm deep tart tin

INGREDIENTS (SERVES 6-8)

Short pastry (see page 424)

250g fresh spinach

1 onion

1 tablespoon olive oil

6 rashers of smoked streaky bacon

50g strong cheddar

2 eggs

200ml single cream

Ground black pepper

METHOD

1. Pre heat the oven to 190°C/gas mark 5.
2. Roll out the pastry and line the tart tin.
3. Prick the base and bake it part blind, (see page 424).
4. Reduce the oven heat to 150°C/gas mark 2.
5. Wash the spinach if necessary and wilt it in a hot pan.
6. Spread the cooked spinach out on to a tray to cool.
7. Chop the onion very finely and fry it in the oil.
8. Cut the bacon into small pieces and cook with the onion. Transfer to a bowl.
9. Squeeze any excess moisture from the spinach, chop it and add to the onions etc.
10. Grate the cheddar and add it with eggs and cream. Season with the black pepper.
11. Spoon the mixture into the pastry case and bake for 30-40 minutes. Serve warm.

INDIVIDUAL RAISED PORK PIES

EQUIPMENT

A metal ring about 7-8cm in diameter. (You can use a plain pastry cutter for this).

INGREDIENTS (MAKES 4-6 DEPENDING ON SIZE)
FOR THE HOT WATER PASTRY

250g plain flour

150g lard

125ml water

Salt

FOR THE FILLING

175g lean shoulder of pork

50g smoked streaky bacon

6 sage leaves

½ teaspoon Aromatic Spice Mix (see page 411)

Salt and ground black pepper

25g fresh white breadcrumbs

TO FINISH

Egg wash (see page 426)

300ml chicken stock

10g leaf gelatine

METHOD

1. To make the pastry, melt the lard in a saucepan without getting it too hot. Place the flour and salt into a bowl and mix in the water and melted lard. mix with a wooden spoon to make a dough. Allow it to cool to a manageable state but use whilst still warm.
2. Heat the oven to 220°C/gas mark 7.
3. Chop finely or mince the pork and bacon.
4. Chop the sage leaves and then combine all the ingredients for the filling. Set aside.
5. Take the metal ring and place it on an oven tray. Line it with the pastry, using your fingers to mould it. Bring the edge up just a bit higher than the rim.
6. Take a quantity of the filling that will fit the space, roll it into a ball and place it in the pie.
7. Take a further piece of pastry, flatten it to make a lid, wet the edges and cover the pie. Trim the edges neatly and crimp them.
8. Make a hole in the centre to let the steam out.
9. Carefully remove the ring and repeat the process until you have used up all the mixture.
10. Make sure they are well spaced on the tray. Brush with egg wash.
11. Bake in the oven for 20 minutes or until the pastry is nicely bronzed.
12. As aspic jelly is virtually unobtainable these days you can make your own using chicken stock and gelatine. Soak the gelatine leaves in cold water to soften them and then drain. Dissolve them in the hot stock and make sure the gelatine is fully melted. Use this to fill the pies using the hole you made to release the steam

HUNTINGDON FIDGET PIE

I found this recipe in a very old cook book and make it often especially around Christmas.

INGREDIENTS (SERVES 4-6)

Double quantity of hot water pastry from the previous recipe.

FOR THE FILLING

350g lean shoulder of pork

110g smoked streaky bacon

1 onion

1 eating apple

12 sage leaves

½ teaspoon Aromatic Spice Mix (see page 411)

1 tablespoon sultanas

Salt and ground black pepper

50g fresh white breadcrumbs

Egg wash (see page 426)

METHOD

1. Heat the oven to 180°C/gas mark 4.
2. Chop finely or mince the pork and bacon. Chop the onion and the apple.
3. Chop the sage leaves and then combine all the ingredients for the filling. Set aside.
4. This pie can be moulded by hand or you can use a pie tin of 1.75lt or larger.
5. Line the tin with two thirds of the pastry, using your fingers to mould it. Bring the edge up just a bit higher than the rim.
6. Place the filling in the pie taking care not to puncture the pastry.
7. Take the remaining third of the pastry, roll it out to make a lid, wet the edges and cover the pie. Trim the edges neatly and crimp them.
8. Make a hole in the centre to let the steam out.
9. Egg wash all exposed pastry.
10. Bake for 45 minutes-1 hour, reducing the oven temperature to 150°C/gas mark 2 once the pastry is golden brown. Allow to cool before serving.
11. If you intend to serve it cold you can pour some aspic jelly into the pie as in the previous recipe.

BACON, LEEK & FUSILLI BAKE

INGREDIENTS (SERVES 2)

2 medium leeks

200g fusilli pasta

1 tablespoon olive oil

110g smoked streaky bacon or lardons

25g butter

20g plain flour

600ml milk

50g sun-dried tomatoes (the ones in oil in jars)

110g strong Cheddar

2 tablespoons double cream

1 teaspoon Dijon mustard

Salt and ground black pepper

50g Parmesan

METHOD

1. Heat the oven to 180°C/gas mark 4.
2. Split the leeks down the middle and shred finely. Wash well and drain.
3. Cook the fusilli, drain well and drizzle with olive oil. Set aside.
4. Stir fry the leeks until they wilt and spread them out on a tray.
5. Chop the bacon, fry it and set aside.
6. Melt the butter and stir in the flour. Allow it to sizzle for a minute then add the milk stirring while it comes to the boil and thickens.
7. Chop up the sun-dried tomatoes and grate both the cheeses
8. Add the cream, mustard, sun-dried tomatoes and grated Cheddar to the sauce.
9. Combine all the ingredients, season and transfer to your dish.
10. Sprinkle over the Parmesan cheese and bake for 20 minutes.

SALAD OF HAM HOCK WITH BUTTER BEANS & CAPERS

INGREDIENTS (SERVES 4)

2 smoked ham hocks weighing about 900g each

1 onion

Ground black pepper

2 bay leaves

4 cloves

1 teaspoon Dijon mustard

½ teaspoon honey

1 teaspoon white wine vinegar

1 tablespoon chopped parsley

110ml olive oil

400g can of butter beans

1 tablespoon capers

1 large cos lettuce or 2-3 little gems

METHOD

1. Soak the ham hocks overnight in cold water to help remove some of the salt.
2. Chop the onion. Heat the oven to 130°C/gas mark ½.
3. Place the ham hocks in a deep casserole with the pepper, bay leaves, cloves and onion.
4. Cover with water, bring to the boil then cook for 2-2½ hours until the meat falls away from the bone.
5. Remove from the oven and lift out the hocks.
6. With a knife and fork, remove the skin and separate the meat from the bone.
7. Break the meat into smallish chunks and put it in a bowl.
8. Mix together the mustard, honey and vinegar. Pour on the olive oil slowly whilst whisking. Add a few turns from the pepper mill and a little of the ham stock.
9. Place the drained butter beans and capers in with the ham then drizzle over the dressing. Serve on crisp lettuce leaves.

PORK WITH MUSTARD, HONEY & TARRAGON

INGREDIENTS (SERVES 2)

4 slices of boneless pork loin (trimmed)

Salt and ground black pepper

Oil for frying

2 teaspoons tarragon vinegar

2 tablespoons dry white wine or vermouth

½ teaspoon of grain mustard

½ teaspoon of Dijon mustard

1 teaspoon clear honey

6 sprigs fresh tarragon

150ml double cream

METHOD

1. Season the pork chops on both sides.
2. Heat a frying pan and sear them on either side so they are nicely coloured then, turn the heat down to cook them through.
3. When the pork is cooked, transfer it to another dish to keep warm.
4. De-glaze the pan with the vinegar and when it is reduced to almost nothing put in the wine, mustards and honey.
5. Now, add the cream and boil until it thickens. Check the seasoning. Chop the tarragon.
6. Finally tip into the sauce any juices that have run from the pork and stir in the chopped tarragon. Place the pork onto the plates and spoon the sauce over.

PORK SAUSAGES

EQUIPMENT

Electric mincer with sausage making attachment

INGREDIENTS (MAKES 16-18 SAUSAGES)

1kg fatty pork shoulder

20g salt

10g freshly ground black pepper

3-5 cloves of garlic (optional) crushed to a purée

Chopped sage, thyme and basil (small bunch of each)

½ a teaspoon each of ground nutmeg, coriander and allspice

150ml red wine

75g fresh brown bread crumbs

Sausage casings

ALTERNATIVE OR ADDITIONAL INGREDIENTS

Smoked paprika, chilli, cayenne, Cajun spice, cumin

METHOD

1. Mince the pork on the fine blade of the mincer.
2. Place the meat in a bowl and add the other ingredients.
3. Mix well. Stuff the casings using the attachment on the mincer.
4. Hang the sausages in a cool dry place to allow them to mature and dry for a day.

SLOW ROAST BELLY OF PORK WITH LENTILS & APPLES

INGREDIENTS (SERVES 4)

900g thick belly of pork with the skin on

Olive oil

Salt and ground black pepper

1 onion

2 cloves garlic

225g Puy lentils

2 bay leaves

Sprig of thyme

450ml water

1 glass of red wine – plus a bit extra

4 eating apples

50g caster sugar

Squeeze of lemon juice

Cooking pork this way is very versatile. With this recipe it is possible to allow the pork to cool completely and perform the second cooking when you are ready to eat it. It can also be cut into squares and roasted again or cut into cubes and fried until crisp to serve in salads or with Eastern dishes such as stir fry or with noodles.

METHOD

1. Heat the oven to 180°C/gas mark 4.
2. Carefully remove the skin from the pork and score it in diagonals. Rub the skin well with a little olive oil and some salt and place it in the oven. Cook in the oven until it is blistered and crisp right through.
3. Reduce the oven temperature to 150°C/gas mark 2.
4. Rub some salt and pepper well into the pork meat. Place it in a separate tray with half a glass of water and cook for 2 hours. The water is to stop the pork getting too dry but should completely evaporate by the end of the cooking time.
5. To make the lentils, chop the onion, crush the garlic and fry in a little oil until they start to brown.
6. Put in the lentils, thyme, water and wine, bring to the boil and then simmer until the lentils are soft and most of the liquid has been absorbed.
7. Peel, quarter and core the apples.
8. Fry them in a little oil until they are golden, then add the sugar and allow it to caramelize before adding the lemon juice. Set aside.
9. When the pork is cooked, remove it from the tray, tip off any excess fat and de-glaze the pan with the extra red wine. When the wine has lifted the juices and flavours from the pan, tip this liquid into the lentils.
10. To serve, spoon the lentils into a mound in the centre of each plate (deep plates are best). Cut the pork into thick strips or cubes and place on the lentils. Break up the crackling and place on top of the pork. Spoon the apples around the dish and garnish with watercress.

APPLE & BLACK PUDDING PASTRIES

INGREDIENTS (SERVES 4)

4 slices from a large black pudding

1 large onion

½ tablespoon olive oil

250g ready-made puff pastry

2 Cox's apples

Salt and ground black pepper

Egg wash (see page 426)

METHOD

1. Heat the oven to 200°C/gas mark 6.
2. Slice the onion, season and fry gently in a little oil until completely soft. Set aside.
3. Cut the pastry into 4 equal pieces and roll out into 4 rectangles roughly 12cm square.
4. Remove any skin from the black pudding and fry briskly in a little oil on both sides, (there is no need to cook it fully at this stage).
5. Peel, quarter and core the apples and cut each quarter into 3 slices.
6. Fry them briefly to prevent them browning.
7. Place a spoonful of the onion onto each pastry square, put a slice of black pudding on top of the onion and top with some slices of apple.
8. Fold the 4 corners of the pastry over the parcel and place them on a baking sheet.
9. Brush the exposed pastry with a little egg wash or milk and bake in the oven until the pastry is puffed and golden (about 15-20 minutes).
10. Serve hot with salad as a brunch or supper dish or pack cold for picnic lunches.

BACON & LEEK SUET PUDDING

EQUIPMENT

1 litre pudding basin or 6 (150ml) individual ones.

INGREDIENTS (SERVES 6)

675g cooked bacon or ham, preferably smoked

2-3 leeks (about 450g in total weight after trimming)

35g butter

25g plain flour

600ml chicken stock (or ham stock if it is not too salty)

2-3 sprigs of thyme

Ground black pepper

Salt (if necessary)

150ml single cream

FOR THE SUET PASTRY:

450g self-raising flour

225g shredded suet

Salt and ground black pepper

Water to bind

METHOD

1. Cut the cooked ham or bacon into cubes.
2. Trim any coarse green from the top of the leeks, split them, wash well to remove any grit, then cut them up small.
3. Melt the butter in a shallow pan and sweat the leeks until they are tender.
4. Sprinkle the flour over the leeks and stir it in.
5. Now, slowly add the hot stock whilst stirring. It will start to thicken as it boils.
6. Turn it down to a simmer, add the thyme stripped from the tough stalk. Then put in the cream and the ham. Stir well, cook for about 2 minutes and set aside.
7. Mix the flour, suet and seasoning together then add enough water to make a dough.
8. Take a 1 litre pudding basin or 6 (150ml) individual ones.
9. Grease them, roll out the pastry and line them.
10. Fill the basin(s) with the ham mixture and cover with pastry lids.
11. Cover with foil and steam for 1 hour and 15 minutes for the larger one or 35 minutes for the individual ones and serve immediately.

STIR-FRIED PORK FILLET

Domestic hobs cannot usually reach the intense heat for stir frying that commercial ones do. It is just about manageable for 2 portions but any more than this, the heat will drop and what should be frying ends up bubbling in its own juices. So, if you want to do a stir fry for more people just cook everything separately or in batches.

INGREDIENTS (SERVES 2)

350g pork fillet (tenderloin)

4 spring onions

2 cloves garlic

1cm cube root ginger

1 red chilli

75g shiitake mushrooms

1 long red pepper

1 tablespoon toasted sesame oil

150g fresh bean sprouts

12 basil leaves

Small bunch coriander

2 tablespoons light soy sauce

Salt and ground black pepper

A pinch of sugar

METHOD

1. Remove any silver membrane or fat from the pork and cut it into slices. Then cut each slice in half.
2. Trim the spring onions and chop finely. Crush the garlic, finely chop or grate the ginger and cut the chilli into fine slices. Slice the mushrooms and red pepper.
3. Heat a large frying pan or wok. Put in half the oil and fry the pork until it is all nicely browned and just cooked, remove from the wok and spread out onto a plate.
4. Return the wok to the heat and put in the rest of the oil. Next fry the onions, mushrooms, red pepper, garlic, ginger, chilli and bean sprouts.
5. Continue frying whilst shaking the pan and stirring.
6. Tear the basil leaves, chop the coriander and add them to the pan along with the soy, a little seasoning and the pinch of sugar.
7. Return the meat to the pan and turn the ingredients several times until all is well coated with the juices.
8. This is now ready to serve and can either be accompanied by some rice or noodles.

HAM HOCK WITH SPLIT PEAS

INGREDIENTS (SERVES 2)

1 smoked ham hock weighing about 900g

250g yellow split peas

1 onion

2 bay leaf

4 cloves

Ground black pepper

1 teaspoon sunflower oil

METHOD

1. Soak the ham hock overnight in cold water to help remove some of the salt. Soak the peas separately to soften them.
2. Heat the oven to 130°C/gas mark ½.
3. Chop the onion and fry it in the oil until it starts to turn translucent.
4. Transfer it to a deep pan or casserole and put in the ham hock, the split peas, pepper, bay leaves and cloves.
5. Cover with the minimum of water and cook in the oven for 2–2½ hours or until the meat falls away from the bone.
6. Remove from the oven and lift out the hock. With a knife and fork remove the skin and separate the meat from the bone.
7. Leaving the meat in largish chunks put it back in with the peas.
8. Take out the bay and cloves and discard.
9. Serve in deep plates with plain boiled potatoes and cabbage or sauerkraut.

CLASSIC CASSOULET

INGREDIENTS (SERVES 6-8)

500g dry cannellini beans (soaked overnight in cold water to soften).

4 duck legs

2 onions

2 large cloves garlic

450g pork belly

450g shoulder lamb

6 Toulouse type sausages

4 sprigs thyme

4 bay leaves

1 can of tomatoes - chopped

1 glass of strong red wine

Salt and ground black pepper

1 teaspoon brown sugar

110g fresh brown breadcrumbs

METHOD

1. Heat the oven to 180°C/gas mark 4.
2. Season the duck legs and roast them for one hour. Remove from the oven and reduce the oven temperature to 150°C/gas mark 2.
3. Chop the onions and crush the garlic. Cut the pork and lamb into cubes.
4. Fry the meat in some of the duck dripping to brown it (you may have to do this in batches)
5. Fry the sausages also, which should then be cut in half.
6. Transfer the cooked ingredients to a casserole as it becomes ready.
7. Fry the onions and garlic and add to this the herbs, beans (drained), tomatoes, wine, seasoning and sugar.
8. Add all this to the casserole and add water or, indeed, more wine if it looks a little dry but don't drown it. Cover with a lid and cook in the oven for 2 hours.
9. Check to make sure the beans are soft and the meat is tender. The next stage can be done immediately or at a later stage, as the dish will now keep quite well.
10. Increase the heat of the oven to 190°C/gas mark 5.
11. Transfer the cassoulet to a shallower dish.
12. Cut the duck meat from the bones and cut into pieces.
13. Lay these over the top of the cassoulet and then sprinkle the whole of the top with breadcrumbs.
14. Put the dish in the oven and bake until the top is brown and crusty and the dish is piping hot. Take it to the table like this.

PORK FILLET WITH SMOKED PAPRIKA & SOUR CREAM

INGREDIENTS (SERVES 2)

350g pork tenderloin

110g button chestnut mushrooms

1 clove garlic

½ tablespoon olive oil

Salt

35ml dry vermouth

1 teaspoon Dijon mustard

1 teaspoon smoked paprika (sweet variety – not the hot)

150ml soured cream

METHOD

1. Trim the pork, remove any silver membrane and cut it into 1cm slices.
2. Slice the mushrooms, crush the garlic.
3. Fry the mushrooms in the olive oil with the garlic and some salt. Set aside.
4. Fry the pork in the same pan until it is nicely browned and just cooked through.
5. Remove from the pan and set aside also.
6. While the pan is still hot put in the vermouth to de-glaze the pan.
7. Stir in the mustard followed by the cream.
8. Stir in the paprika and any juices that have come out of the pork and mushrooms.
9. Reduce the sauce if necessary until thick before returning the pork and mushrooms to the pan.
10. Continue long enough to heat the pork etc. and serve immediately with rice or noodles.

PORK FILLET WRAPPED IN PARMA HAM WITH MUSHROOM, CREAM & MADEIRA SAUCE

INGREDIENTS (SERVES 6)

1kg pork tenderloin

25g dried porcini mushrooms

1 small onion

25g butter

300g chestnut button mushrooms

2 teaspoons plain flour

425ml chicken or veal stock

2 teaspoons Dijon mustard

1 sprig of thyme

Salt and ground black pepper

6 sage leaves

6 slices of Parma ham

Olive oil for brushing

1 small wine glass of Madeira

150ml double cream

2-3 drops of sherry or white wine vinegar

650g baby spinach

METHOD

1. Pour 150ml of boiling water over the dried porcini and press them down.
2. To make the sauce, chop the onion very fine and sweat it in the butter until it starts to colour.
3. Slice the mushrooms and cook these with the onion. Sprinkle over the flour and stir until it disappears.
4. Heat the stock and add it a little at a time.
5. Bring to the boil, season and add the chopped porcini mushrooms along with the water they were soaked in, the mustard and the thyme.
6. Season with salt and pepper and simmer for 2-3 minutes. Set aside.
7. Heat the oven to 220°C/gas mark 7.
8. Trim the pork of any membrane and cut into 6 portions. Lay a sage leaf on each piece and wrap Parma ham around each one. Place on a tray, brush lightly with oil and cook in the oven for 20-25 minutes. Transfer the pork to another dish and keep warm.
9. Put the Madeira into the roasting tray and place it over a low heat to melt all the deposits.
10. Transfer this to the mushroom sauce.
11. Take out any thyme sprigs, put the cream in the sauce and bring to the boil.
12. Taste for seasoning and add a few drops of wine vinegar.
13. To serve, wilt the spinach and place a portion in the centre of each plate. Slice the pork at an angle and arrange on the spinach. Spoon the sauce around the meat.

BEEF & VEAL

BOBOTIE

This South African dish is an amalgamation of Cottage Pie, Curry and Moussaka – it is sweet, hot, spicy and delicious.

INGREDIENTS (SERVES 4)

500g minced beef

1 large onion

2 cloves of garlic

2cm cube root ginger

1 long red pepper

110g chestnut button mushrooms

25g butter

½ teaspoon turmeric

1 teaspoon ground cumin

1 teaspoon ground coriander seed

2 teaspoons sweet paprika

½ teaspoon ground cardamom

Salt and ground black pepper

1 teaspoon plain flour

1 eating apple

50g sultanas

1 large tablespoon mango chutney

25g flaked almonds

150ml beef stock

2 eggs

200ml milk

1 tablespoon fresh white breadcrumbs

METHOD

1. Heat the oven to 150°C/gas mark 2.
2. Chop the onion and crush the garlic. Peel and grate the ginger.
3. Chop the red pepper and the mushrooms.
4. In a saucepan large enough to take all the ingredients fry the onion and garlic in the butter.
5. When the onions start to colour add the ginger, red pepper and mushrooms.
6. Continue frying until the mushrooms etc. cook then put in the meat.
7. Keep stirring over the heat, breaking up the mince so it doesn't form lumps.
8. Put in the spices and the seasoning then the flour and stir them in.
9. Peel, core and grate the apple and add it along with the sultanas, chutney and almonds.
10. Finally add the stock and bring the whole pan to the boil.
11. Transfer to an ovenproof dish and press the mixture down.
12. Cover with foil or a lid and cook in the oven for 30 minutes.
13. Beat together the eggs, breadcrumbs and milk and pour over the top.
14. Bake in the oven for 30-45 minutes until the top is brown and set.

BRAISED STEAK WITH ONIONS

INGREDIENTS (SERVES 4)

800g braising steak (blade or 'feather' steak or even rump or topside)

1 tablespoon sunflower oil

2 onions

25g plain flour

150ml red wine

300ml beef stock or water

1 tablespoon tomato purée

Thyme

1 bay leaf

Salt and ground black pepper

METHOD

1. Heat the oven 150°C/gas mark 2.
2. Trim the steak but leave it in portion size pieces.
3. Fry them in oil until nicely browned on both sides and transfer to a casserole.
4. Slice the onions and fry until they begin to colour (you may need a bit more oil).
5. Sprinkle the flour over the onions and stir until it coats them.
6. Add the wine, stock and tomato purée and bring to the boil.
7. Put in the thyme and bay leaf and season with the salt and pepper.
8. Pour this over the steaks and transfer the dish to the oven.
9. Cook until the meat is tender 1-1½ hours or until the fibres part easily with a fork.

STEAK & KIDNEY PIE

EQUIPMENT

A pie dish of 1.5kg capacity or 6 individual pie dishes.

INGREDIENTS (SERVES 6)

900g of blade or chuck steak

225g beef kidney or chestnut button mushrooms if you don't like kidney

2 onions

1 tablespoon beef dripping or oil

2 teaspoons plain flour

200ml beer

200ml beef stock

1 teaspoon tomato purée

A tied bundle of fresh herbs (bouquet garni)

1 tablespoon Worcestershire sauce

Salt and ground black pepper

Short pastry (see page 424)

Egg wash (see page 426)

METHOD

1. Heat the oven to 150°C/gas mark 2.
2. Cut the steak and kidney into cubes removing any excess fat or gristle.
3. Chop the onions and fry them in the dripping until they start to colour.
4. Remove the onion from the pan and fry the steak and kidney/mushrooms, getting them nicely browned. (You may need to do this in batches.)
5. Transfer the meat etc. to a deep pan or casserole. Sprinkle the flour over the meat and stir it in.
6. De-glaze the frying pan with the beer and pour it over the meat.
7. Add the beef stock, tomato purée, bouquet garni, Worcestershire sauce to the casserole and season well with the salt and pepper., Bring to the boil and transfer to the oven.
8. Cook for 1–1½ hours or until the meat is tender.
9. Test the meat and check the seasoning. Remove the bouquet garni.
10. Transfer the mixture to your pie dish or dishes.
11. Increase the oven temperature to 190°C/gas mark 5.
12. Roll out the pastry to 1cm in thickness, cover the dish, crimp the edges, and brush with egg wash. (Remember if your pie mixture is still hot, egg wash your pastry before it goes on top of the pie.)
13. Bake in the oven for 25–35 minutes until the pastry is cooked and golden.
14. The flavour will improve if you leave the mixture overnight before assembling the pie with the pastry. It also makes life easier to assemble it when the filling is cold. The mixture will heat through as the pastry cooks.

BOLOGNAISE SAUCE

You can use this recipe for Spaghetti Bolognaise or the Lasagne in the next recipe or you can add a can of red kidney beans and some chilli for Chilli con Carne.

INGREDIENTS (SERVES 4-6)

450g lean ground beef

2 onions

1 small red pepper

75g button mushrooms

4 cloves of garlic

A bunch of mixed herbs (choose from thyme, basil, sage, marjoram, bay)

50g smoked streaky bacon

2 tablespoons olive oil

Salt and ground black pepper

25g plain flour

2 x 400g cans of tomatoes

1 tablespoon tomato purée

1 teaspoon sugar

150ml red wine

METHOD

1. Heat the oven to 150°C/gas mark 2.
2. Chop the onion, pepper and mushrooms.
3. Crush the garlic. Chop the herbs. Finely chop the bacon.
4. Fry the onions and garlic in olive oil until they begin to brown.
5. Transfer to a deep pan.
6. Fry the pepper, mushroom, herbs and bacon in the pan for 6–8 minutes.
7. Transfer these ingredients to the pan with the onions.
8. Now fry the meat until browned (it may be necessary to do this in several batches). Add to the pan as each batch becomes ready.
9. Season with the salt and pepper.
10. De-glaze the frying pan with the red wine to gather all the flavours.
11. Sprinkle the flour over the meat and vegetables and stir it in.
12. Place the pan over the heat. Put in the tomatoes, tomato purée, red wine and add a pinch of sugar to balance the flavour.
13. Bring to the boil, taste, and add more seasoning if necessary.
14. Cover and cook over a very low heat for 1-1½ hours. This is best done in a casserole in the oven.

LASAGNE AL FORNO

Use the bolognaise sauce from the previous recipe. You will also need a rectangular dish to assemble and complete this recipe. I know the Cheddar cheese is not terribly authentic but I like the combination of it with the Parmesan.

INGREDIENTS (SERVES 4)

Bolognaise sauce (from previous page)

6 sheets of fresh lasagne

6 slices of Mozzarella cheese

110g Cheddar cheese - grated

50g grated Parmesan

FOR THE CREAM SAUCE

1 small onion

600ml milk

5 cloves

1 bay leaf

35g butter

25g plain flour

1 teaspoon Dijon mustard

Salt and ground black pepper

50ml double cream

METHOD

1. To make the cream sauce, chop the onion and simmer in the milk with cloves and bay leaf.
2. In another pan melt the butter and stir in the flour. Cook for a few moments before adding the milk slowly.
3. Mix to a smooth sauce (it will thicken as it boils).
4. Whisk in the mustard and season with the salt and pepper.
5. Finally add the cream and strain.
6. Heat the oven to 170°C/gas mark 3.
7. Place a spoonful of cream sauce over the base of your dish and spread it out.
8. Place a layer of lasagne over the top followed by a layer of the Bolognaise sauce.
9. Place slices of Mozzarella over this followed by another layer of pasta and bolognaise sauce.
10. Finish with a layer of pasta and cream sauce.
11. Scatter Cheddar cheese and Parmesan over the top and bake for 1 hour until the cheese is browned.
12. For a deluxe version you can also add chopped hard-boiled egg, thin slices of Milano salami and slices of plum tomato.

BEEF BOURGUIGNON

INGREDIENTS (SERVES 4)

1kg chuck steak

1 tablespoon beef dripping or oil

225g button onions or one large onion

2 cloves garlic

225g button mushrooms

110g smoked bacon lardons

25g plain flour

300ml red wine

300ml beef stock

1 tablespoon tomato purée

Salt and ground black pepper

2 bay leaves

4 sprigs thyme

METHOD

1. Heat the oven to 150°C/gas mark 2.
2. Cut the beef into chunks and fry in the oil to brown.
3. Place in a deep casserole.
4. Peel the button onions (or chop if using a large onion). Crush the garlic.
5. Fry the mushrooms, bacon and onions until they colour then add the garlic and continue frying for 5 minutes. Add this to the beef.
6. Sprinkle the flour into the pan and make a roux with the remaining fat (you may need a bit extra) and cook for a couple of minutes.
7. Add the wine and the stock and bring to the boil before adding the tomato purée and the herbs. Season with the salt and pepper.
8. Bring to the boil and pour over the meat etc..
9. Slow cook the casserole (covered) in the oven until the meat is tender – 1–1½ hours.
10. Both the flavour and the texture of the meat will improve if eaten the following day.
11. Serve with creamy mash and a green vegetable.

BRAISED SHORT RIBS OF BEEF

This cut is sometimes called Jacob's ladder. Cooking it on the bone adds extra flavour.

INGREDIENTS (SERVES 4)

4 short ribs of beef

15g dried porcini mushrooms

1 tablespoon beef dripping or oil

1 large onion

250g button chestnut mushrooms

5 cloves garlic

25g plain flour

½ bottle red wine

400g can chopped tomatoes

Salt and ground black pepper

Soy sauce

Worcestershire sauce

A few drops of red wine vinegar

Some sprigs of thyme and bay tied together

METHOD

1. Heat the oven to 150°C/gas mark 2.
2. Pour 150ml of boiling water over the dried porcini mushrooms.
3. Sear the surface of the ribs in a pan with dripping or oil until they are nicely browned on all sides.
4. Transfer to a deep casserole as they become ready.
5. Chop the onions and fry them in the same pan until they start to brown.
6. Chop the button mushrooms and the garlic and fry them with the onions.
7. When cooked transfer them to the casserole with the meat.
8. Add a little more oil or dripping to the pan if it is dry and put in the flour to make a roux.
9. Cook and stir for a couple of minutes.
10. Add the wine and the tomatoes. Chop the porcini and add these along with the water.
11. Add the seasoning and sauces/vinegar to get the right balance of flavour then add the herbs.
12. Pour the resulting sauce over the ribs, cover and place the casserole in the oven.
13. Slow cook for about 2 hours until the meat is tender.
14. As with previous recipes, this improves if left for 24 hours before eating.

SHIN OF BEEF 'OSSO BUCCO' STYLE WITH RICE PILAF

INGREDIENTS (SERVES 6)

1350g slices of shin of beef with plenty of meat on*

1 onion

2 carrots

3 sticks of celery

2 cloves garlic

1 lemon

2 tablespoons olive oil

300ml white wine

400g can chopped tomatoes

Salt and ground black pepper

A pinch of sugar

A sprig of rosemary

2 bay leaves

*Shin and oxtail take the longest of all the beef cuts to become tender but because of the amount of connective tissue the meat is meltingly soft when you get it right. As with previous slow-cooked dishes this is better left for 24 hours.

FOR THE RICE PILAF

1 medium onion

½ tablespoon sunflower oil

1 cup of basmati or long grain rice

½ teaspoon turmeric

1 star of star anise – crushed

Salt and ground black pepper

METHOD

1. Heat the oven to 150°C/gas mark 2.
2. Chop the onion, carrot and celery into fine dice. Crush the garlic. Grate or pare the lemon zest.
3. Sweat the vegetables and garlic in 1 tablespoon of the olive oil for 5–10 minutes without colouring. Place them in a deep casserole.
4. Fry the pieces of beef in the olive oil until browned and place on top of the vegetables.
5. De-glaze the pan with the white wine and add the chopped tomatoes, seasoning, herbs and lemon zest.
6. Taste the liquid and if it is too acidic add a pinch of sugar.
7. Pour this mixture over the beef, cover and cook in the oven for 3½-4½ hours. Test the meat with a knife and fork – the fibres of the meat should part with no pressure. Top up the liquid with water or wine, if it reduces too much.

FOR THE RICE PILAF

1. Chop the onion very finely and cook gently in the oil until cooked but not coloured.
2. Add the rice, seasoning and spices and 2 cups of water.
3. Cook gently without a lid until all the water is absorbed.
4. Remove from the heat and put a lid on the saucepan.
5. After 5 minutes fluff the rice up with a fork. It is now ready to serve.

BRAISED OXTAIL WITH ONIONS & RED WINE

INGREDIENTS (SERVES 4)

2 whole oxtails

1 tablespoon sunflower oil

3 onions

4 cloves garlic

2 medium carrots

110g chestnut button mushrooms

50g smoked bacon lardons

2 teaspoons plain flour

2 bay leaves

4 sprigs thyme

Salt and ground black pepper

300ml strong red wine

1 tablespoon Worcestershire sauce

1 tablespoon tomato purée

METHOD

1. Heat the oven to 130°C/gas mark ½.
2. Trim any excess fat from the oxtails and cut them into sections. Sear them in a pan using the sunflower oil until they are browned all over. Transfer to a casserole.
3. Chop the onions finely and crush the garlic.
4. Peel the carrots and cut them into dice.
5. Quarter the mushrooms.
6. Fry all of these plus the lardons adding more oil if necessary.
7. When they are starting to colour, sprinkle in the flour and stir to incorporate. Put in the wine, Worcestershire sauce, tomato purée, herbs and seasoning and enough water so that the resulting sauce will eventually cover the oxtail.
8. Cover the casserole and cook in the oven for between 3-4 hours.
9. Test that the meat falls away from the bone.
10. Serve in deep dishes with creamy mashed potatoes. (See page 264).

OXTAIL PIE

INGREDIENTS (SERVES 4)

Use the oxtail recipe opposite and when the meat is tender, allow it to cool and remove the meat from the bone. Discard the bone and mix the meat back into the sauce.

FOR THE PASTRY:

75g butter

250g plain flour

75g shredded suet

1 tablespoon of finely chopped herbs (say parsley sage and thyme) or a pinch of dried

Salt and ground black pepper

1 egg

2 tablespoons water

Egg wash (see page 426)

METHOD

1. Place the meat filling into a suitably sized pie dish.
2. Heat the oven to 180°C/gas mark 4.
3. To make the pastry, rub the butter into the flour and then add the suet. Add the herbs and salt and pepper.
4. Mix in the egg and water until you have a dough.
5. Roll out the pastry and cover the pie.
6. Brush with egg wash and bake for 40 minutes until the pastry is golden brown.

VEAL STEAKS WITH TARRAGON & PEPPERCORN SAUCE

INGREDIENTS (SERVES 2)

2 veal loin steaks about 200g each

20 leaves of French tarragon plus some sprigs for garnishing

1 teaspoon of whole green peppercorns

25g butter

1 teaspoon black peppercorns

Salt

½ tablespoon olive oil

A few drops of tarragon vinegar

75ml dry white vermouth

½ teaspoon Dijon mustard

110ml double cream

METHOD

1. Chop the 20 leaves of tarragon and the green peppercorns quite fine and mash them into the butter.
2. Crush the black peppercorns and pat them onto the veal steaks and season with salt.
3. Heat a frying pan and fry the steaks in the olive oil until seared and browned on both sides and cooked how you like them – medium-rare is recommended.
4. Remove the steaks from the pan and set aside. Put the vinegar and vermouth into the pan.
5. Stir the mustard into the liquid and when it has mixed in, add the cream.
6. Boil this sauce until it starts to thicken then stir in the butter.
7. By now you will have some juices that have run out of the steaks – add these to your sauce.
8. Serve the steaks and spoon the sauce over part of the steak leaving some of the meat visible. Garnish with sprigs of tarragon.

CASSEROLE OF VEAL WITH SHERRY & WILD MUSHROOMS

INGREDIENTS (SERVES 4)

1kg stewing veal (shoulder cut)

1 onion

1 clove garlic

12g dried porcini mushrooms

300ml chicken stock

25g butter

25g plain flour

A small glass white wine

Salt and ground black pepper

1 sprig of rosemary

2 bay leaves

100ml double cream

2 tablespoons dry sherry

METHOD

1. Heat the oven to 150°C/gas mark 2.
2. Cut the veal into cubes, chop the onion finely and crush the garlic.
3. Soak the dried porcini in the (hot) chicken stock.
4. Sweat the onions and garlic in the butter without colouring, then put in the mushrooms. When the mushrooms have started to cook transfer everything to a casserole.
5. Now fry the veal in batches transferring the meat to the casserole as it becomes ready.
6. Place the casserole over the heat.
7. Sprinkle the flour over the meat until it coats it and disappears.
8. Add the wine and the chicken stock (with the porcini – chopped up a bit if they are large pieces).
9. Bring to the boil, season with the salt and pepper and add the herbs.
10. Cover the casserole and cook in the oven for one hour until the meat is tender.
11. Stir in the cream and sherry and bring to the boil.
12. Serve with noodles and a green vegetable.

CHILLI CON CARNE WITH CHOCOLATE

The addition of chocolate to this very tasty recipe for chilli gives it a superb lift. The sweetness balances the acidity of the tomato and the bitterness gives an extra angle to the flavour with the smoothness adding a velvety texture. The secret is to keep it subtle, it won't actually taste of chocolate but it makes a difference.

INGREDIENTS (SERVES 4)

500g minced lean beef

1 red pepper

1 onion

50g smoked streaky bacon

110g chestnut button mushrooms

1 tablespoon olive oil

2 cloves garlic

2 teaspoons plain flour

2 teaspoons Cajun spice mix

½ teaspoon Cayenne pepper – more or less depending on how hot you like it.

400g can chopped tomatoes

1 tablespoon tomato purée

1 tablespoon sweet chilli sauce

400g can red kidney beans

Salt and ground black pepper

50g plain chocolate

Soured cream and rice to serve

METHOD

1. Chop the red pepper, onion, bacon and mushrooms and crush the garlic.
2. Fry the onion in the oil to give it a head-start before adding the pepper, garlic, bacon, and mushrooms.
3. Transfer them to a saucepan large enough to take all the ingredients.
4. Fry the minced beef in the same pan (best done in batches) and transfer to the saucepan as it becomes ready.
5. Now place the saucepan over the heat and sprinkle over the flour and the spices.
6. Stir it in well then add the tomatoes, tomato purée, sweet chilli and the beans.
7. Season well with the salt and pepper and bring to the boil.
8. Simmer for 45 minutes to one hour over a low heat or in a low oven.
9. Break up the chocolate and stir until it melts into the sauce.
10. Serve it on rice (see page 115) topped with a spoonful of soured cream.

FILLET STEAKS IN PUFF PASTRY WITH PESTO & A TOMATO SAUCE

EQUIPMENT

Pastry lattice cutter

INGREDIENTS (SERVES 6)

6 x 110-150g fillet steaks preferably taken from the middle section

25g fresh basil

25g fresh flat leaf parsley

50g freshly grated Parmesan

50g pine nuts

2 cloves of garlic

Ground black pepper

Olive oil for frying

400g ready-made puff pastry

Egg wash (see page 426)

FOR THE TOMATO SAUCE

350g ripe, well flavoured tomatoes

50ml olive oil

Salt and ground black pepper

METHOD

1. Heat the oven to 230°C/gas mark 8.
2. For the pesto, place the herbs, Parmesan, pine nuts, garlic and black pepper into the food processor and process to a paste. If it is a little dry add a few drops of olive oil.
3. Season the fillet steaks and sear them briefly in a hot pan.
4. Transfer to a plate to cool down.
5. Cut the pastry in to 6 equal size pieces and roll each one out to a rectangle 15x10cm.
6. Cut with a lattice cutter along the 15cm length then turn the pastry over.
7. Spread a thick layer of pesto on 1 side of the steaks and invert them onto a piece of pastry.
8. Wet the edges of the pastry, gather them up around the steak and seal.
9. Now turn the whole parcel over onto a baking sheet and brush lightly with egg wash. (Don't place the parcels too close together to allow the heat to circulate.)
10. Bake in the oven for 15 minutes until the pastry is golden brown. This should produce a rare steak. If any person wishes a more cooked steak turn the oven down and leave for a further 5-10 minutes.
11. Serve immediately with fresh tomato sauce to the side.

FOR THE TOMATO SAUCE

1. Peel the tomatoes and chop them up.
2. Stew in the olive oil with the seasoning until the tomato pulps and goes to a sauce like consistency.

FILLET OF BEEF WITH MUSHROOMS AU GRATIN

INGREDIENTS (SERVES 4)

4 x 175g 'tournedos' fillet steaks

½ an onion

1 clove of garlic

1 tablespoon olive oil

200g mixed wild mushrooms

Salt and ground black pepper

2 tablespoons Madeira

110ml double cream

1 egg yolk

1 tablespoon chopped parsley and chives

50g grated fresh Parmesan

METHOD

1. Chop the onion and crush the garlic.
2. Heat a frying pan and sweat these in the olive oil until they begin to colour.
3. Chop the mixed mushrooms, add to the pan and continue frying until they are cooked. Season with the salt and pepper and put in the Madeira.
4. Continue cooking until the Madeira is reduced to almost nothing and transfer these ingredients to a plate to cool down thoroughly.
5. Whip the cream lightly and fold the mushrooms into it along with the egg yolk and herbs. Chill well.
6. Season the fillet steaks and sear on both sides until nicely browned. Allow to cool.
7. All the previous preparation can be done in advance.
8. To complete the dish, heat the oven to 220°C/gas mark 7.
9. Place the fillet steaks onto an aluminium tray and spoon the mushroom mix on to the tops of them.
10. Sprinkle with the Parmesan cheese and bake for 6-8 minutes, or longer if you like your beef cooked a bit more. Serve immediately.

STEAK & PORTER PIE

EQUIPMENT

A four portion pie dish or four individual pie dishes

INGREDIENTS (SERVES 4)

900g of blade steak

2 onions

110g chestnut button mushrooms

1 tablespoon beef dripping or oil

2 teaspoons plain flour

300ml stout or Guinness

300ml beef stock

1 tablespoon Worcestershire sauce

A tied bundle of fresh herbs (bouquet garni)

Salt and ground black pepper

Short pastry (see page 424)

Egg wash (see page 426)

METHOD

1. Heat the oven to 150°C/gas mark 2.
2. Cut the steak into cubes. Chop the onions and mushrooms.
3. Fry the onions in some dripping until they start to colour. Add the mushrooms and continue frying. Transfer these to a saucepan when done.
4. Fry the pieces of steak, getting them nicely browned. (You may need to do this in batches.)
5. Stir the flour into the last batch taking care not to burn it. Transfer the meat to the pan with the onions and mushrooms.
6. Put the Guinness into the frying pan and stir to dissolve all the tasty residues from the pan. Add this to the meat with the beef stock, the Worcestershire sauce and the herbs. Bring to the boil and season with the salt and pepper.
7. Simmer, covered, for 1–1½ hour in the oven. Check the flavour at the end of the cooking time. Add a pinch of sugar if it tastes a little bitter (that'll be the stout).
8. Increase the oven temperature to 190°C/gas mark 5.
9. Transfer the mixture to your pie dish or dishes. Roll out the pastry to 1cm in thickness, cover the dish, crimp the edges, decorate with pastry leaves if you are feeling artistic.
10. Egg wash the pastry. Remember if your pie mixture is still hot, decorate and egg wash your pastry before it goes on top of the pie.
11. Bake in the oven for 25–35 minutes, or until the pastry is burnished a golden brown. Take to the table to serve.
12. The flavour will improve if you leave the mixture overnight before assembling the pie with the pastry. It also makes life easier to assemble it when the filling is cold. The mixture will heat through as the pastry cooks.

FILLET STEAK WITH AN OXTAIL PUDDING

The best of both worlds – a rare fillet steak with a mini oxtail pudding.

EQUIPMENT

6 x 100ml aluminium pudding basins

INGREDIENTS (SERVES 6)

6 x 75g fillet steaks

1kg oxtail

2 medium onions

1 teaspoon plain flour

1 large glass red wine

1 tablespoon tomato purée

1 bay leaf

A sprig of thyme

Salt and ground black pepper

Oil for frying

FOR THE SUET PASTRY

225g self-raising flour

110g beef suet

Salt

Water to mix

METHOD STAGE 1

1. Heat the oven to 130°C/gas mark ½.
2. Trim any excess fat from the oxtail.
3. Brown the oxtail pieces in a frying pan in the oil and transfer to a deep casserole.
4. Chop the onion and fry it gently until it begins to colour then sprinkle over the flour and stir until it is dispersed.
5. Add the wine, tomato purée, herbs and seasoning and ½ a pint of water. Bring to the boil, check the seasoning then pour it over the oxtail. Using a casserole that just fits the oxtail will mean your sauce should now cover the meat.
6. Place a lid on the casserole and cook in the oven for 4-5 hours.
7. Remove from the oven and allow to cool.

METHOD STAGE 2

8. For the suet pastry, mix the flour, suet and salt together then mix it to a dough with cold water. Set aside.
9. Remove the meat of the oxtail from the bone and cartilage, which is discarded. Chop the meat into small pieces.
10. Grease the pudding basins and line them with the suet pastry.
11. Fill the puddings with the oxtail meat and just a little sauce to fill any gaps. Seal the puddings with pastry lids, cover with tin foil and steam for about 30 minutes.

METHOD STAGE 3

12. Heat the gravy from the oxtail in a saucepan and reduce to thicken it if necessary.

13. Heat a large frying pan with a little oil.
14. Season the steaks and fry them to medium-rare or however you like your steak done.
15. Put the steaks in the centre of the plates.
16. Turn out an oxtail pudding onto each steak and spoon the sauce around. Serve with mashed potato and a green vegetable.

OPEN BEEF WELLINGTON

INGREDIENTS (SERVES 4)

4 x 110-150g fillet steaks (centre cut)

4 flat mushrooms

Salt and ground black pepper

Olive oil

400g ready-made puff pastry

110g Gruyere cheese (as 4 slices)

METHOD

1. Heat the oven to 230°C/gas mark 8.
2. Season the mushrooms and either fry them in a little oil or bake them in the oven, drizzled with oil.
3. Place them on kitchen paper to soak up excess moisture and allow them to cool.
4. Season the fillet steaks and sear them in a hot pan to just colour the exterior. Allow to cool.
5. Divide the pastry into 4 and roll out each piece so it is roughly 5cm bigger all round than the steak and about the thickness of a pound coin.
6. Make sure the mushroom and steak are quite cold and place a mushroom on to each pastry base followed by a steak and topped with a slice of cheese.
7. Bake in the oven for 10–15 minutes or a bit longer if you like your steak cooked more.
8. As the puff pastry cooks it will rise around the edges of the steak trapping any juices and melting cheese.

CLASSIC BEEF WELLINGTON

INGREDIENTS (SERVES 6)

900g trimmed fillet of beef (centre cut, i.e. not the scraggy tail end or the rump fillet that is sometimes called the 'chateau-briand'). Properly trimmed means the sinewy bit or 'chain' down the side has been removed and all the silver skin from the surface.

150g good quality smooth pâté

500g butter puff pastry

Ground black pepper

Egg wash (see page 426)

METHOD

1. Heat the oven to 220°C/gas mark 7.
2. Roll out the pastry to a rectangle large enough to encase the whole piece of beef.
3. Season the beef well with black pepper. Do not use salt - the pâté should season it well enough.
4. Spread the pâté onto the top of the fillet covering it from end to end.
5. Invert it onto the pastry so the pâté is underneath.
6. Brush the edges of the pastry with egg wash and fold the 2 sides over to meet and encase the whole piece of meat.
7. Turn the whole thing over so the join is now underneath.
8. Crimp the ends as neatly as possible so the parcel is completely sealed.
9. Place on a tray and brush with egg wash.
10. Bake for 35-45 minutes depending how you like your beef cooked. (It also depends on the thickness of the piece of beef.)
11. Allow to rest for at least 15 minutes before carving into thick slices.
12. Serve with a red wine jus or gravy.

VARIATIONS

A mushroom duxelle stuffing can be used in place of the pâté or as a layer underneath the beef.

The beef can be wrapped in herb pancakes before wrapping in pastry.

BEEF RENDANG

This is an Indonesian curry and, unlike other coconut milk-based curries, it is quite dark. The technique for this is to cook it slowly and for quite a long time so it becomes almost dry. The flavour develops with keeping. It can also be made with mutton, venison or goat.

INGREDIENTS (SERVES 4)

650g chuck steak cut into cubes

1 onion

2 tablespoons sunflower oil

25g root ginger – peeled

6 cloves of garlic

1 stalk of lemon grass

1 teaspoon turmeric

2 teaspoons ground coriander

2 teaspoons ground cumin

½ teaspoon ground cinnamon

The seeds from 6 cardamom pods - crushed

1-4 green chillies – depending on how hot you like it

½ teaspoon salt

Zest and juice of a lime

1 teaspoon tamarind paste

2 teaspoons sun-dried tomato purée

400ml can full-fat coconut milk

METHOD

1. Chop the onion and fry it in one tablespoon of oil until it starts to colour.
2. Add the beef and keep frying to seal the meat – you may need more of the oil.
3. Place the meat and onions in a saucepan.
4. Chop the ginger, garlic, lemon grass and chillies coarsely and place in a food processor along with the spices and salt to make a paste.
5. In a bowl, mix the paste with the lime zest, tamarind, tomato purée and coconut milk.
6. Place it all in the saucepan with the beef and onions.
7. Bring to the boil and cook slowly until the beef is tender. This may take up to 1½ hours.
8. The sauce should reduce to produce a thick consistency.
9. This is best eaten the following day served with plain boiled rice.

LAMB

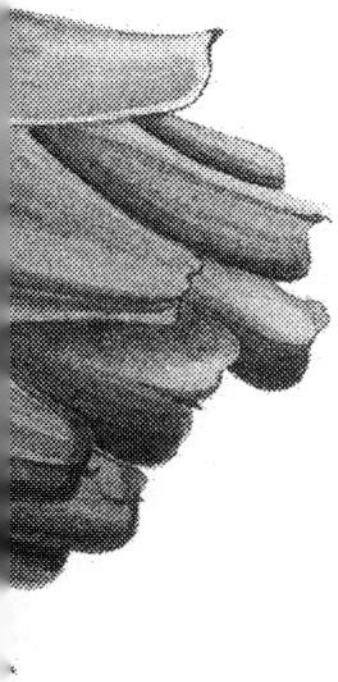

LAMB SAMOSAS

INGREDIENTS (MAKES 6-8)

200g minced lamb

1 tablespoon sunflower oil

1 teaspoon black mustard seeds

1 small onion

2cm cube root ginger

1 clove garlic

½ teaspoon ground coriander

½ teaspoon ground cumin

Pinch of chilli powder (optional)

1 teaspoon garam masala

25g cooked peas

Salt and ground black pepper

Small bunch fresh coriander

1 tablespoon mango chutney

5 leaves filo pastry

Melted butter

Sesame seeds

METHOD

1. Heat the oven to 200°C/gas mark 6.
2. Heat the oil in a shallow pan and fry the mustard seeds until they start to pop.
3. Chop the onion, ginger and garlic and fry with the mustard seeds until they begin to colour.
4. Add the lamb and continue frying until the meat starts to colour.
5. Put in the spices, peas and seasoning and stir well.
6. Chop the coriander and stir it in with the chutney. Set aside to cool.
7. Make strips of the filo pastry about 8cm wide and brush with the melted butter.
8. Place a dessertspoonful of the mixture at one end of the strip and fold up in triangles.
9. Brush each one with melted butter and sprinkle with sesame seeds.
10. Bake for 10-15 minutes.

LAMB GOULASH

INGREDIENTS (SERVES 6)

1kg of boneless shoulder of lamb, cut into cubes (or, if you prefer beef, use blade steak)

2 large onions

2 red peppers

2 cloves garlic

1 tablespoon vegetable oil

300ml red wine

2 teaspoons plain flour

4 teaspoons paprika (smoked if you like but not the hot one)

400g tin of tomatoes, chopped

Salt and ground black pepper

1 small carton of soured cream

METHOD

1. Heat the oven to 150°C/gas mark 2.
2. Chop the onions and peppers and crush the garlic.
3. Fry the onions and peppers in a little oil until golden.
4. Add the garlic and fry for a further 2 minutes.
5. Transfer them to a casserole.
6. Fry the cubes of meat in small batches so they are nicely browned and place in the casserole with the onions.
7. De glaze the pan with the red wine.
8. Sprinkle the flour and paprika over the meat and onions and stir it in until it disappears.
9. Add the wine and tomatoes to the casserole, season and bring to the boil whilst stirring.
10. Cover and cook in the oven for one hour or until the meat is tender.
11. Stir in the soured cream and check the seasoning.
12. Serve with noodles, rice or new potatoes.

SHEPHERD'S OR COTTAGE PIE

INGREDIENTS (SERVES 4)

450g of lean minced lamb or beef

A little dripping or oil

2 onions

1 carrot

110g chestnut mushrooms

110g smoked streaky bacon

1 level tablespoon plain flour

1 tablespoon chopped fresh herbs (or you can use a pinch of dried)

Grated nutmeg

1 tablespoon tomato purée

Salt and ground black pepper

300ml meat stock

FOR THE TOPPING

900g potatoes

50g butter

METHOD

1. Pre heat the oven to 150°C/gas mark 2.
2. Chop the onion finely and the carrot into small dice.
3. Cut the mushrooms and bacon up small.
4. Fry the onion and carrot in a little dripping or oil until they are starting to brown.
5. Add the mushrooms and bacon and cook for a further 2-3 minutes.
6. Add the meat breaking up the lumps with a fork while it colours.
7. Sprinkle over the flour and stir it in followed by the herbs, nutmeg, tomato purée and seasoning.
8. Bring to the boil and transfer it to the dish you will be serving it in.
9. Cover with a lid or tin foil and place it in the oven for 45 minutes.
10. Peel and boil the potatoes in salted water. Drain and mash them.
11. Add the butter and a little milk to make them creamy. Correct the seasoning.
12. Pipe or spread the potato over the meat in the dish and cook for a further 20-30 minutes until the top is golden brown.

LAMB CASSEROLE

INGREDIENTS (SERVES 4)

600g lamb (use boneless neck or shoulder).

1 onion

2 medium carrots

1 medium turnip

1 tablespoon olive oil

25g plain flour

400g can tomatoes

A small glass of red wine

Salt and ground black pepper

1 sprig of rosemary

2 bay leaves

METHOD

1. Heat the oven to 150°C/gas mark 2.
2. Cut the lamb it into 2½cm cubes.
3. Chop the onion. Peel the carrots and turnip and cut them into neat dice.
4. Fry the vegetables in a little oil until they begin to colour.
5. Transfer to a deep casserole.
6. Sear the pieces of lamb in the same pan and add to the casserole when nicely coloured.
7. Now place the casserole over the heat.
8. Sprinkle over the flour and stir until everything is coated and the flour virtually disappears.
9. Add the tomatoes and the wine, seasoning and herbs and enough water to cover.
10. Bring to the boil, cover with a lid, and then transfer to a low oven for about 1 hour.
11. Test the meat with a knife and fork to see if the fibres part easily.
12. Serve with noodles, gnocchi, rice or mashed potato.
13. Variations: add a spice of your choice: smoked paprika/Cajun spice.

LOIN OF LAMB WITH LEMON, HERB & GARLIC STUFFING

INGREDIENTS (SERVES 2-3)

1 boned loin of lamb (without the chump end) trimmed of excess fat

1 small onion

1 clove of garlic

1 tablespoon olive oil

A good size bunch of herbs (choose from marjoram, thyme, savory, parsley and rosemary)

Grated zest of a lemon

50g fresh brown bread crumbs

Salt and ground black pepper

METHOD

1. Heat the oven to 200°C/gas mark 6.
2. To make the stuffing chop the onion and garlic and fry it in the olive oil until golden.
3. Transfer the onions and garlic to a bowl. Chop the herbs and add these along with the lemon zest.
4. Stir in the breadcrumbs and seasoning and set aside to cool. Add a few drops of water if the stuffing is a little dry.
5. Place the stuffing down the centre of the loin of lamb and roll the lamb around it. Tie it in three places. Season with salt.
6. Roast in the oven for 30–40 minutes depending on the size of the loin and how well cooked you like your lamb.
7. Allow it to rest for at least 15 minutes before carving into thick slices.
8. Serve with a little gravy or jus.

LAMB EN CROÛTE

This recipe uses just the 'eye' of the meat taken from either the best end or the loin of lamb. Allow 150g of this meat per person (trimmed weight).

EQUIPMENT

Pastry lattice cutter

INGREDIENTS (SERVES 4)

Loin or best end fillet of lamb

Salt and ground black pepper

Olive oil for frying

1 medium onion

1 clove of garlic

25g butter

110g chestnut button mushrooms

A small bunch of mixed herbs (basil / thyme / parsley)

1 teaspoon Dijon mustard

250g puff pastry

Egg wash (see page 426)

METHOD

1. Heat the oven to 200°C/gas mark 6.
2. Take the 'eye' meat from whichever cut you are using and remove all fat and membrane from it.
3. Season with salt and black pepper and sear quickly in a hot pan to colour the meat all over. Set aside.
4. Chop the onion and crush the garlic.
5. Melt the butter in a pan – preferably the one you seared the lamb in and fry the onion and garlic until they start to colour.
6. Chop the mushrooms very fine and add them to the pan. If any liquid appears, continue cooking until it has all evaporated. Chop the herbs.
7. When the mushrooms are cooked remove from the heat and add the chopped herbs and mustard. (The mixture should be quite dry).
8. Seasoning with salt and pepper and allow to cool.
9. Roll out the pastry to a rectangle large enough to encase the lamb and cut it through with a lattice cutter.
10. Make a bed of the stuffing on the pastry the same size as the lamb, lay the lamb fillet on it and place some more stuffing on the top.
11. Roll the lamb and stuffing up in the pastry and seal it well.
12. Brush with egg wash and bake in the oven for 15-20 minutes. (Timing will depend on the thickness of the lamb fillet and how you like your lamb cooked.)
13. Allow to rest for 10 minutes before carving into thick slices.
14. Serve with a little jus and perhaps redcurrant or similar jelly.

ROAST RUMP OF LAMB WITH CREAMED ONIONS & CAPERS

This is sometimes called the chump and is usually a nice joint of lamb for 2 unless it is early in the season and they are small in which case have one each.

INGREDIENTS (SERVES 2)

1 rump of lamb with the bone removed

2 cloves garlic

2 sprigs rosemary

Salt and ground black pepper

2 large onions

50g butter

2 tablespoons cream

A small glass red wine

1 tablespoon capers – rinsed

METHOD

1. Heat the oven to 180°C/gas mark 4.
2. Smash the garlic cloves and place them in the bottom of the roasting tray with the rosemary. Sit the lamb on top and season with the salt and pepper.
3. Roast in the oven for 35-45 minutes depending on how you like your lamb cooked. Allow to rest before carving.
4. To make the sauce, peel and chop the onions and stew them in the butter with some salt and pepper until soft. Do not allow them to colour.
5. Purée the onions with a stick blender or food processor then return to a clean pan and add the cream.
6. De-glaze the roasting tin with the red wine to make a little jus.
7. Place a spoonful of the onion sauce on the plate, carve the lamb into thick slices and place them on the sauce. Scatter the capers over the sauce. The sweetness of the onion sauce works well with the salty sour capers as a contrast.
8. Serve the jus separately.

ROAST RACK OF LAMB WITH A HERB CRUST & MINT SALSA

Mint salsa is a very intense savoury relish. Once you've tried it with roast lamb you won't want to go back to plain old mint sauce that swims around your plate in a vinegary wash wiping out any flavour of the lamb.

The lamb serves two, the mint salsa makes more than enough for two but it will keep in the fridge for next time. Leave out the mint to serve this sauce with fish or replace the mint with tarragon to give a wow factor to roast beef, steak or even fresh tuna (see page 88).

INGREDIENTS (SERVES 2)

1 rack of lamb, French trimmed

A small bunch of fresh herbs (choose from parsley, thyme, rosemary, oregano, tarragon)

1 clove garlic

2 tablespoons fresh wholemeal breadcrumbs

Salt and ground black pepper

1 teaspoon Dijon mustard

1 egg yolk

A small glass of red wine

FOR THE MINT SALSA

1–2 cloves of garlic

A bunch each of basil, parsley and mint

2 tablespoons capers (rinsed)

1 tablespoon Dijon mustard

A few drops of white wine vinegar

75ml olive oil

METHOD

1. Heat the oven to 200°C/gas mark 6.
2. Chop the herbs very fine, crush the garlic to a purée and combine these with the breadcrumbs and the salt and pepper.
3. Mix together the egg yolk with the Dijon mustard.
4. Dry the surface of the lamb well and paint the mustard mixture over the surface of the lamb except the exposed rib bones and the underside.
5. Then coat the lamb with the breadcrumb mixture generously, pressing them on with gentle pressure.
6. Roast for 20-30 minutes. (20 for pink, 30 for more cooked.)
7. Allow the lamb to rest in a warm place for 10 minutes before carving into individual chops. De-glaze the roasting tin with the red wine to make a little jus.
8. Serve the salsa separately.

FOR THE MINT SALSA

1. Place all the ingredients, except the oil, into a food processor.
2. Run the machine, stopping occasionally to press the ingredients down from the sides.
3. Finally add the olive oil slowly with the machine still running.

SPICED LAMB FILLET WITH FRUITED COUSCOUS & MINTED YOGURT

INGREDIENTS (SERVES 2)

1 lamb fillet (either from the best end or the loin) about 350g/12oz trimmed weight

2 teaspoon Moroccan spice blend or 'Ras-el-Hanout' or make your own with a mixture of ginger (powder), cumin, coriander, pepper, cinnamon, nutmeg, allspice, cloves and cardamom

1 tablespoon olive oil

FOR THE COUSCOUS

1 small onion

1 small red pepper

1 eating apple

3 tablespoons olive oil

1 cup of couscous

1 cup of boiling water

Juice of ½ a lemon

1 tablespoon sultanas

6 dried apricots (quartered)

Salt and ground black pepper

Small bunch of fresh coriander

FOR THE MINTED YOGURT

200ml plain yoghurt

6 mint leaves

Salt and ground black pepper

FOR THE COUSCOUS

1. Make the couscous first to allow the grains time to swell.
2. Finely chop the onion and the pepper. Chop the apple into small dice.
3. Gently fry the peppers and onion in one tablespoon of the olive oil without colouring.
4. Add the chopped apple towards the end of the cooking time.
5. Remove from the heat, add the couscous followed by the water, lemon juice, sultanas, apricots and the rest of the olive oil.
6. Season and allow the grains to swell. Fluff occasionally with a fork whilst this happens. Check the seasoning.
7. Chop the coriander and fold it into the couscous.

FOR THE LAMB

1. To cook the lamb, make sure it is free from all fat and sinew then coat it generously in the spices.
2. Heat the olive oil in a heavy-based pan and sear the lamb fillets like you would cook a steak. Turn the heat down and continue cooking until it has reached the stage of 'doneness' you like. Set aside to let it rest.

TO SERVE

1. To make the minted yogurt, chop the mint leaves finely and stir into the yoghurt with the seasoning.
2. Make a pile of the couscous onto the plates (if it has cooled you can reheat in the oven or microwave), carve the lamb in thick slices and arrange around the couscous.
3. Serve the minted yoghurt separately.

LAMB TAGINE

INGREDIENTS (SERVES 2)

250g diced lean lamb – shoulder or neck

1 tablespoon olive oil

1 onion

2 cloves garlic

1 teaspoon ground ginger

1 teaspoon ground coriander

1 teaspoon ground cinnamon

1 teaspoon ground turmeric

1 teaspoon ground cumin

400g can of tomatoes

2 slices of preserved lemon (see page 406)

10 dried apricots

1 tablespoon honey

Salt and ground black pepper

METHOD

1. Heat the oven to 170°C/gas mark 3.
2. Fry the pieces of lamb in the olive oil until they start to colour.
3. Transfer them to an oven-proof dish or casserole.
4. Chop the onion and crush the garlic.
5. Tip out any excess fat and fry the onions and garlic until they are soft.
6. Sprinkle the spices over the onions etc. and stir them in.
7. Liquidize the tomatoes and add these along with the quartered apricots and the honey.
8. Chop the preserved lemon and add it along with a teaspoonful of the liquid from the jar.
9. Add a little water if it seems too thick and check the seasoning – it should require little salt as the preserved lemon will be quite salty.
10. Stir the sauce into the lamb.
11. Cover the casserole and put in the oven and cook for 1 hour or until the meat is tender.
12. Serve with flat bread, rice or couscous.

LAMB KOFTAS

These spicy little meat balls are fantastically versatile and there are several ways of cooking them.

In Morocco they thread them on skewers and grill them over charcoal. You can also shallow fry them slowly until crisp on the outside and serve them with dipping sauces or in pita bread with lettuce and minted yoghurt.

They are also delicious cooked in a tomato sauce and served with either couscous or pasta.

INGREDIENTS (SERVES 6-8)

225g lean lamb – neck fillet or shoulder

A small bunch each of parsley and coriander

1 small onion

1 clove of garlic

1 teaspoon Ras el Hanout spice mixture

Salt

METHOD

1. Mince the lamb twice or grind in a food processor.
2. Finely chop the onion, crush the garlic and chop the herbs.
3. Mix together all the ingredients and shape into balls about the size of a quail's egg.
4. Cook the koftas by your preferred method (see introduction to the left).
5. Serve with flat bread, rice or couscous.

LANCASHIRE HOT POT

Middle neck and scrag-end of lamb are old-fashioned cuts that you rarely see these days probably due to the word 'scrag'. They used to be, along with breast of lamb, the cheaper cuts. Nowadays supermarkets sell the neck as fillets and charge quite a lot for them. Some supermarkets sell stewing lamb in packs and an old-fashioned butcher will cut proper 'middle neck' chops if you give him some notice.

INGREDIENTS (SERVES 4)

12 middle neck chops of lamb

6 large potatoes

2 large onions

2 lambs kidneys

Salt and ground black pepper

METHOD

1. Heat the oven to 180°C/gas mark 4.
2. Peel and thinly slice the potatoes and onions. Trim any excess fat from the chops.
3. Skin and remove the 'core' from the kidneys and slice them.
4. Layer all the ingredients into a deep casserole, seasoning as you go and finishing with a layer of potato.
5. Pour in enough water to cover everything except the final layer of potato.
6. Cover and cook in the oven for 1 hour, then reduce the oven to 150°C/gas mark 2 for a further hour.
7. Half an hour before the end of the cooking process, remove the lid and brush the top layer of potato with a little oil to help the potatoes to brown.

LAMB STEW WITH PEARL BARLEY

INGREDIENTS (SERVES 4)

12 middle neck chops
(see previous recipe).

1 large onion

1 tablespoon sunflower oil

2 medium carrots

2 medium, white turnips

2 bay leaves and a sprig of thyme

2 tablespoons pearl barley

Salt and ground black pepper

METHOD

1. Heat the oven to 180°C/gas mark 4.
2. Chop the onion. Peel the carrot and turnip and cut into neat dice.
3. Fry the onion in a little oil and place it in the bottom of a casserole large enough to take all the ingredients.
4. Put the bay leaves and thyme on top of the onions.
5. Fry the lamb chops in oil to brown them on both sides and transfer them to the casserole as they become ready.
6. Layer them with the vegetables, pearl barley, seasoning and herbs.
7. Pour water into the casserole until it just covers the ingredients.
8. Cover the casserole with a lid and place in the oven. Cook for one hour then reduce the heat to 140°C/gas mark 1 for a further hour.
9. Serve in deep plates with boiled or mashed potatoes.

GAME

GAME TERRINE

You can mostly use what game you have, but you will need about 800g (not including the bacon) of prepared meat for this capacity terrine dish. It also needs the pork as other game is low on fat.

EQUIPMENT

1200ml capacity terrine dish, preferably loaf shaped.

Mincer or food processor

INGREDIENTS (SERVES 8-10)

1 pheasant

175g belly of pork or wild boar

175g rabbit, hare or grouse meat

110g liver (either from pheasant or rabbit)

225g smoked streaky bacon, cut thin and without rind

2 tablespoons brandy

Small bunch each of basil and thyme

1 sprig rosemary

6 bay leaves

Zest of ½ an orange

2-3 cloves garlic

Salt and ground black pepper

½ teaspoon Aromatic Spice Mix (see page 411)

150ml double cream

2 eggs

50g fresh white bread crumbs

METHOD

1. Remove the legs from the pheasant and strip the meat from them. Cut the breasts from the carcass, remove the skin, cut the meat into long strips and marinate in the brandy.
2. Cut up the pork, the liver and other meats (except the bacon) and place in a bowl along with the pheasant leg meat.
3. Chop the basil, thyme and rosemary and crush the garlic then put all these in with the meat. Season with salt and add the pepper, ground spices and orange zest.
4. Mince this mixture twice or process in a food processor briefly.
5. Put the mixture back into the bowl and work in the cream, eggs and breadcrumbs.
6. Heat the oven to 150°C/gas mark 2.
7. Line the terrine dish with the streaky bacon, leaving enough hanging over the sides to fold back over the finished dish. (The ends of the terrine dish do not need lining.)
8. Place a layer of the meat mixture along the bottom of the dish and then arrange some strips of pheasant breast on top of this.
9. Spread in another layer of meat and some more pheasant strips. Continue like this until the terrine is full.
10. Fold the bacon over the top of the meat thus enclosing the mixture then place a line of bay leaves along the top of the terrine.
11. If the dish has a lid, put this on it or alternatively cover with 4 layers of tin foil. Place the terrine in a shallow pan of water and then cover the whole thing in tin foil.
12. Put it in the oven for 1½-2 hours.

13. Test with a temperature gauge, probe or visually (press the centre if the juices that rise are clear the terrine is cooked). Allow to cool to room temperature then refrigerate overnight with a weight on the top.
14. It will keep for a week and can be eaten the following day although after 2-3 days the flavour will develop.
15. Turn out the terrine and cut into slices and serve with herb or quince jelly or Cumberland sauce.

POT-ROASTED PHEASANT

Browning the birds first in this recipe ensures they have a nice burnished colour but transferring to the casserole with all the other bits gives you a moist, flavoursome dish all in one pot with a super, natural gravy to serve with it.

INGREDIENTS (SERVES 4)

2 pheasants

50g butter

1 onion

2 cloves garlic

1 tablespoon sunflower oil

150g chestnut mushrooms

75g smoked bacon lardons

2 sprigs thyme

2 bay leaves

250g peeled fresh chestnuts

Salt and ground black pepper

Large glass of white wine

METHOD

1. Set the oven 200°C/gas mark 6.
2. Smear the butter over the pheasants, season them and place in a roasting tray.
3. Roast for 20–30 minutes until nicely browned and remove from the oven. Reduce the temperature of the oven to 180°C/gas mark 4.
4. Chop the onion and garlic and fry them in the oil.
5. Quarter the mushrooms if they are large or leave smaller ones whole. Add them to the pan with the onions and put in the lardons.
6. When they are cooked tip them into a large casserole with the thyme, bay leaf and chestnuts. Season well.
7. Remove the pheasants from the roasting tray and place them on top of the mushrooms etc Pour the white wine into the roasting tray, place it over the heat and stir to gather all the flavour and juices from the pan. Then tip this into the pheasant casserole.
8. Cover with a lid , place in the oven and cook for a further 45-55 minutes depending on the size of the birds. Check to see they are cooked by pulling a leg away from the body.
9. Carve the pheasants and serve them with the juices and other ingredients from the casserole.

PIGEON BREASTS WITH CHILLI & CHOCOLATE

INGREDIENTS (SERVES 2)

2 young pigeons

1 small glass of port

½ a small red chilli

2 sprigs of thyme

Salt and ground black pepper

Oil for frying

25g plain dark chocolate (70% cocoa solids minimum)

12g butter

FOR THE STOCK

1 onion

1 carrot

2 sticks celery

6 parsley stalks

10 black peppercorns

A splash of red wine

1 tablespoon sunflower oil

METHOD

1. Remove the 4 breasts from the pigeons and set them aside. The legs being very small go in the stock with the carcasses.
2. Chop the chilli very fine, bruise the thyme and marinate the pigeon breasts in the port with the chilli and thyme for 3-4 hours.
3. Chop up the carcasses and chop the vegetables for the stock.
4. Heat a little oil in a pan and sear the pigeon carcasses, the legs and the vegetables before putting in the parsley stalks, peppercorns and red wine.
5. Put in enough water to just cover the ingredients and bring to the boil. Do not season at this stage.
6. Reduce the heat to a simmer, cover and cook the stock for a good 2 hours.
7. Strain and then put the liquid back in the pan and boil rapidly to reduce it to 150ml.
8. Remove the pigeon breasts from the marinade and pat dry with kitchen paper.
9. Season them with salt and pepper and fry them in a little oil so they are cooked but moist in the centre (they can be cooked less if you prefer them like that). Keep the pigeon warm while you make the sauce.
10. Strain the marinade and tip it into the pan you used to fry the breasts.
11. Bring to the boil and add the pigeon stock.
12. Chop the chocolate and add this swirling it around as it melts.
13. Do the same with the butter.
14. Spoon the sauce onto warm plates, slice the pigeon breasts and lay them on the sauce.
15. Garnish with extra chilli rings if you like it hot.

BRAISED VENISON IN RED WINE WITH CHERRIES & CHESTNUTS

INGREDIENTS (SERVES 6)

1kg lean shoulder of venison cut into cubes

75g dried cherries

½ bottle strong red wine

110g smoked bacon lardons

2 onions

1 tablespoon olive oil

25g plain flour

225g fresh or vacuum-packed chestnuts

4 bay leaves

2-3 sprigs each of rosemary and thyme

Salt and ground black pepper

10g tomato purée

1 teaspoon of Aromatic Spice Mix
(see page 411)

METHOD

1. Soak the cherries in the red wine overnight.
2. Heat the oven to 150°C/gas mark 2.
3. Chop the onions and fry them in the oil until they start to colour then add the lardons and fry for 2-3 minutes. Transfer these to a deep casserole.
4. Fry the venison until nicely browned in the same pan, this may need to be done in batches. Transfer the meat to the casserole with the onions and bacon.
5. De-glaze the pan with some of the red wine to get all the tasty bits from it.
6. Sprinkle the flour evenly over the meat.
7. Place the casserole over the heat then add the herbs, spices, seasoning, all the red wine, the cherries and tomato purée.
8. Use water or stock to top up the liquid level so it just covers the meat. Bring to the boil stirring occasionally then test the seasoning. Cover with a lid and place in the oven.
9. The cooking time will vary depending on the type of venison you are using, the age of the animal and how long it has been hanging.
10. Test the meat after 1 hour to see how tender it is and cook longer if necessary.
11. If you are using fresh, raw chestnuts add them after one hour; if you are using the vacuum-packed ones add them at the end of the cooking time.
12. If you require the sauce a little thicker this can be done with cornflour.
13. This dish is best eaten the next day to allow the flavours to develop. This is lovely served with very creamy mashed potato and a simple green vegetable or even red cabbage.

RABBIT PIE

INGREDIENTS (SERVES 6)

2 young rabbits

2 medium onions

75g butter

2 bay leaves

2 sprigs thyme

6 juniper berries

1 glass dry white wine

1 carrot

1 stick celery

1 lemon

Salt and ground black pepper

35g plain flour

50ml double cream

3 hard-boiled eggs

Short pastry (see page 424)

Egg wash (see page 426)

METHOD

1. Heat the oven to 180°C/gas mark 4.
2. Joint the rabbits and put them in a deep casserole.
3. Chop the onion finely and stew it gently in 25g butter with the bay, thyme, and juniper. Put in the white wine and tip this over the rabbit.
4. Peel the carrot and cut into chunks with the celery then add to the casserole.
5. Cut 2 wide strips of lemon zest with a potato peeler. Add this to the rabbit. Now season and cover with just enough water.
6. Cover the casserole and cook in the oven for 45 minutes. Check to see if the rabbit is tender and cook for longer if necessary.
7. Remove the rabbit and strain the stock.
8. Remove all the meat from the bones. Set aside.
9. Measure out 425ml of the stock.
10. Melt the remaining 50g of butter in a pan and then put in the flour. Let it sizzle for a bit, and then slowly start adding the stock until you have a thick sauce.
11. Add the cream and a squeeze of lemon juice. Check the seasoning.
12. Chop the hard-boiled eggs and add to the sauce along with the rabbit meat.
13. Increase the heat of the oven to 200°C/gas mark 6.
14. Place the mixture into the pie dish. Roll out the pastry to a thickness of about 1cm and lay this over the top.
15. Crimp the edges and brush with egg wash.
16. Bake in the oven for 25–35 minutes until the pastry is golden brown. Serve immediately.

RAISED GAME PIES WITH BLACKBERRY JELLY

EQUIPMENT

4 x 150ml aluminium pudding basins

INGREDIENTS (MAKES 4)
FOR THE HOT WATER PASTRY

150g lard

225g plain flour

125ml water

Salt

FOR THE FILLING

1 partridge

150g lean shoulder of pork

50g smoked streaky bacon

Pinch each of ground allspice, grated nutmeg & ground juniper

4 sage leaves

Salt and ground black pepper

25g fresh white breadcrumbs

25ml cold water

FOR THE TOPPING

300ml chicken or game stock

10g of gelatine

½ jar of blackberry jelly

METHOD

1. Heat the oven to 220°C/gas mark 7.
2. Strip all the meat from the partridge then chop finely or mince the partridge, pork and bacon.
3. Chop the sage leaves and then combine all the ingredients for the filling. Set aside.
4. Place a strip of parchment paper 2cm wide and 23cm long in the tins to eventually ease the removal of the pies.
5. To make the pastry, melt the lard without getting it too hot. Place the flour and salt into a bowl then pour in the water and the lard.
6. Mix with a wooden spoon to make a dough. Use whilst warm.
7. Roll out a piece of the pastry and line the basins.
8. Trim the edges at the lip of the basin.
9. Take a quantity of the filling that will fit the space and place it in each pie. (The pastry around the edges should be slightly proud of the meat.)
10. Bake in the oven for 15 to 20 minutes until cooked through.
11. Soak the gelatine leaves in cold water then, when they are softened, dissolve them in the warm stock.
12. When the pies come out of the oven and have cooled, pour a little jellied stock into each one to fill the spaces where the meat has shrunk.
13. Refrigerate until cold and the jellied stock has set.
14. Melt the blackberry jelly and spoon onto the top of the pie.
15. Refrigerate to set the blackberry jelly again.

ROAST WILD DUCK WITH SWEET POTATO & GINGER MASH AND MARQUISE SAUCE

INGREDIENTS (SERVES 4)

2 mallard ducks (there are several species of wild duck but mallard is the most common)

1 onion

1 carrot

2 sticks celery

6 bay leaves

6 sprigs of thyme

Salt and ground black pepper

1 tablespoon olive oil

FOR THE MASH

2 medium sweet potatoes

Salt and ground black pepper

2 cloves garlic

2½cm cube root ginger

25g butter

FOR THE MARQUISE SAUCE

1 teaspoon flour

150ml good red wine

150ml good rich game stock or beef stock if you don't have game

Pared zest and juice of an orange

1 teaspoon tomato purée

1 teaspoon soy sauce

METHOD

1. Heat the oven to 190°C/gas mark 5.
2. Chop the onion, carrot and celery roughly and scatter in the roasting tray with the herbs. Toss them with a little oil. Season the ducks inside and out. Place them on top of the vegetables and rub a little olive oil into the uppermost skin.
3. Roast for 1 hour then remove from the oven to rest.
4. Peel and cut up the sweet potato and cook in boiling salted water until soft.
5. Drain well and mash with the back of a fork.
6. Peel and chop the ginger and garlic very fine and stir it into the mash with the butter and lots of black pepper. Set aside.
7. Once you have removed the ducks from the roasting tray sprinkle the flour over the vegetables and stir it in over a moderate heat.
8. Add the rest of the ingredients for the sauce and bring to the boil stirring the mixture to release all the tasty bits from the tray.
9. Transfer to a saucepan, check the seasoning and simmer for 10 minutes. Strain to serve.
10. Increase the oven to 200°C/gas mark 6.
11. Joint the ducks removing as much of the carcass as possible.
12. Place the joints skin-side up in a clean roasting tray and place in the oven to get the duck hot and crisp.
13. To serve: place a small heap of the sweet potato mash on one side of the plate and place the duck leg onto this.
14. Pour a little of the sauce onto the other side of the plate and serve the breast on this.

ROAST LOIN OF VENISON WITH CAFÉ DE PARIS BUTTER

INGREDIENTS (SERVES 8)
FOR THE CAFÉ DE PARIS BUTTER

2 cloves of garlic

25g anchovies

A small bunch of herbs to include any or all of the following parsley, chives, basil, tarragon

250g salted butter

1 teaspoon Dijon mustard

1 teaspoon sweet smoked paprika

Ground black pepper

FOR THE VENISON

1.5 kg of boneless venison loin

1 glass red wine

Salt and ground black pepper

2 teaspoons Aromatic Spice mix (see page 411)

25g butter

Soy sauce

Olive oil for frying

METHOD

1. To make the butter, mash the garlic to a paste and do the same with the anchovies. Chop the herbs very fine. Soften the butter (don't throw the wrapper away).
2. Beat all the butter ingredients together or you can put the whole lot in the food processor. Reform the butter into a cylinder, then wrap it in the paper and then again in cling film and refrigerate.
3. Trim any fat and/or silver membrane from the loin. Rub it with the spice mix and place it in a dish with the red wine for 2 hours.
4. Heat the oven to 200°C/gas mark 6.
5. Remove from the marinade and pat dry. Sprinkle with salt and black pepper.
6. Heat a heavy-based pan and put in a little olive oil.
7. Sear the outside of the venison until it is browned all over.
8. Transfer to the oven and roast for 10 minutes, then remove and allow the meat to rest.
9. De-glaze the pan with the red wine, add the soy sauce and bring to the boil. When bubbling, add the 25g of butter a little at a time to thicken the jus.
10. To serve: carve the venison loin into thick slices, drizzle the sauce around and top with slices of the café de Paris butter.

STUFFED RABBIT WITH CREAMED CABBAGE

INGREDIENTS (SERVES 2)

1 medium-sized wild rabbit

8 slices of pancetta

FOR THE STUFFING

1 medium onion – chopped finely

½ red pepper

1 clove garlic

5 sage leaves -chopped

3 sprigs of thyme - chopped

25g butter

50g fresh breadcrumbs

50g minced pork

25g pistachios

Salt and ground black pepper

FOR THE CREAMED CABBAGE

1 medium 'tenderheart' cabbage

2 carrots

Salt and ground black pepper

Nutmeg

25g butter

100ml double cream

METHOD

1. Heat the oven to 180°C/gas mark 4.
2. Chop the rabbit in half separating it just below the ribcage and put aside the top half for a stew, pie or terrine.
3. Bone out the legs and the loin keeping the leg meat joined to the loin.
4. Chop the onion, dice the red pepper, crush the garlic and chop the herbs.
5. Melt the butter and sweat the onion, garlic and pepper until soft. Stir in the herbs and set aside to cool.
6. Mix together with the breadcrumbs, minced pork and pistachios. Season with the salt and pepper.
7. Lay the 2 boned joints of rabbit onto your work surface. Make a sausage with half the stuffing and place it on the leg meat roughly where the bone was removed.
8. Reform the leg/loin around the stuffing to form a parcel and turn it over. Repeat with the other leg.
9. Lay 4 slices of pancetta over each parcel overlapping each slice slightly and tucking the ends underneath. Place on an oiled baking sheet and brush with a little oil.
10. Place in the oven and roast for 25–30 minutes. Allow to rest in a warm place before carving.
11. For the cabbage, remove any coarse outer leaves and cut the cabbage in quarters lengthways.
12. Remove the core and shred the cabbage as finely as possible.
13. Peel and grate the carrot and place it in a pan with the cabbage.
14. Season with the salt, pepper and nutmeg. Put in

the butter with one tablespoon of water. Put a lid over the cabbage and place it on a very high heat.

15. When you see a lot of steam coming out from under the lid remove the pan from the heat.
16. Tip off any excess water and stir in the cream. Replace the lid.
17. To serve: Place a pile of the cabbage/carrot onto each plate. Slice the rabbit leg through and arrange it on top of the cabbage.

PHEASANT BREASTS FLAMED IN WHISKY WITH SOUR CREAM & PAPRIKA

Choose perfect pheasant breasts that have no shot in them and remove the skin. If you have a lot of pheasants or got them cheap or you don't fancy all that plucking and eviscerating just peel off the skin, feathers and all and remove the legs and the breasts.

Use the legs for sausages, pies or a terrine and use the breasts for this recipe. This dish only takes a short time to cook and can be done at the last minute.

INGREDIENTS (SERVES 2)

2 good sized pheasant breasts

10g clarified butter (see page 426)

1 double measure of whisky

1 tablespoon concentrated game or chicken stock

½ teaspoon Dijon mustard

150ml full-fat soured cream

1 level teaspoon paprika

Salt and ground black pepper

METHOD

1. Season the breasts and fry in the clarified butter until they are just cooked and nicely golden all over. Remove them from the pan and put them somewhere to keep warm.
2. Put the whisky into the hot pan and ignite it (watch your eyebrows).
3. Before it has time to completely evaporate, put in the stock and then whisk in the mustard.
4. Add the cream and bring to the boil until it thickens. Tip in any juices that have come out of the meat, sprinkle in the paprika and adjust the seasoning if necessary.
5. Serve the pheasant breast with the sauce either over the meat or to one side, however you prefer it.
6. Serve with rice pilaf or new potatoes and some courgettes or beans.

PHEASANT, PORK AND HAM PIE WITH CHESTNUTS & CRANBERRIES

EQUIPMENT

Spring form cake tin of 20cm diameter and 8cm deep

INGREDIENTS (SERVES 4)
FOR THE FILLING

1 pheasant

1 onion

1 carrot

1 stick celery

Bouquet garni

500g minced pork

110g cubed smoked ham or bacon

A small bunch each of basil and thyme

2 cloves garlic

110g cranberries

75ml white wine

50g fresh white breadcrumbs

150g cooked peeled chestnuts

Salt and ground black pepper

12g leaf gelatine

FOR THE PASTRY

500g plain flour

200g lard

50g butter

2 eggs

100ml cold water

Salt

Egg wash (see page 426)

METHOD

1. Heat the oven to 170°C/gas mark 3.
2. Bone the pheasant and remove the skin.
3. Make a strong stock from the bones with onion, carrot, celery and bouquet garni.
4. Mince the pheasant leg meat and combine with the pork and bacon.
5. Cut the pheasant breasts into strips and set aside.
6. Chop the basil, thyme and garlic and add these to the meat mixture.
7. Heat the cranberries in a dry pan until they just start to pop.
8. Mix the white wine, breadcrumbs, chestnuts and cranberries into the meat mixture.
9. Season with the salt and pepper.
10. Make the pastry by rubbing the lard and butter into the flour and salt and then make into a pastry with the eggs and water. Chill for half an hour.
11. Roll out the pastry and line the tin leaving enough for a lid.
12. Arrange the meat into the pastry layering it with strips of pheasant breast.
13. Wet the edges of the pastry and cover with a pastry lid.
14. Trim and crimp the edges, make a design on the top if you wish and cut a hole in the top as a steam vent that will later be used to fill with the jelly. Brush with egg wash.
15. Bake for 1–1½ hours lowering the temperature if the pastry is brown before the allotted time.
16. Soak the gelatine leaves in cold water to soften them.

17. Measure out 600ml of the strained stock, season it and heat it if it is not already hot.
18. Drain the gelatine and stir it into the hot stock making sure it melts.
19. Allow to cool fully before pouring in your jelly to fill the gaps left by the shrinking meat.
20. Leave 24 hours before serving. Serve cold for salads and picnics.

GAME SAUSAGES

EQUIPMENT

Electric mincer with sausage making attachment

INGREDIENTS (MAKES 18-20)

500g mixed game (choose from rabbit, pigeon, pheasant and venison)

500g pork (on the fatty side) or even wild boar if you can get it

2 cloves garlic

25g chopped fresh herbs – sage, thyme, basil

20g salt

6g freshly ground black pepper

50g breadcrumbs

Small glass of red wine

½ teaspoon each of ground allspice and juniper

Sausage casings

METHOD

1. Crush the garlic and chop the herbs.
2. Mince the meats and place in a bowl with the rest of the ingredients. Mix well.
3. Pack the mixture into the casings using a sausage maker.
4. To prevent the sausages bursting, they should be slowly fried rather than grilled, and never prick them.

ROAST GUINEA FOWL WITH POTATO & CHORIZO STUFFING

INGREDIENTS (SERVES 2)

1 guinea fowl (with giblets)

50g butter

275g peeled potatoes (preferably King Edwards)

1 small onion

2 sticks of celery

1 clove of garlic

4-5 sage leaves

½ teaspoon Cajun spices

110g soft chorizo (whole)

1 tablespoon olive oil

A small glass of port

Salt

METHOD

1. Heat the oven to 200°C/gas mark 6.
2. Remove the giblets from the guinea fowl, season it inside and out and smear the breasts with butter.
3. Roast it in the oven for 25–40 minutes depending on the size of the bird.
4. Boil the potatoes and drain. Chop the onion and the celery.
5. Crush the garlic, cut the sage leaves into thin strips and chop the chorizo into small pieces.
6. Clean the liver from the giblets, removing any sinew or dark patches and cut into pieces.
7. Fry the chorizo in a little of the olive oil and when it starts to cook add the onion and celery.
8. When the onion starts to soften add the potato, cut into chunks, and continue frying until the potato starts to brown and has absorbed the reddish oil from the chorizo. Set aside.
9. In a clean pan fry the liver in the rest of the olive oil and when it is nearly cooked add the sage and garlic. When cooked add this to the potato mix and season it all well with the salt and Cajun spice.
10. When the guinea fowl is cooked allow it to rest before cutting it in half or into joints.
11. De-glaze the roasting tray with the port making sure you lift all the tasty bits in the tray. You can also add a little stock to make a bit more gravy but this dish only needs a little.
12. Put the joints of the bird back in the oven if they have cooled a bit. Make a bed of the stuffing in the centre of each plate and arrange the joints on top. Drizzle the jus around the plate.

POT-ROASTED GUINEA FOWL WITH TRUFFLES & FIGS

INGREDIENTS (SERVES 2)

1 guinea fowl

50g butter

1 small truffle thinly sliced

2-3 shallots

Sprig of thyme

2 bay leaves

½ tablespoon olive oil or dripping

Salt and ground black pepper

150ml veal or chicken stock

4 fresh figs

50ml white wine

10g cornflour

METHOD

1. Preheat the oven to 180°C/gas mark 4.
2. Loosen the skin covering the breast of the bird taking care not to tear it. Remove the wish bone with a small, sharp knife.
3. Soften the butter and push it over the breast under the skin.
4. Slide truffle slices under the skin, arranged over the breast meat.
5. Tie the legs with a piece of string.
6. Finely chop the shallots and fry them in a little dripping or oil. When they are sizzling add the bay leaves and thyme and season with the salt and pepper.
7. Place this in the bottom of a deep casserole, de-glaze the pan with the wine and add this, then sit the guinea fowl on top. Sprinkle a little salt over the breast.
8. Cook for 45 minutes--1 hour depending on the size of the bird.
9. Remove from the oven and allow it to rest. Take the guinea fowl out of the casserole, allowing the juices to drain back into it. Cut in half or into joints, the truffle should be showing nicely now under the burnished skin. Put the guinea fowl somewhere to keep warm.
10. Cut the figs into quarters, drizzle with a little oil and roast in the oven for 10 minutes.
11. Remove the bay leaves and any thyme stalks from the casserole and place it over a high heat.
12. Add the veal/chicken stock and bring to the boil. Mix the cornflour with a little water and add this to thicken the sauce.
13. Spoon the sauce onto the plates and place the guinea fowl on top and decorate with the quartered figs.

SQUAB PIGEONS WITH APPLES & CHESTNUTS

INGREDIENTS (SERVES 2)

2 oven-ready squab pigeons

16 chestnuts

2 Cox apples

½ tablespoon olive oil

50ml Marsala or medium sherry

150ml game stock

10g butter

Salt and ground black pepper

METHOD

1. Heat the oven to 220°C/gas mark 7.
2. Rub the pigeons with a little olive oil and season them inside and out.
3. Roast in the oven for between 25–35 minutes. The shorter time means that the meat will be slightly underdone.
4. If you are using fresh chestnuts, cut a slit in them and cook in boiling water for 10 minutes and then refresh under cold water. They can now be peeled and the inner skin should come away also.
5. Peel, quarter and core the apples and then sauté both the apples and chestnuts in a pan in a little oil. Add these to the roasting tray with the pigeons 10 minutes before the end of the cooking time.
6. At the end of the cooking time, transfer the pigeon, apple and chestnuts to another tray to allow the pigeon to rest. Tip any juices from the inside of the birds back into the original roasting tray and put in the Marsala (or sherry).
7. Put the tray back over the heat and stir to melt and release all the residue of the pan.
8. Add the game stock, reduce it down until it begins to thicken then whisk in the butter. Place the apple and chestnuts into the sauce including any juices that have exuded from the pigeon.
9. Divide the sauce between two warm plates, then halve or carve the pigeon and arrange it on top of the sauce.

PHEASANT WITH CREAM & TARRAGON

I find roasting pheasants difficult to get right; if you cook them so the breast is cooked just right the legs are not cooked enough and if you cook the legs properly the breast can be dry. To cook and serve them separately seems to be the answer and casseroling the legs means you get extra flavour to your sauce.

INGREDIENTS (SERVES 4)

2 oven-ready pheasants

1 tablespoon olive oil

1 onion

1 carrot

2 bay leaves

1 clove of garlic

6 juniper berries

1 teaspoon plain flour

150ml dry white wine

4-5 sprigs tarragon

Salt and ground black pepper

50g butter

2 teaspoons of tarragon vinegar

2–3 tablespoons double cream

METHOD

1. Heat the oven to 150°C/gas mark 2.
2. Remove the legs from the pheasants, and then cut the breasts from the carcass leaving the wing bone attached.
3. Heat the olive oil in a frying pan and brown the pheasant legs all over. Transfer them to a casserole.
4. Chop the onion and carrot and crush the garlic clove (keeping the skin on). Fry these with the juniper berries and, when they are beginning to colour, sprinkle over the flour.
5. When the flour has been absorbed, tip in the white wine and an equal quantity of water. Strip the tarragon leaves from the stems, reserve the leaves and put the stems in the sauce with the bay leaves. Season the sauce and pour it over the pheasant legs. Add more liquid if it does not cover the legs.
6. Cook the pheasant legs in the oven for 45 minutes–1 hour until tender.
7. Melt the butter in a shallow pan, season the pheasant breasts and start to cook them skin-side down.
8. Cook them gently in the butter so that it does not burn, turning once to cook both sides. Putting a lid on the pan will speed the cooking process. Remove the breasts from the pan and keep warm.
9. Put in the vinegar and reduce to almost nil.
10. Strain the sauce from the pheasant legs and add this to the pan. Bring to the boil and reduce until it thickens, if necessary.
11. Add the cream and check the seasoning.
12. Chop the tarragon leaves and add these and return the pheasant legs to the sauce.
13. To serve, place a leg with sauce on one side of the plate and the breast on the other.

WHITE GAME PITHIVIER

This is a useful dish for using a mixed bag of game. You can also make individual versions of this by making smaller parcels.

EQUIPMENT

Pastry lattice cutter (optional)

28cm wide baking sheet

INGREDIENTS (SERVES 4)

1 pheasant

1 partridge

1 rabbit

(or a similar combination of game)

1 tablespoon sunflower oil

1 carrot

1 onion

1 stick celery

2 bay leaves

2 sprigs thyme

150ml dry white wine

Salt and ground black pepper

25g butter

20g flour

1 tablespoon double cream

1 teaspoon Dijon mustard

Grated nutmeg

500g puff pastry

Egg wash (see page 426)

METHOD

1. Heat the oven to 150°C/gas mark 2.
2. Cut the game up a bit so it will fit into a casserole.
3. Fry the pieces in the oil to give them a bit of colour.
4. Roughly chop the carrot, onion and celery then place with the bay, thyme, wine and seasoning in a casserole with the game.
5. Add enough water to just cover the game. Cover with a lid.
6. Simmer in the oven until the meat is tender.
7. Melt the butter in a pan and stir in the flour. When the flour has cooked out a little, add enough of the strained game stock to make a thick sauce.
8. Bring it to the boil then add the cream, mustard and nutmeg to the sauce. Set aside.
9. Remove all the meat from the bones and cut into smallish pieces.
10. Bind the meat together with the sauce (you may not need all the sauce).
11. Check the seasoning as this needs to be quite highly flavoured. Allow to get completely cold.
12. Heat the oven to 220°C/gas mark 7.
13. Cut the pastry in 2, one piece slightly larger, and roll them both out to roughly 28cm diameter.
14. Cut to a perfect circle using a plate. Place the smaller (i.e. thinner) piece on the baking sheet and spoon the filling in the centre leaving a 5cm border.
15. Wet this border and place the other piece of pastry over the top. (You can run a lattice cutter through the pastry first if you have one.)
16. Press the edges down well and make a hole in the top for the steam to escape (if not using the lattice cutter) and score decorative lines in the pastry.

17. Brush the top of the pastry with egg wash taking care not to let it dribble over the edge.
18. Bake for 40–45 minutes until well browned. Reduce the heat of the oven if it is getting too dark before the time has been reached.

SPATCHCOCK PARTRIDGE WITH CABBAGE & BLACK PUDDING

This is an easy and quick dish to do and brings out the best in this game bird.

INGREDIENTS (SERVES 2)

2 partridge

Salt and ground black pepper

4 slices good quality black pudding

Olive oil

1 onion

1 small pointed cabbage

METHOD

1. First spatchcock the partridge: Turn the bird over so its backbone is uppermost and the parson's nose is pointing away from you. Cut down either side of the backbone with a sharp (serrated) knife or poultry shears.
2. Discard the backbone and flatten the carcass with the heel of your hand.
3. Sprinkle it liberally with the salt and pepper.
4. The partridge can now be pan fried, grilled, roasted in a hot oven or even barbecued. But do not overcook it.
5. Cut the black pudding slices into quarters and fry them in a little hot oil. Set aside.
6. Slice the onion and fry gently until it turns translucent. Remove any of the coarse or damaged outer leaves of the cabbage, cut it into quarters lengthways and remove the central stalk. Shred it very thinly (you may not need all the cabbage).
7. Put the cabbage into the pan with the onion and turn up the heat.
8. Season with salt and pepper and keep stirring whilst it cooks.
9. At the point the cabbage is tender fold in the black pudding.
10. Place the cabbage on to the plates and serve the partridge on top.

CASSEROLE OF WILD BOAR WITH FRIED POLENTA

INGREDIENTS (SERVES 6)

1kg lean shoulder of wild boar cut into cubes

18 small onions – pickling size or shallots

110g smoked streaky bacon

1 tablespoon olive oil

½ bottle strong red wine

25g plain flour

4 bay leaves

2-3 sprigs each of rosemary and thyme

1 tablespoon dried wild mushrooms

1 tablespoon redcurrant jelly

Salt and ground black pepper

10g tomato purée

1 teaspoon Aromatic Spice mix (see page 411)

FOR THE POLENTA

700ml water

200g quick cook, coarse polenta flour

Salt and ground black pepper

Nutmeg

25g butter

25g grated Parmesan

*The cooking time will vary depending on the cut of the meat you are using, the age of the animal and how long it has been hanging.

METHOD

1. Heat the oven to 150°C/gas mark 2.
2. Peel the onions and cut the bacon into lardons. Fry them until they are golden and place in a deep casserole.
3. Fry the boar meat until nicely browned in the same pan, this may need to be done in batches. Transfer the meat to the casserole with the onions and bacon.
4. De-glaze the pan with the red wine to get all the tasty bits from it.
5. Sprinkle the flour evenly over the meat, then add the red wine, herbs, wild mushrooms (chopped up a bit), tomato purée, redcurrant jelly and spice.
6. Use water or stock to top up the liquid level so it just covers the meat and season with the salt and pepper.
7. Bring to the boil, stirring occasionally, and make sure the redcurrant jelly has melted. Cover with a lid and place in the oven.
8. Test the meat after 1½ hours to see how tender it is and cook longer if necessary.* De-fat the surface if necessary and if you require the sauce a little thicker this can be done with cornflour.
9. This dish is best eaten the next day to allow the flavours to develop.
10. To Make the polenta, bring the water to the boil in a saucepan. Pour in the polenta flour and beat as it thickens. (It goes a bit like porridge.)
11. Reduce the heat and let it bubble while you add the seasoning, butter and cheese. Pour the mixture into a loaf tin and allow it to cool. As it cools it will solidify.
12. Remove from the loaf tin and cut it into thick slices. Fry in hot olive oil until crisp and brown. Serve on the side with the casserole.

This is a selection of dishes made without meat. Some are main courses, some are snacks and salads, some are ways of cooking vegetables to accompany main courses (these ones are at the end of the section). I have not given portion indications for all the recipes as it depends on how you are going to serve the dishes.

VEGETARIAN

DHAL SAAG (LENTILS WITH SPINACH)

INGREDIENTS (SERVES 4)

1 onion

2 cloves garlic

1 tablespoon sunflower oil

1 teaspoon black mustard seeds

1 teaspoon each of ground cumin, coriander and turmeric

½ teaspoon asafetida

Seeds from 10 cardamom pods

Salt and ground black pepper

2cm cube root ginger

150g red lentils

1 teaspoon sun-dried tomato purée

600ml water

100g baby leaf spinach

METHOD

1. Chop the onion small and crush the garlic.
2. Heat the oil in a saucepan. Place in the mustard seeds and heat until they begin to pop.
3. Put the onion and garlic into the pan and fry until the onion begins to soften and colour lightly.
4. Put in the spices and seasoning and fry briefly.
5. Grate or finely chop the ginger and add it along with the lentils, tomato purée and water.
6. Bring to the boil and cook gently until the lentils are soft (about 30 minutes).
7. Prior to serving, wilt the spinach in a separate pan and stir into the dhal.
8. Serve with beetroot and mango salad (see next page).

BEETROOT & MANGO SALAD

This salad can be used as a side dish for any vegetarian curry.

INGREDIENTS

4 medium size cooked beetroot (not the vinegared variety)

1 ripe mango

1 handful of rocket

110g walnuts

A small bunch fresh coriander

1 clove of garlic

1cm cube root ginger

1 tablespoon cider vinegar

1 tablespoon walnut oil

1 tablespoon sunflower oil

Salt and ground black pepper

METHOD

1. Cut the beetroot into wedges.
2. Peel and slice the mango.
3. Arrange both onto the rocket and scatter with the walnuts.
4. To make the dressing, purée the garlic and ginger. Chop the coriander.
5. Place them in a bowl with the vinegar and whisk in the two oils.
6. Season with the salt and pepper and spoon it over the salad.

PANEER IN CHILLI TOMATO SAUCE

Paneer is a light Indian cheese and is available on the cheese counter of most supermarkets.

INGREDIENTS (SERVES 4)

250g paneer

4 tablespoons sunflower oil

1 onion

4 cloves garlic

1 red chilli

25g root ginger

2 bay leaves

2 teaspoons ground coriander

½ teaspoon ground turmeric

Seeds from 5 cardamom pods

½ teaspoon salt

400g can chopped tinned tomatoes

100ml water

150g cooked peas

1 teaspoon garam masala

2 tablespoons single cream

Small bunch fresh coriander – chopped

METHOD

1. Cut the paneer into cubes and fry it in 2 tablespoons of hot oil until browned on all sides – remove from the pan.
2. Chop the onion, garlic, chilli and ginger finely.
3. Fry them in the rest of the oil until the onion starts to colour then add the bay leaves, ground coriander, turmeric, cardamom seeds (crushed), salt and tomatoes.
4. Simmer for 4-5 minutes adding a little of the water if it becomes too thick.
5. Add the paneer and peas and simmer for a further 5 minutes.
6. Just prior to serving add the garam masala, cream and fresh coriander.
7. Serve with rice or flat bread.

TAGINE OF SWEET POTATOES WITH CARROT & ORANGE SALAD

None of the spices in this recipe (except the ginger) are hot so you can be liberal with them to increase the flavour.

INGREDIENTS (SERVES 4)

450g sweet potatoes

1 onion

2 cloves of garlic

2cm cube root ginger

½ teaspoon ground black pepper

2 teaspoons ground cumin seed

2 teaspoons ground coriander seed

1 teaspoon paprika (plain or smoked)

½ teaspoon ground cinnamon

1 tablespoon sunflower oil

4 pieces of preserved lemon (see page 406)

600ml water

Salt – the preserved lemon is salty so take care not to over season

50g ground almonds

6 dried apricots (cut in quarters)

FOR THE CARROT AND ORANGE SALAD

1 medium carrot

2 oranges

A small bunch of coriander

Black pepper

1 lime or lemon

METHOD

1. Chop the onion. Crush the ginger and garlic.
2. Peel the sweet potato and cut it into medium size chunks.
3. Sprinkle the spices, ginger and garlic over the sweet potato.
4. Fry the onion in the oil until it begins to brown.
5. Put in the sweet potato etc. and fry for a little longer.
6. Chop the preserved lemon and add with the water, seasoning, almonds and apricots.
7. Bring to the boil, reduce the heat and simmer until the potato is soft and the sauce has thickened.
8. Serve with the fruited couscous (see page 196) and the Carrot and Orange Salad below.

FOR THE CARROT AND ORANGE SALAD

1. Peel and grate the carrot.
2. Remove the skin and fillet the orange with a sharp knife.
3. Chop the coriander very fine.
4. Combine all the ingredients and squeeze over the lemon / lime juice.

IMAM BYALDI

INGREDIENTS (MAKES 2)

2 medium aubergines

75ml olive oil

Salt and ground black pepper

200g fresh ripe tomatoes

1 onion

2 cloves garlic

200g canned chopped tomatoes

Juice of ½ a lemon

½ teaspoon sugar

METHOD

1. Heat the oven to 200°C/gas mark 6.
2. Top and tail the aubergines and cut in half, so you have 4 'drum' shapes.
3. Slash the flesh (but not the skin) in a criss-cross with a sharp knife.
4. Season with salt and pepper, coat liberally with olive oil and cook in a hot oven until soft for about 15-20 minutes.
5. Skin the fresh tomatoes and chop them.
6. Chop the onion very fine and crush the garlic.
7. Fry the onion and garlic in olive oil until they begin to colour then add the chopped and canned tomatoes.
8. Season well and add the lemon juice and sugar.
9. Simmer slowly for about 15 minutes.
10. When the aubergines are cooked, remove them from the oven and press down the flesh with the back of a spoon.
11. Fill this well with the tomato sauce then pour the rest in the dish around the aubergines.
12. Reduce the oven to 170°C/gas mark 3.
13. Pour a little more olive oil into the dish and return it to the oven for a further 20-30 minutes.
14. Baste occasionally with the juices in the tray.

VEGETABLE SAMOSAS

INGREDIENTS (MAKES 6-8)

1 small onion

1 clove garlic

1cm cube root ginger

1 tablespoon vegetable oil

1 teaspoon black mustard seeds

1 teaspoon ground coriander

1 teaspoon ground cumin

Pinch of chilli powder (optional)

1 teaspoon garam masala

Salt and ground black pepper

50g cooked peas

200g cooked sweet potato

Small bunch fresh coriander – chopped

5 sheets filo pastry

Melted butter

Sesame seeds

METHOD

1. Heat the oven to 200°C/gas mark 6.
2. Chop the onion, crush the garlic and ginger.
3. Heat the oil in a shallow pan and fry the mustard seeds until they start to pop.
4. Add the onion, ginger and garlic and fry until they begin to colour.
5. Add the spices and seasonings, the peas and potatoes and continue frying until the potatoes start to colour.
6. Stir in the coriander and set aside to cool.
7. Make strips of the filo pastry about 6cm wide brushing each one with melted butter.
8. Place a teaspoonful of the mixture at one end of the strip and fold up in triangles.
9. Brush each one with melted butter and sprinkle with sesame seeds.
10. Place in the oven and bake for 25–35 minutes.

ONION TART WITH MELTED GOAT'S CHEESE

EQUIPMENT

4 individual tart tins

INGREDIENTS (SERVES 4)

Short Pastry (see page 424)

3 large onions

1 tablespoon olive oil

Salt and ground black pepper

1 teaspoon sugar

A few drops of wine vinegar

1 egg

200g goat's cheese (Capricorn from Somerset is ideal)

METHOD

1. Heat the oven to 190°C/gas mark 5.
2. Chop the onions finely and fry in the oil with the seasoning until they begin to colour.
3. Put in the vinegar and sugar, reduce the heat, cover with a lid and cook slowly to a jam-like consistency. (It may be necessary to remove the lid and reduce the liquid content if the onions make a lot of liquid.) Allow to cool.
4. Line the tart tins with the pastry.
5. Add the egg to the onion mix and spoon the filling into the tart cases.
6. Bake for about 15-20 minutes until the filling is set. Allow to cool.
7. Take the tarts out of the tins and place on a flat oven tray.
8. Slice the cheese into 4 rounds and place a round on each tart.
9. Increase the heat of the oven to 220°C/gas mark 7 and bake the tarts until crisp and the cheese is nicely melting.

POTATO FLAMMEKUECHE

INGREDIENTS

FOR THE BREAD DOUGH

(You may have more than you need here so you can make some rolls with what you have over).

15g fresh yeast

½ teaspoon sugar

150ml warm water

250g white bread flour

1 teaspoon salt

1 tablespoon olive oil

FOR THE TOPPING

2 medium potatoes – about 350g (Desiree reds or Maris Piper)

Salt and ground black pepper

1 small onion

3 tablespoons olive oil

150g crème fraiche or sour cream

50g grated Parmesan

Rosemary or thyme – a few sprigs

METHOD

1. To make the bread, dissolve the yeast and sugar in the warm water.
2. Warm the flour (see page 353) and add the salt and oil.
3. Make a well in the centre. When the water/yeast mixture is fizzing, mix it into the flour to form a dough.
4. Knead until smooth and elastic.
5. Cover with a cloth and put in a warm place.
6. Allow to prove until double in size.
7. Heat the oven to 230°C/gas mark 8.
8. Peel the potatoes and slice them very thinly.
9. Wash the potato slices in cold water and then drain in a colander.
10. Season with the salt and leave them to drain further.
11. Roll out your dough into two rounds and place them onto greased baking sheets.
12. Pat the potato slices dry and mix with 1 tablespoon of the olive oil.
13. Spread the crème fraiche across the two dough bases and sprinkle with pepper.
14. Slice the onions and scatter them over the bases then arrange the potato in an overlapping layer on top.
15. Dress with the herbs tucking some of them under the potato slices.
16. Drizzle them with more olive oil and a bit more pepper.
17. Bake for 15 minutes then scatter over the Parmesan and return them to the oven for a further 5 minutes. Serve immediately.

STUFFED BUTTERNUT SQUASH

EQUIPMENT

Pastry lattice cutter

INGREDIENTS (SERVES 2)

1 medium sized butternut squash

1 tablespoon olive oil

1 onion

50g celery

1 small red pepper

1 tablespoon olive oil

10 sage leaves

8 dried apricots (the soft ones)

50g fresh brown breadcrumbs

Salt and ground black pepper

250g ready-made puff pastry

Egg wash (see page 426)

Smoked pepper sauce (see next page)

METHOD

1. Heat the oven to 180°C/gas mark 4.
2. Cut the squash in half to leave you with the bulbous end (the straight end can be used for other dishes, see page 249).
3. Peel the squash and cut it in half across the circumference.
4. Hollow out the seeds and discard them.
5. Place the bulbous portions of the squash in a roasting tray, brush with oil, sprinkle with a little salt and pepper and roast in the oven for about 20 minutes until they are soft. Allow to cool.
6. Make the stuffing while the squash is roasting. Chop the onion, celery and red pepper and fry in a little oil until they begin to soften.
7. Chop the apricots into quarters and add with the chopped sage.
8. Season and stir in the breadcrumbs. Set aside.
9. Cut the pastry into 2 equal pieces and roll into rectangles about 15 x 10cm.
10. Cut them with the lattice cutter along the 15cm length and turn them over.
11. Fill the cavity of the roasted squash with the stuffing and place each one in the centre of a piece of the pastry, upside down.
12. Wet the pastry edges and gather them around the squash to create a parcel. It doesn't matter if it is not too neat as you won't see this side.
13. Turn the parcels over onto a baking tray and egg wash the pastry.
14. Bake in the oven for 20-25 minutes until the pastry is nice and golden.
15. Serve immediately with a border of the smoked pepper sauce.

SMOKED PEPPER SAUCE

INGREDIENTS (SERVES 2)

1 onion

2 red peppers (as dark red as you can pick out)

2 cloves garlic

1 tablespoon olive oil

3-4 tomatoes (again, as red as possible)

Salt and ground black pepper

A few drops of red wine vinegar

2 teaspoons of smoked paprika (the sweet – not the hot)

1 tablespoon sweet sherry

METHOD

1. Slice the onion and peppers, crush the garlic.
2. Sweat them in the olive oil until they begin to soften.
3. Cut up the tomatoes and add these along with the salt, pepper and vinegar.
4. Cover with a lid and cook until everything is very soft.
5. Add the paprika and whizz in the food processor or liquidizer.
6. Sieve the resulting sauce into a clean pan.
7. Bring to the boil and reduce if it is a little thin or loosen with a few drops of water if it is too thick.
8. Add the sherry just before serving.

GREEK SALAD WITH FRIED HALOUMI

INGREDIENTS (SERVES 2)

2 ripe tomatoes

½ cucumber

1 small red onion

Juice of ½ a lemon

2 tablespoons olive oil

A small bunch each of mint and flat leaf parsley

12 Kalamata olives

Salt and ground black pepper

150g Haloumi cheese

METHOD

1. Cut the tomatoes into quarters and then each quarter in half.
2. Cut the cucumber into chunks roughly the size of the tomato pieces.
3. Slice the onion finely.
4. Mix the lemon juice with 1 tablespoon of the olive oil.
5. Tear or cut the herbs coarsely and place in a bowl with the tomatoes cucumber and onion.
6. Add the olives and season with salt and pepper. Pour over the dressing.
7. Cut the Haloumi cheese into strips. Heat a frying pan with a little olive oil and fry the cheese until it is golden. Place the strips on top of the salad.

RED ONION & FETA TART

INGREDIENTS (SERVES 4)

3-4 large red onions

1 tablespoon olive oil

Salt and ground black pepper

1 teaspoon brown sugar

1 teaspoon balsamic vinegar

250g ready-made puff pastry

110g feta cheese

METHOD

1. Peel and chop the onions and fry in the olive oil until they start to colour.
2. Lower the heat, season with the salt and pepper and add the sugar and vinegar.
3. Continue cooking until the onions take on a jam like consistency and any liquid has evaporated. Allow to cool.
4. Heat the oven to 200°C/gas mark 6.
5. Cut the puff pastry into 4 and roll out each piece until you can cut a circle 10cm in diameter.
6. Place them on a baking sheet or tray.
7. Place a spoonful of the onion mixture into the centre of each circle and spread it out with the back of the spoon but leave a 1cm border.
8. Bake in the oven until the edges are well risen and golden. Crumble the feta cheese over the top of the tarts and return to the oven for 5 minutes before serving.

SWEETCORN & PEA FRITTERS WITH AVOCADO SALSA

INGREDIENTS (MAKES 6)

200g can of sweetcorn

1 small red onion

110g cooked peas

2 eggs

110g plain flour

1 teaspoon baking powder

Salt and ground black pepper

A small bunch of mixed herbs, choose from mint, parsley, tarragon, oregano and basil

Sunflower oil for frying

FOR THE AVOCADO SALSA

2 medium size ripe tomatoes

2 teaspoon cider vinegar

1 teaspoon mango chutney juice (i.e. the chutney without the bits)

½ teaspoon Dijon mustard

75ml olive oil

1 small avocado

Small bunch tarragon

METHOD

1. Drain the sweetcorn.
2. Chop the onion and place it in the food processor with ¾ of the sweetcorn, the peas, eggs, flour, baking powder and seasoning.
3. Process to a batter, transfer to a bowl and add the rest of the sweetcorn.
4. Chop the herbs and stir them into the batter.
5. Heat a non-stick frying pan with a little of the vegetable oil in it and spoon in one tablespoon of mixture per fritter.
6. Allow the mixture to become firm before turning them over. Cook the fritters in batches of 3 for 1 minute each side.

FOR THE SALSA

1. Skin the tomatoes and cut them into quarters.
2. Remove the seeds and place them in a sieve over a bowl.
3. Cut the remaining tomato flesh into neat dice.
4. Press the juices from the tomato seeds and discard the seeds.
5. Into the bowl, with the tomato juice, place the vinegar, chutney and mustard.
6. Whisk together whilst pouring on the olive oil.
7. Peel and cut the avocado into small dice and add this along with the tomato pieces.
8. Finally chop the tarragon and add this.
9. Serve with the sweetcorn fritters and a little salad.

MUSHROOM PANCAKES

INGREDIENTS (SERVES 6 AS A STARTER OR 3 AS A MAIN COURSE).
FOR THE PANCAKES:

75g plain flour

2 eggs

250ml milk (approximately)

Salt

Sunflower oil

FOR THE MUSHROOM MIXTURE

375g mixed wild mushrooms

15g dried porcini mushrooms

25g butter

A sliver of garlic

Salt and ground black pepper

1 teaspoon plain flour

150ml double cream

A sprig of thyme

½ teaspoon Dijon mustard

A few drops of Marsala or medium sherry

50g Parmesan cheese - grated

METHOD

1. To make the pancake batter, make a well in the flour, put in the egg and a little of the milk and beat to a smooth paste.
2. Add more milk until you have the consistency of single cream.
3. Add salt and a little oil and allow to stand.
4. Heat a heavy, flat, preferably non-stick pan and make 6 pancakes.
5. Pick over the mushrooms, brushing away any dirt but try to avoid washing them.
6. Pour 150ml of boiling water over the dried mushrooms.
7. Chop the fresh mushrooms roughly. Crush the garlic.
8. Melt the butter in a pan and gently fry the mushrooms with the garlic, salt and pepper.
9. If there is any liquid in the pan when the mushrooms are cooked, drain this off and reserve it.
10. Return the pan to the heat and sprinkle over the flour. Stir until the flour disappears then add the liquid from the porcini, and any liquid you drained from the mushrooms.
11. When the mixture thickens add the cream, thyme, mustard and Marsala.
12. Check the seasoning, add the reconstituted porcini and allow the mixture to bubble gently for a couple of minutes.
13. Lightly butter an ovenproof dish. Lay out the pancakes and divide the mushroom mixture between the pancakes reserving some of the sauce.
14. Roll or fold the pancakes and arrange in the dish.
15. Spoon the remaining sauce over, and sprinkle with the grated cheese.
16. Brown under a hot grill and serve immediately.

SAVOURY CORN BREAD

In the deep south of the USA corn bread is traditionally served with sticky ribs; a good carbohydrate foil for their richness. I have added more bits and pieces into it to make it more exciting. It is also delicious buttered as a savoury snack or as something a bit different for picnics.

EQUIPMENT

1 litre loaf tin

INGREDIENTS

3 spring onions

110g (prepared weight) sweet potato or squash

½ a red pepper

2 cloves garlic

1 tablespoon olive oil

4 halves sun dried tomato

10 black olives

A few sprigs of thyme and rosemary

75g canned sweetcorn

50g Parmesan or strong Cheddar

110g butter

50g ground almonds

110g plain flour

110g corn meal

2 teaspoons baking powder

4 eggs

Salt and ground black pepper

METHOD

1. Heat the oven to 180°C/gas mark 4.
2. Slice the spring onions, cut the sweet potato and red pepper into small dice and crush the garlic.
3. Sweat all these in the olive oil until they begin to soften. Allow to cool.
4. Chop the sun-dried tomatoes, olives and herbs and put them with the cooked vegetables along with the sweetcorn (drained). Set aside.
5. Grate the cheese and place it in a food processor with the butter, ground almonds, flour, corn meal and baking powder. Process until it looks like crumble then add the eggs.
6. Process again until you have a smooth batter.
7. Remove the batter from the machine and fold in the vegetables.
8. Mix well and season with salt and pepper.
9. Line a the loaf tin with baking parchment and spoon in the batter.
10. Bake for 1 hour. Reduce the heat to 150°C/gas mark 2 for the last 15 minutes if it is looking a bit dark.
11. Cool for 15 minutes before removing from the tin and cooling on a wire rack.

A COUPLE OF VEGETARIAN PASTA RECIPES

Use the fillings below to make either ravioli or cannelloni. Fresh pasta does not keep well in the fridge overnight - it discolours and can go sticky (supermarket fresh pasta is partially dried), so it is best to cook your dishes on the same day. You will also need a pasta rolling machine.

SPINACH & RICOTTA FILLING

INGREDIENTS (MAKES 8-10 RAVIOLI OR 4-5 CANNELLONI)

1 onion

25g butter

225g fresh spinach

50g Ricotta cheese

25g grated Parmesan

Salt and ground black pepper

METHOD

1. Finely chop the onion and sweat in the butter until soft. Set aside.
2. Steam or wilt the spinach and lay it on a tray to cool.
3. Squeeze out the excess moisture and chop.
4. Combine these ingredients with the Ricotta and Parmesan and season.

MUSHROOM & CHEESE FILLING

INGREDIENTS (MAKES 8-10 RAVIOLI OR 4-5 CANNELLONI)

1 onion

1 clove of garlic

110g button chestnut mushrooms

12g dried porcini mushrooms (optional)

A few sprigs each of parsley, marjoram and basil

Salt and ground black pepper

50g Ricotta cheese

25g freshly grated Parmesan

METHOD

1. Chop the onion, crush the garlic and chop the herbs.
2. Pour a little boiling water on the porcini.
3. Fry the onion in a little oil then chop the mushrooms finely and add these along with the herbs and seasoning.
4. Squeeze the excess moisture from the porcini, chop them and add to the pan.
5. Keep cooking the mixture until all the moisture has evaporated. Cool then stir in the two cheeses.

PASTA DOUGH

EQUIPMENT

Pasta rolling machine

INGREDIENTS

250g pasta flour

2 whole eggs

2 egg yolks

Salt

1 tablespoon olive oil

METHOD

1. Place the flour in a bowl and make a well in the centre.
2. Put in the salt and the oil and then place the eggs and yolks in the well. (Hold back one egg white and only use it if needed, as eggs vary in size.)
3. Start mixing with a table knife and only use your hand when the mixture ceases to be sticky – you can also use a food processor for making this dough.
4. When the dough is made, wrap it in cling film and refrigerate for 30 minutes before rolling.

TO MAKE THE RAVIOLI

1. Roll out the pasta in the machine to the finest setting.
2. Cut out rounds of the pasta dough with the largest pastry cutter. Place a teaspoonful of the mixture on one round, dampen the edges and place another round on the top. Crimp the edges together trying to expel any air. Place the raviolis on a lightly-floured tray prior to cooking. Do not pile them up as they will stick together.
3. Cook in boiling salted water without crowding the pan for 3-5 minutes.
4. Remove with a slotted spoon.
5. Serve drizzled with olive oil and sprinkled with a little Parmesan or on a bed of the tomato sauce or with the sage butter sauce (see overleaf).

TO ASSEMBLE THE CANELLONI

1. Heat the oven to 180°C/gas mark 4.
2. Roll out the pasta using the pasta machine at the thinnest setting and then cut it into rectangles approximately 14x18cm.
3. Butter a shallow ovenproof dish. (You can place a layer of the tomato sauce as a base if you wish at this point.)
4. Spoon the filling in a line across the 14cm width of the pasta sheets and roll into a tube, sealing the join with a little moisture.
5. Lay the tubes in the dish and spoon over the cream sauce (see overleaf).
6. Sprinkle with the grated Parmesan and bake for 25–35 minutes.

PASTA SAUCES

INGREDIENTS - CREAM SAUCE

50g butter

35g plain flour

600ml milk

1 small onion

5 cloves

1 bay leaf

Salt and ground black pepper

50ml double cream

METHOD

1. Chop the onion and simmer in the milk with the cloves and bay leaf.
2. In another pan, melt the butter and stir in the flour.
3. Cook for a few moments before adding the milk slowly.
4. Mix to a smooth sauce (it will thicken as it boils).
5. Season with the salt and pepper.
6. Finally add the cream and strain.

INGREDIENTS - TOMATO SAUCE

2 medium onions

1 tablespoon olive oil

2 cloves of garlic

A few sprigs each of basil, thyme and oregano

Small glass of white wine

400g tin of tomatoes or 450g of fresh tomatoes

½ teaspoon sugar

1 teaspoon sun-dried tomato paste

Salt and ground black pepper

METHOD

1. Chop the onions finely and fry in the olive oil.
2. Crush the garlic and chop the herbs and add them to the pan.
3. Chop the tomatoes (if you are using fresh remove the skin) and add them together with the white wine, sugar, tomato paste and seasoning.
4. Bring to the boil and simmer for at least 10-15 minutes.

INGREDIENTS - SAGE BUTTER SAUCE (FOR 2 PORTIONS)

8 small sage leaves

2 tablespoons liquid – you can use the liquid from the dried porcini or white wine or vegetable stock

75g unsalted butter

Salt and ground black pepper

METHOD

1. Shred the sage leaves and place them in a pan with the liquid.
2. When it is simmering add the butter a small piece at a time whilst stirring.
3. To serve spoon over the drained ravioli

FALAFEL

INGREDIENTS (MAKES 8)

250g dried chick peas

1 small onion

1 clove of garlic

Seeds from 10 cardamom pods

1 tablespoon chopped flat leaf parsley

1 tablespoon chopped fresh coriander

½ teaspoon ground coriander seed

½ teaspoon ground cumin

Pinch cayenne pepper

½ teaspoon baking powder

40g plain flour

Salt

Sunflower oil for deep frying

METHOD

1. Soak the chick peas overnight in plenty of cold water.
2. Drain well and grind in a food processor until finely chopped but not mushy.
3. Chop the onion very fine or grate it. Crush the garlic and cardamom and chop the herbs.
4. Place the ground chick peas in a bowl and combine with the other ingredients adding a little water if it is too dry. Season with the salt.
5. Form into balls compressing the mixture well.
6. Deep fry at 180°C for 4 minutes.
7. Drain on kitchen paper.

COURGETTE & FETA FRITTERS

INGREDIENTS (MAKES 6)

1 onion

250g courgettes

2 tablespoons sunflower oil (plus extra for frying)

2 eggs

50g plain flour

2-3 sprigs mint

2-3 sprigs dill

Black pepper

110g Feta cheese

METHOD

1. Chop the onion and courgettes up very fine.
2. Fry the onion in the oil until it starts to colour.
3. Add the courgettes and cook until soft.
4. Mash the Feta cheese with a fork.
5. In a bowl beat the eggs into the flour until smooth.
6. Chop the herbs and add these together with the black pepper and the Feta cheese.
7. Add the onions and courgettes.
8. Heat a non-stick frying pan and cook 1-2 tablespoons of the mixture at a time. Turn the fritters once making sure they are brown on both sides. Drain on kitchen paper.

SAVOURY CHELSEA BUNS

Great for picnics

INGREDIENTS (MAKES 6)
FOR THE BREAD DOUGH

15g fresh yeast

150ml warm water

½ teaspoon sugar

250g strong white bread flour

½ teaspoon salt

2 tablespoons olive oil

Egg wash (see page 426)

FOR THE FILLING

1 medium onion

2 cloves garlic

110g chestnut button mushrooms

1 tablespoon olive oil

Salt and ground black pepper

Small bunch mixed herbs – sage, basil, thyme

1 teaspoon of sun-dried tomato purée

1 tablespoon grated Parmesan

Sesame seeds

METHOD

1. To make the dough, crumble the yeast into the warm water with the half teaspoon of sugar and wait for it to start bubbling.
2. Warm the flour with the salt, then add the oil.
3. Add the yeast/water mixture to the flour and mix to form a dough.
4. Knead briefly and put to prove in a warm place.
5. When it has doubled in bulk it is ready for the next stage.
6. Chop the onion, crush the garlic and chop the mushrooms.
7. Fry the onion in the oil until it begins to colour.
8. Add the garlic, seasoning and mushrooms and continue frying until the mushrooms are cooked and there is no liquid in the pan. Remove from the heat.
9. Chop the herbs and add along with the tomato purée and cheese.
10. Allow to fully cool.
11. Heat the oven to 220°C/gas mark 7.
12. Knead the bread dough briefly then roll it out to a rectangle roughly 25x30cm.
13. Spread the mixture over the surface of the dough and roll up into a cylinder.
14. Cut in slices about 3cm thick with a sharp knife.
15. Oil a deep tray and place the buns in it leaving some space between them for expansion.
16. Brush with egg wash and scatter with sesame seeds.
17. Prove until doubled in size then bake in the oven for 20-25 minutes.

ASIAN COLESLAW

Great with falafel, Thai fish cakes, koftas, chicken, tuna steak – you name it!

You can use other raw vegetables that you either have or like – red cabbage, spinach, pak choi, fennel, celery.

INGREDIENTS

½ of a sweetheart (pointy) cabbage

1 medium carrot

½ a long red pepper

1 small eating apple

1 ripe tomato

A small bunch of fresh coriander

1 tablespoon roasted peanuts or cashew nuts

A handful of beansprouts – optional

FOR THE DRESSING

1 tablespoon sweet chilli sauce

Juice of ½ a lime

1 teaspoon Nam Pla (fish sauce)

1 teaspoon Dijon mustard

1 tablespoon sesame oil

2½cm cube root ginger

2 tablespoon plain yoghurt

METHOD

1. Remove any damaged outer leaves of the cabbage, remove the core and shred it finely.
2. Grate the carrot (you can also grate the core of the cabbage to save wasting it).
3. De-seed and slice the pepper. Peel, core and chop the apple. Chop the tomato.
4. Chop the coriander and mix all the vegetables together except the nuts.

FOR THE DRESSING

5. Peel and grate the ginger and place it in a bowl with the rest of the ingredients for the dressing. Go easy on the lime if you don't want it too sour. Whisk them together.
6. Combine the dressing with the vegetables and finally add the nuts. Best eaten the same day.

TWICE BAKED GOAT'S CHEESE SOUFFLÉS

This easy recipe means you can serve savoury soufflés having done the tricky bit some time earlier. The corn meal that coats the exterior gives it a lovely crust. Instructions are given for serving it two ways.

EQUIPMENT

6 medium ramekins

INGREDIENTS (MAKES 6)

Corn meal

300ml milk

½ an onion

6 cloves

1 bay leaf

50g butter (plus extra for greasing the ramekins)

45g flour

Salt and ground black pepper

150g of hard goat's cheese

3 eggs

300ml double cream

Leaves from 2 sprigs of thyme

50g freshly grated Parmesan

ALTERNATIVE SERVING METHOD
(Does not require the last 3 ingredients above).

After removing the soufflés from the ramekins place them on a lightly oiled baking sheet. Return them to the oven where they will puff up to their original size. Serve them on a bed of dressed salad leaves.

METHOD

1. Heat the oven to 180°C/gas mark 4.
2. Butter the insides of the ramekins and dust with the cornmeal.
3. Place the milk into a saucepan with the onion (chopped), the cloves and bay leaf. Bring to the boil and then take off the heat and allow it to stand for about 20 minutes to infuse.
4. Melt the butter in a saucepan then add the flour. Let it sizzle for a few moments before adding the strained milk, slowly.
5. Stir as the mixture thickens and until all the milk is added. Remove from the heat and season with salt and pepper.
6. Grate the goat's cheese and put it into the sauce and beat until it is melted. Allow to cool. Separate the eggs. Beat the yolks into the sauce and in a separate bowl whip the egg whites to a stiff foam.
7. Fold one third of the egg whites into the mixture to lighten it, then the other two thirds.
8. Spoon the mixture into the ramekins.
9. Place them in a shallow roasting tray half filled with boiling water and bake for 15-20 minutes until risen and lightly golden.
10. Remove from the oven and allow to cool. The soufflés will collapse as they cool – this is meant to happen. When they are completely cool they can be removed from the ramekins gently. On re-heating they will puff up to their original size
11. Take 6 individual shallow dishes. Gently remove the cold soufflés from the ramekins and place them in the dishes.
12. Pour the cream over the soufflés, sprinkle with the thyme leaves and Parmesan and return them to the oven. Bake for 15 minutes until puffed up and golden. Serve immediately.

TOMATO & PESTO TART

EQUIPMENT

A 20cm metal flan tin

INGREDIENTS (SERVES 4)

200g butter puff pastry

3-4 ripe red tomatoes

3-4 cherry tomatoes

Coarse sea salt

FOR THE PESTO

A bunch of fresh basil – approximately 25g

1 tablespoon pine kernels

75g grated Parmesan

1 clove garlic

Ground black pepper

1 tablespoon olive oil

METHOD

1. To make the pesto, place the basil, pine kernels, Parmesan, garlic and black pepper into a food processor and blend to a paste. Finally add the olive oil.
2. Heat the oven 200°C/gas mark 6.
3. Roll out the pastry until it roughly fits the flan tin. It needs to be kept reasonably thick and the sides don't need to come right to the top of the tin.
4. Spread the base with the pesto.
5. Slice the tomatoes thickly discarding the top and bottom slice and lay them in a single layer over the pesto.
6. Cut the cherry tomatoes in half and use them to fill any gaps between the tomato slices.
7. Sprinkle with sea salt.
8. Bake in the oven for 25-35 minutes until the sides are brown and crispy.
9. Serve straight away.

GRATIN OF ROOT VEGETABLES

INGREDIENTS

1kg root vegetables (choose from carrot, parsnip, swede, celeriac, turnip)

2 cloves of garlic

50g butter

300ml double cream

150ml vegetable stock

Salt and ground black pepper

Nutmeg

METHOD

1. Heat the oven to 150°C/gas mark 2.
2. Peel and slice all the vegetables thinly (use a mandolin or food processor if you have either of these). Crush the garlic.
3. Use half the butter to butter an oven dish large enough to take all the vegetables.
4. In a bowl, mix the sliced vegetables with the garlic, cream, stock, and seasoning.
5. Pack them into your dish saving a few nice slices to layer on the top.
6. Melt the rest of the butter and pour it over the top of the vegetables.
7. Cover the dish with foil and cook for 1½-2 hours. Test with a skewer after 1 hour. Remove the foil and increase the heat to 190°C/gas mark 5 for the final 30 minutes to brown the top.

PEAR & STILTON TART

EQUIPMENT

25cm diameter by 4cm deep tart tin

INGREDIENTS (SERVES 6-8)

Short pastry (see page 424)

FOR THE FILLING

150g Stilton (minus any rind)

2 eggs

Ground black pepper

150ml single cream

2 large ripe pears

8 sage leaves

METHOD

1. Heat the oven to 180°C/gas mark 4.
2. Line the flan tin and bake the pastry blind (see page 424).
3. Reduce the heat of the oven to 150°C/gas mark 2.
4. Mash the Stilton with the eggs, then add the cream and pepper. Alternatively do this in a food processor.
5. Peel, quarter and core the pears and lay them cut side down in a fan around the pastry base.
6. Shred the sage leaves and scatter over the pears.
7. Pour over the Stilton mix and bake for 25-35 minutes until the egg filling is just set.
8. Serve warm preferably the same day with a little dressed salad.

PUMPKIN, WALNUT & PECORINO SALAD

INGREDIENTS (SERVES 4)

1450g (prepared weight) squash or pumpkin

2 tablespoons olive oil

Salt and ground black pepper

1 bag of mixed salad leaves

24 fresh walnuts (shelled)

150g Pecorino cheese in the piece

Salad dressing

METHOD

1. Heat the oven to 180°C/gas mark 4.
2. Peel and de-seed the pumpkin and cut it into thick strips, toss in a little oil and season.
3. Transfer to a roasting tray and cook in the oven until they are soft. Set aside.
4. Arrange the salad leaves onto the plates and distribute the walnuts amongst the leaves. Pare the Pecorino into shavings with a peeler and arrange with the salad. Fry the pumpkin slices in a little oil to get them hot again and deliciously golden.
5. To serve, dress the salad just prior to placing the pumpkin pieces in with the leaves.

LEEK & STILTON LASAGNE

You can make your own pasta from the recipe on page 241 or buy fresh lasagne sheets from the supermarket.

EQUIPMENT

20 x 26cm lasagne dish

INGREDIENTS (SERVES 4)

2 medium leeks

1 tablespoon olive oil

2 large tomatoes

110g smoked bacon lardons (optional)

600ml milk

50g butter

40g plain flour

Salt and ground black pepper

1 teaspoon Dijon mustard

50ml double cream

225g Stilton cheese

50g strong Cheddar cheese

50g grated Parmesan

METHOD

1. Heat the oven to 150°C/gas mark 2.
2. Split the leeks down the middle, wash well and then shred finely.
3. Stir fry the leeks using olive oil until they are just beginning to collapse then lay them out on a tray.
4. Skin and de-seed the tomatoes. Cut the flesh into strips and reserve the seeds.
5. Fry the bacon lardons in a little oil if you are using them.
6. To make the white sauce, heat the milk and in another pan melt the butter then stir in the flour. Let it bubble for a few moments before adding the hot milk.
7. Bring to the boil and mix with a whisk or wooden spoon until smooth.
8. Season and add the mustard and cream.
9. Sieve the tomato pips and add the resulting juice to the sauce. Set aside.
10. Crumble or dice the Stilton, grate the Cheddar.
11. Roll out the pasta if you are using home-made and cut it into rectangles to fit your dish.
12. Spread a little of the white sauce over the bottom of the dish and make your first layer of pasta. Over this place half of the leeks, bacon, Stilton and tomato.
13. Pour over a little more sauce, then more pasta. Add another layer of the leeks, bacon etc., then a little more sauce reserving enough for the top over the final layer of pasta.
14. Sprinkle with the Parmesan and Cheddar cheese and place in the oven for 1 hour.

ASPARAGUS & POTATO FRITTATA

INGREDIENTS (SERVES 2)

250g Jersey Royal or Charlotte potatoes

1 onion

1 Romano (long) red pepper

1 tablespoon olive oil

A small bunch fresh asparagus

A few sprigs of basil, tarragon and parsley

4 eggs

Salt and ground black pepper

25g butter

½ a lemon

METHOD

1. Boil the potatoes, drain and allow them to cool.
2. Slice the onion and pepper and fry in a little oil until soft.
3. Trim the woody ends off the asparagus and discard. Cut off the tips to about 6cm lengths and set aside.
4. Cut the rest of the asparagus into small pieces and add to the pan.
5. Remove the skins of the potatoes, mash slightly with the back of a fork and add to the pan also.
6. Chop the herbs. Break the eggs into a bowl and beat with the salt, pepper and herbs.
7. When the potato is beginning to colour remove the pan from the heat. Allow the contents to cool a little before tipping it into the egg mixture. Stir to mix evenly.
8. Heat a clean non-stick pan, put in a little oil then tip in the egg mixture.
9. Turn down the heat and cook until the egg is beginning to set.
10. Place the pan under a hot grill to finish cooking the top.
11. Melt the butter in a separate pan and quickly sauté the asparagus tips.
12. Squeeze the lemon juice into the pan and when the butter froths, tip it over the frittata.
13. Serve in wedges.

CHEESE & HERB SOUFFLÉ

EQUIPMENT

4 medium ramekins

INGREDIENTS (SERVES 4)

30g butter

25g plain flour

150ml milk

75g grated Gruyère cheese

25g grated Parmesan cheese

½ teaspoon English mustard

Salt and ground black pepper

Extra butter for greasing the ramekins

Corn meal or semolina

3 large eggs

A small bunch of mixed herbs, choose from parsley, marjoram, basil, tarragon

METHOD

1. Heat the oven to 190°C/gas mark 5.
2. Melt the 25g of butter in a pan and stir in the flour.
3. Cook the flour out for about a minute and then pour in the milk.
4. Stir with a whisk over the heat until the mixture thickens.
5. Remove from the heat and beat in the cheeses, mustard and seasoning. Don't put in too much salt as the cheese will be quite salty.
6. Allow the mixture to cool while you butter the ramekin dishes and line them with the corn meal/semolina.
7. Separate the eggs, putting the yolks in with the cheese sauce and the whites in a clean bowl. Beat the yolks into the cheese sauce. Chop the herbs and add these.
8. Whisk the egg whites. When the whites are stiff mix about one third of the amount into the cheese mixture then fold the remaining amount in carefully to retain as much air as possible.
9. Spoon the mixture into the ramekins and place in a deep tray.
10. Pour boiling water into the tray about half way up the sides of the ramekins.
11. Bake for about 20–25 minutes until the soufflés are well risen. Serve immediately.

WILD MUSHROOMS WITH TARRAGON & MUSTARD

INGREDIENTS (SERVES 2)

2-4 slices of bread from a French stick or similar

Olive oil

110g either parasol, puff ball, field mushrooms, or porcini

20-25 tarragon leaves

50g butter

Salt and ground black pepper

1 teaspoon Dijon mustard

Squeeze of lemon juice

METHOD

1. Brush the slices of bread with olive oil and crisp them in a hot oven.
2. Clean the mushrooms by brushing them to remove any dirt (avoid washing them as they tend to absorb water).
3. Cut up any mushrooms that are large.
4. Chop the tarragon and knead it into the butter with the black pepper.
5. Heat a shallow pan and start to fry the mushrooms in oil (if they release a lot of liquid keep cooking to reduce the quantity to almost one tablespoon).
6. Stir the mustard into the remaining liquid in the pan then add the tarragon butter a little at a time stirring it in as it melts. Add a squeeze of lemon and a little salt if necessary.
7. Serve straight from the pan onto the hot toast.

CASSEROLE OF CHESTNUTS, MUSHROOMS & RED WINE

Looks so rich and dark and tasty it could be a beef casserole but it is totally vegetarian.

Like most stews and casseroles this is better if kept for 24 hours before consumption. It is also delicious made into a pie or served as an accompaniment to grilled meat for carnivores.

INGREDIENTS (SERVES 4)

2 red onions

3 cloves garlic

1 tablespoon olive oil

400g wild mushrooms or a mixture of cultivated ones

1 teaspoon plain flour

200ml red wine

300ml water or vegetable stock

Small bunch of thyme

25g tomato purée

A little soy or mushroom ketchup

200g peeled chestnuts

Salt and ground black pepper

METHOD

1. Heat the oven to 150°C/gas mark 2.
2. Peel and chop the onion keeping it chunky. Peel and chop the garlic. Fry them in the oil to a golden colour.
3. Brush any dirt off the mushrooms and cut any large ones into smaller chunks. Fry these with the onions and season.
4. Sprinkle the flour over evenly.
5. Add the wine and stock slowly keeping everything in the pan moving.
6. When all the liquid is added put in the thyme, tomato purée and the soy or ketchup. Finally add the chestnuts. Taste the sauce and adjust the seasoning. Transfer to a casserole and cook in the oven for 35–45 minutes.

CABBAGE & SPINACH CAKE

EQUIPMENT

20cm diameter cake tin

INGREDIENTS (SERVES 4)

450g spinach

1 tablespoon sunflower oil

450g green cabbage (not Savoy)

50g butter

Salt and ground black pepper

Nutmeg

METHOD

1. Wash the spinach well then drain in a colander.
2. Heat a large saucepan, add the oil and stir fry the spinach in the oil until it collapses then spread it out on a tray to cool.
3. To prepare the cabbage, remove any damaged leaves and discard. Remove 4 or 5 nice green leaves and keep these whole. Then cut the rest into quarters and remove the stalk.
4. Cook all the cabbage in boiling salted water until it is just tender, then lift it out of the water and spread it on a tray to cool.
5. Take a flan dish or tin of about 20cm in diameter and line it with cling film. Next, remove any large stalks from the green leaves that were kept whole and line the flan dish, overlapping the leaves and leaving the upper half hanging over the edge of the dish.
6. Remove any large stalks from the rest of the cabbage, squeeze it gently to remove any excess moisture and chop it up. Do the same with the spinach and put them together in a bowl.
7. Melt the butter and add it to the bowl along with the seasoning and nutmeg and mix well.
8. Spoon the mixture into the flan dish and fold the overhanging leaves over the top.
9. Cover with cling film and stand a plate on top.
10. To serve, remove the cling film turn the cabbage out onto a board and cut it into wedges. Steam, or microwave to serve.

SWEET PEPPER MOUSSE WITH WARM CHIVE DRESSING

EQUIPMENT

4 x 150ml aluminium pudding basins or 6 dariole moulds

INGREDIENTS (MAKES 4 MEDIUM OR 6 SMALL MOUSSES)

1 large or 2 medium red onions

3 large, deep red peppers

2 cloves of garlic

Olive oil

Salt and ground black pepper

3 eggs

FOR THE DRESSING

1 large ripe tomato

½ teaspoon Dijon mustard

1 teaspoon white wine vinegar

½ teaspoon honey

50ml olive oil

Small bunch chives

METHOD

1. Heat the oven to 150°C/gas mark 2.
2. Peel then chop the onions.
3. Remove the stalk and seeds from the peppers and cut into chunks. Peel the garlic.
4. Place all these ingredients into a casserole, drizzle with olive oil and season well.
5. Cover and cook in the oven until all the vegetables are soft.
6. Allow to cool then drain off any excess liquid, (set aside). Process the cooled vegetables in a food processor with the eggs. Sieve the mixture and pour into the lightly greased pudding basins or dariole moulds. Stand these in a shallow pan in an inch of boiling water. Cover with a sheet of foil. Place the pan in the oven (same heat) for 15 to 20 minutes until the mousses are just set.
7. To make the dressing, skin and de-seed the tomato. Press the seeds through a sieve into a bowl. Discard the seeds. Chop the flesh into neat dice and set aside.
8. Put the mustard, vinegar and honey in a bowl with the saved tomato juice and any cooking juices from the peppers.
9. Whisk whilst adding the oil in a thin stream to get a perfectly emulsified sauce.
10. Chop the chives. Warm the dressing in a pan and add the tomato and chives. Turn the mousses out onto plates and dress with the sauce.

BAKED STUFFED MUSHROOMS

INGREDIENTS (SERVES 4)

4 large flat 'Portobello' mushrooms

Olive oil

Salt and ground black pepper

1 onion

1 clove garlic

50g butter

250g mixed wild mushrooms or a selection of cultivated ones

A small bunch of basil, tarragon and thyme

1 teaspoon Dijon mustard

2 tablespoons double cream

25g fresh brown bread crumbs

25g grated Parmesan

A small bunch of parsley

METHOD

1. Heat the oven to 180°C/gas mark 4.
2. Place the large flat mushrooms in a baking tray, drizzle with olive oil and season with salt and pepper. Bake in the oven for 15-20 minutes.
3. Chop the onion, crush the garlic and sweat them gently in the butter.
4. Chop the wild mushrooms quite small and add these along with some seasoning.
5. If a lot of liquid results from the mushrooms, continue cooking until the pan becomes quite dry.
6. Chop the herbs and add along with the mustard and cream. Cook until the mixture becomes thick then remove from the heat.
7. Making sure the flat mushrooms have the gills uppermost, spoon the wild mushroom mixture onto the flat mushrooms.
8. Chop the parsley and mix together with the bread crumbs and Parmesan.
9. Sprinkle liberally over the mushrooms.
10. Increase the oven temperature to 200°C/gas mark 6 and bake the mushrooms for 10-15 minutes until they are nicely browned.
11. Serve with a few simple dressed leaves or just some leaves of chicory.

WILD MUSHROOM RISOTTO

INGREDIENTS (SERVES 4)

1 medium onion

2 cloves garlic

25g dried porcini mushrooms

600ml vegetable stock

100g chestnut button mushrooms

50g butter

Salt and ground black pepper

200g risotto rice

2 tablespoons dry white vermouth

50g grated Parmesan

50ml double cream

A small bunch of parsley basil and chives

METHOD

1. Finely chop the onion and crush the garlic.
2. Soak the dried mushrooms in a little of the hot stock. Slice the button mushrooms.
3. Sweat the onion and garlic in the butter without colouring then add the button mushrooms and season.
4. Drain the porcini, chop them and add to the pan.
5. Continue cooking until the mushrooms are soft then add the rice.
6. Get the rice hot in the pan and well coated in the butter, then add half the stock and the vermouth. Bring to the boil and turn to a simmer.
7. As the rice absorbs the stock keep adding 50ml of the stock at a time and continue cooking and stirring.
8. This is now the moment of judgement. As you reach the final stages keep testing the rice which should be tender but firm and the liquid 'saucy' for want of a better word. As it reaches that stage, correct the seasoning and add the Parmesan and cream, and a little extra butter if you like.
9. Finally chop the herbs and add them.
10. Serve the risotto straight away. (If it is delayed at this point it will carry on absorbing liquid and become over cooked and stodgy).

WHOLE BRIE BAKED IN FOCACCIA BREAD

Extravagant but great for a centre piece at a buffet.

INGREDIENTS (SERVES LOTS!)

500g white bread flour

300ml warm water

25g fresh yeast

½ teaspoon sugar

Salt and ground black pepper

2 cloves of garlic

2 sprigs rosemary

2 tablespoons olive oil

1 whole mini Brie

A jar of apricot chutney or similar

Egg wash (see page 426)

METHOD

1. Pre heat the oven to 200°C/gas mark 6.
2. Warm the flour (see page 353) and add the salt and pepper to it.
3. Dissolve the yeast in the warm water and add the sugar.
4. Wait for the mixture to fizz. Chop the garlic and the rosemary and add to the flour.
5. Make a well in the centre and put in the oil.
6. Add the yeast mix to the flour and mix with a table knife until the water is absorbed.
7. Add a little more water if it is too dry or some flour if it is too wet.
8. Turn it out on to your work surface and knead to a smooth dough. Put in a warm place to prove.
9. When it has doubled in bulk, knead until smooth and elastic.
10. Roll out the bread dough to a large circle big enough to enclose the whole brie.
11. Place the Brie in the centre and spread the chutney generously over it.
12. Wet the edges of the dough and fold it over the Brie and chutney.
13. Turn the whole parcel over onto an oiled baking sheet, brush with egg wash and put in a warm place to prove.
14. When the dough has again risen place it in the oven for 35–45 minutes. Serve warm cut into wedges.

SPINACH, RICOTTA & HERB TART

EQUIPMENT

6 individual fluted tart tins

INGREDIENTS (SERVES 6)

Short pastry (see page 424)

FOR THE FILLING

225g fresh leaf spinach

Olive oil

110g Ricotta cheese

2 eggs

150ml single cream

A small bunch of herbs: basil, tarragon, marjoram

Salt and ground black pepper

METHOD

1. Set the oven to 180°C/gas mark 4.
2. Line the tart tins with the pastry.
3. Wash the spinach, drain well then wilt it in a hot pan with a teaspoon of olive oil.
4. Spread it out onto a tray to cool then drain and chop it.
5. Beat the cheese with the eggs and when smooth add the cream.
6. Chop the herbs and fold them into the eggs etc. along with the spinach.
7. Season well then spoon it into the pastry cases.
8. Bake for 15-20 minutes until the filling is just set. Allow to cool.
9. Remove them from the tins and place upside down on a baking sheet. Increase the heat of the oven to 200°C/gas mark 6 and bake until the pastry is crisp and golden (about 8-10 minutes).
10. Serve (the right way up) onto a bed of salad.

GOAT'S CHEESE & RED ONION PIZZA

INGREDIENTS (MAKES 2 X 20CM PIZZAS)

250g white bread flour

2 tablespoons olive oil

150ml warm water

12g fresh yeast

1 teaspoon honey

½ teaspoon salt

FOR THE TOPPING

2 large red onions

1 tablespoon olive oil

12 sage leaves

Salt and ground black pepper

2 'Capricorn' or similar type drum-shaped goat's cheeses

METHOD

1. Heat the oven to 230°C/gas mark 8.
2. Dissolve the yeast in the water and add the honey.
3. Warm the flour and add the salt.
4. When the yeast mixture is bubbling, add it to the flour with the oil and mix with a table knife.
5. When it becomes a rough dough, turn it out onto the work surface and knead until smooth. Put it back in the bowl, cover with a cloth and put it in a warm place to prove.
6. Slice the onions and fry in the olive oil until they begin to colour.
7. Reduce the heat and continue cooking until the onion is really soft. Chop the sage leaves and add to the onion with the salt and pepper and set aside.
8. Slice the goat's cheese.
9. Take the proved dough and knead again on the work surface.
10. Cut the dough in half and roll out each half to a circle about 20cm diameter with a rolling pin and place it on an oiled baking sheet or pizza tin.
11. Divide the onion mixture between the two pizzas then place sliced goat's cheese on top. Prove until the edges are puffing up and place it in the hot oven for 10-15 minutes.
12. Serve immediately.

HASSELBACK POTATOES

INGREDIENTS (SERVES 2-4)

450g medium sized Desiree red potatoes

Salt and ground black pepper

4-5 bay leaves

300ml chicken stock

Olive oil or butter

METHOD

1. Heat the oven to 190°C/gas mark 5.
2. Peel the potatoes and make a series of cuts nearly all the way through but leaving them joined at the base. (You can place a small piece of thin plywood behind the potato to stop the knife going all the way through).
3. Place them in roasting tray and sprinkle with salt and pepper.
4. Tear up the bay leaves and scatter them around the potatoes, placing a few bits into the cuts.
5. Pour over the stock and brush the tops with melted butter or oil.
6. Bake them in the oven for 45-55 minutes until the tops are browned and the potatoes have absorbed all the stock.
7. It may be necessary to check throughout the cooking and maybe brush them again with butter or oil.

CARROT & PARSNIP PURÉE

INGREDIENTS (SERVES 6-8)

450g carrots

450g parsnips

1 clove of garlic crushed

50g butter

Salt and ground black pepper

METHOD

1. Peel and chop the carrots and parsnips.
2. Cook in salted water until soft. Drain well.
3. Add the crushed garlic, butter and some black pepper.
4. Mash with a potato masher or for a very smooth purée finish in a food processor.

SWEET & SOUR RED CABBAGE

Very good with pork or game.

INGREDIENTS (SERVES 4-6)

1 medium red cabbage

1 onion

1 tablespoon sunflower oil

½ teaspoon crushed star anise (optional)

1 cooking apple

1 small glass red wine

1 teaspoon sugar

A few drops red wine vinegar

1 tablespoon of sunflower oil

Salt and ground black pepper

METHOD

1. Shred the cabbage finely. Chop the onion.
2. Fry the onion in the oil with the star anise.
3. Place the cabbage in a pan. Peel and grate the apple and add it to the cabbage.
4. Add the cooked onion, the wine, wine vinegar and sugar.
5. Season well and cook on a slow heat or in a low oven.
6. The cabbage can be served fully cooked or slightly 'al dente'.

DAUPHINOISE POTATOES

EQUIPMENT

Casserole or shallow baking dish.

INGREDIENTS (SERVES 4-6)

1kg waxy potatoes such as reds

300ml single cream

Salt and ground black pepper

2 cloves garlic

50g butter

METHOD

1. Heat the oven to 180°C/gas mark 4.
2. Peel and slice the potatoes and place them in a bowl with the cream.
3. Season well with the salt and pepper. Crush the garlic and mix this in well.
4. Transfer the potatoes into the dish and press them down until they are level.
5. Melt the butter and brush it over the top of the potatoes.
6. Bake in the oven for 45 minutes to 1 hour.

POTATO ROSTI

For a parsnip or celeriac rosti replace 50% of the potato with the other vegetable and proceed as normal. It doesn't work without the potato as it needs the starch to stick together.

INGREDIENTS (MAKES 6 SMALL OR 1 LARGE)

450g peeled potatoes (King Edward or Maris Piper)

Salt and ground black pepper

2 tablespoons olive oil

METHOD

1. Grate the potatoes and make sure they get tossed in salt and half the oil immediately and before they have time to discolour.
2. Leave to stand for 5 minutes (the salt will draw moisture from the potato) then drain the potato well.
3. Place it in another bowl and sprinkle over the black pepper.

COOKING METHOD 1

Heat a pan with a little oil in it and make small potato cakes with the grated potato about the thickness of a pound coin. Tidy up the edges with a fork and use it also to press down the potato to compact it. Turn them over to cook the other side when the first side is browned.

COOKING METHOD 2

Heat a pan with a little oil and place all the potato into the pan, pressing it down with the back of a fork. Cook slowly until browned, shaking the pan to prevent it sticking. Turn over to cook the other side. Slide it out of the pan and finish cooking in a hot oven for 10-15 minutes depending on thickness. Serve in wedges.

CREAMY MASH

For really superb creamy mash I always use King Edward potatoes or at a pinch Desiree Reds. Boil the potatoes in the usual way, drain them and put them back into the pan to let the steam rise from them and ensure they become quite dry. Next, mash thoroughly and if you have a potato ricer use that for faultless, lump-free mash. Next, add a knob of butter, a pinch of freshly ground black pepper, a little grated nutmeg and check the salt content. Finally beat in as much milk as will make the mash quite creamy.

CAJUN MACAIRE POTATOES

INGREDIENTS (MAKES 4)

4 medium size potatoes

50g butter

Pinch salt

1 teaspoon Cajun spices

1 tablespoon sunflower oil

METHOD

1. Cook the potatoes in their skins either by baking or boiling.
2. Cool and peel.
3. Mash the flesh with the butter using a fork and season with the salt and spices.
4. Form into flat cakes with your hands.
5. Fry to a golden brown on both sides.

STEAMED CABBAGE

Use a tender cabbage such as the pointed cabbage. This is really quick to do and a lovely way of keeping all the flavour and texture of fresh cabbage.

INGREDIENTS (SERVES 4-6)

1 medium cabbage

1-2 carrots

12g butter

Salt and ground black pepper

Nutmeg

1 tablespoon water

METHOD

1. Remove any coarse or damaged leaves from the cabbage. Cut it into quarters and remove the stalk.
2. Shred the cabbage and peel and grate the carrot, (you can also grate the cabbage stalk if you wish).
3. Place all the vegetables in a shallow pan and season well.
4. Put in the butter, nutmeg and the tablespoon of water.
5. Put a lid on the pan and place it over a high heat.
6. Stand over it and when there is a lot of steam coming out from under the lid remove the pan from the heat and stir the contents well.
7. It is now ready to serve.

DESSERTS

HOT FIG SANDWICH

A fantastically quick pudding to make especially if you buy the brioche and custard ready-made.

INGREDIENTS (SERVES 4)

4-6 fresh ripe figs

8 slices of brioche loaf

300ml thick custard

Clear honey for drizzling

METHOD

1. Set the oven to 220°C/gas mark 7.
2. Cut the figs into thick slices.
3. 'Butter' the brioche slices with the custard and lay fig slices on four of them.
4. Place the other brioche slice on top to make four sandwiches.
5. Place the sandwiches on a baking sheet and place in the oven.
6. Cook for 10 minutes until golden brown.
7. To serve, place a spoonful of warmed custard onto each plate, cut the sandwiches in half diagonally and arrange on top of the custard.
8. Drizzle with honey.

PITHIVIER

INGREDIENTS (SERVES 6)

350g ready-made butter puff pastry

Flour for rolling

FOR THE ALMOND CREAM

125g ground almonds

125g caster sugar

25g plain flour

125g butter

1 egg

A couple of drops of almond essence or a little Amaretto (both optional)

FOR THE GLAZE

Egg wash (see page 426)

METHOD

1. Heat the oven to 180°C/gas mark 4.
2. To make the almond cream, place the almonds, caster sugar and flour into a bowl and add the butter chopped into small pieces.
3. Rub the butter into this mixture until it resembles crumble.
4. Add the egg and the essence / Amaretto if you are using them and beat the mixture to a paste. Set aside.
5. Cut the pastry in half and roll out each one large enough to cut out a 20cm in diameter circle from each one.
6. Place one circle on a baking sheet and spoon the almond cream into the centre. Spread it evenly leaving a 2cm border.
7. Wet this border with water and place the other circle over the top bringing the edges together, taking care not to trap any air.
8. Press the edges down with a fork to create a tight seal.*
9. Brush with egg wash thoroughly taking care not to dribble any over the cut edges of the pastry.
10. Bake the pithivier for 15 minutes at 180°C/gas mark 4 then reduce the heat to 150°C/gas mark 2 for a further 20-25 minutes.
11. Transfer the baked pithivier to a wire cooling rack.
12. Serve warm, if possible, with clotted cream.
13. *You can decorate this dessert by cutting a design on the edge and you can also drag a fork in a spiral through the egg wash for a pretty decoration.

PEACH CLAFOUTIS TART

You can use other fruits in season, for example, apricots, plums, cherries, nectarines, gooseberries.

EQUIPMENT

25cm diameter x 4cm deep tart tin

INGREDIENTS (SERVES 6-8)

Sweet pastry (see page 425)

FOR THE FILLING

25g butter

2 eggs

50g plain flour

75g caster sugar

200ml full cream milk

50ml double cream

3 ripe peaches

METHOD

1. Heat the oven to 180°C/gas mark 4.
2. Line the tart tin with the pastry and part bake it blind (see page 424).
3. Reduce the oven temperature to 150°C/gas mark 2.
4. To make the filling, first melt the butter.
5. Whisk the eggs together with the flour and sugar to make a smooth paste.
6. Slowly add the milk beating all the time.
7. Finally beat in the cream and the melted butter.
8. Pour boiling water over the peaches and leave for 5 minutes before peeling them (This is optional as sometimes they do not peel as well as one would like them to.)
9. Halve the peaches, removing the stone, and cut each half into three pieces.
10. Lay them in the tart case.
11. Pour over the batter filling, taking care not to overfill.
12. Transfer to the oven and bake for 20-25 minutes until the filling is set.

TIRAMISU

Literally translated as 'pick-me-up' it was invented in Italy in the seventies as a mid-morning calorie boost to go with that espresso!

EQUIPMENT

It is important to use the right size dish for this – it should be the size of 5 of your biscuits laid side by side and the depth of over 2 of the same biscuits

INGREDIENTS (SERVES 4)

1 teaspoon of instant coffee made up with 75ml boiling water

2 tablespoons brandy

25g dark 70% chocolate

2 medium eggs

2 tablespoons caster sugar

125g mascarpone

10 sponge fingers or Savoiardi biscuits

1 heaped teaspoon cocoa powder

METHOD

1. Mix the coffee and brandy together.
2. Chop the chocolate up small.
3. Place the eggs in a clean glass or china bowl, add the sugar and whisk until light and pale.
4. Fold the mascarpone into this mixture until smooth.
5. Dip the sponge fingers into the coffee/brandy mixture tuning once and make a layer in your dish using five of the biscuits - do not leave them too long in the mixture otherwise they become soggy.
6. Spread half the mascarpone mixture over the biscuits.
7. Scatter the chocolate over the top and then repeat with the remaining biscuits and mascarpone.
8. Place the cocoa powder in a sieve and shake a layer over the top of the finished pudding.
9. Cover with cling film and refrigerate.

PIEMONTESE STUFFED PEACHES

INGREDIENTS (SERVES 4)

4 large ripe peaches

12 Amaretti biscuits – the crisp ones

25g ground almonds

40g caster sugar

2 teaspoons cocoa powder

A few drops of Amaretto

150ml sweet white wine, preferably Italian!

25g unsalted butter

METHOD

1. Heat the oven to 200°C/gas 6.
2. Halve the peaches and remove the stone. Enlarge the hole in the peach where the stone was by scooping out a little more of the flesh.
3. Chop this flesh and place it in a bowl.
4. Crumble in the Amaretti biscuits and add the almonds, sugar and cocoa to the mix.
5. Add the Amaretto and some of the wine if necessary to make a cohesive stuffing.
6. Place the peach halves flat-side up in a baking dish.
7. Fill the cavities with the stuffing and dot each one with butter.
8. Sprinkle a little extra sugar over the peaches and pour the rest of the wine in the baking dish.
9. Bake for 20-25 minutes and serve at room temperature with a dollop of mascarpone or clotted cream.

DANISH CHOCOLATE GÂTEAU

This defies description as it is not really a gâteau, more a type of refrigerator cake (but it is not really a cake either). Having said that, it is delicious and can be served as a dessert with cream or in fingers to go with coffee or as a sneaky fridge raid.

EQUIPMENT

750ml loaf tin or similar

INGREDIENTS (SERVES 6 AS A DESSERT)

75g butter

75g golden syrup

200g dark chocolate

2 shots of rum or brandy

75g digestive biscuits or Hobnobs

50g whole toasted almonds

50g raisins (preferably soaked in sherry overnight)

50g glacé cherries (natural colour)

METHOD

1. Line the tin with parchment paper.
2. Heat the butter and syrup together in a saucepan and whisk to amalgamate them. Remove from the heat and break the chocolate into it.
3. Stir until the chocolate is melted, then add the rum or brandy.
4. Break the digestive biscuits into a bowl and then add the nuts and fruit.
5. Pour over the chocolate and mix well.
6. Spoon the mixture into the loaf tin, packing it down well with the back of a spoon. Smooth the top and place in the refrigerator overnight.
7. To serve, turn out of the loaf tin and cut into thick slices.

CRÈME BRÛLÉE

EQUIPMENT

Blow torch

4 medium ramekins

INGREDIENTS (SERVES 4 DEPENDING ON RAMEKIN SIZE)

5 egg yolks

50g caster sugar

1 vanilla pod or ½ teaspoon vanilla paste

450ml double cream

50g caster sugar

Extra caster sugar for glazing the top

METHOD

1. Heat the oven to 150°C/gas mark 2.
2. Place the egg yolks in a bowl with the sugar and beat them together.
3. Cut a slit in the vanilla pod lengthways and place it in a saucepan with the cream.
4. Bring the cream to the boil then whisk it into the egg / sugar mix. Scrape a few seeds from the vanilla pod and remove it from the mix.
5. Strain the mixture and pour it into the ramekins.
6. Stand them in a shallow pan of hot water, cover with foil and place in the oven for 30 - 40 minutes. (Cooking time is crucial, they should be just set, overcooking will scramble them so keep checking). Allow to cool.
7. Spread a thin layer of caster sugar over the top of the brûleé taking care not to get any on the edges, caramelize with a blow torch, chill before serving.

LAYERED RASPBERRY CRÈME BRÛLEÉ

A variation on the previous recipe.

EQUIPMENT

Blow torch

6 medium ramekins and a 600ml volume Pyrex dish or similar

INGREDIENTS (SERVES 4 DEPENDING ON RAMEKIN SIZE)

Crème brûleé mix from the previous recipe

Caster sugar for glazing the top

150g fresh raspberries

10 crisp Amaretti biscuits

Liqueur of your choice (Amaretto/Grand Marnier/Kirsch)

METHOD

1. Heat the oven to 150°C/gas mark 2.
2. Make the brûleé custard as in the previous recipe but place the mixture into a suitably sized Pyrex dish or similar.
3. Stand it in a shallow pan of hot water, cover with foil and place in the oven for 45 minutes. (Cooking time is crucial, it should be just set, overcooking will scramble them so keep checking.) Allow to cool then refrigerate overnight.
4. Take a ramekin and spread a thin layer of custard over the bottom of the ramekin and spread it flat with the back of a spoon.
5. Place 3-4 raspberries onto the custard and then crumble over some of the biscuit.
6. Sprinkle sparingly with some of the liqueur and then make another layer of custard. Repeat the process until you reach the top of the ramekin with a layer of custard which should be spread as flat as possible.
7. Repeat with the remaining ramekins.
8. Spread a thin layer of caster sugar over the top of each brûleé.
9. Caramelize with a blow torch and chill before serving.
10. Needs to be served within 1 hour or the biscuit starts to go a bit soggy.

POTTED CHOCOLATE

This is a very rich chocolate dessert, small portions are recommended.

EQUIPMENT

6 small ramekins or pots

INGREDIENTS (SERVES 6)

225g good quality plain chocolate (70% cocoa solids)

90ml strong coffee i.e. espresso or similar

60ml Brandy (or liqueur of your choice)

3 eggs

METHOD

1. Break the chocolate up into a bowl and pour over the hot coffee. When the chocolate has melted, stir until smooth then mix in the liqueur.
2. Separate the eggs and stir the yolks into the chocolate.
3. Whisk the egg whites to a light foam (do not over whip or they become chalky) then fold into the chocolate with a spatula. Pour into the ramekins and chill until set.

VARIATIONS

For a non-alcoholic variety use 150ml of strong coffee.

For a Chocolate Orange Pot use orange zest and 150ml of concentrated orange juice or a combination of coffee and orange liqueur.

Amaretto liqueur gives a pleasant almondy flavour.

Also, looks nice served in glasses with cream poured on the top just before serving so they look like Irish coffees.

PROFITEROLES

INGREDIENTS (SERVES 4)

300ml double cream

TO MAKE THE CHOUX PASTRY

85ml water

85ml milk

65g butter

100g plain flour

2 large eggs

Chocolate fudge sauce (below)

METHOD

1. Heat the oven to 220°C/gas mark 7.
2. Place the water, milk and butter into a saucepan and bring to the boil.
3. Tip the flour into the pan and beat over the heat until the mixture is smooth and ceases to be sticky - about 1-2 minutes.
4. Cool slightly, transfer to a bowl and beat in the eggs one at a time. (This can be done in a food processor).
5. Pipe out onto baking sheets in pieces about the size of your first finger joint.
6. Bake for 20 minutes or until puffed up and golden brown.
7. Make a hole on the base or side of each one with the point of a knife.
8. Put back in the oven for 2 minutes to drive out the steam. Allow to cool.
9. Whip the cream and place it in a piping bag with a small nozzle. Fill the profiteroles with the cream using the hole you made earlier.
10. Serve in a dish with the warm chocolate sauce below.

CHOCOLATE FUDGE SAUCE

INGREDIENTS (SERVES 6)

150ml single cream

75ml milk

75ml golden syrup

25g butter

150g caster sugar

½ teaspoon vanilla paste

110g plain chocolate (70% cocoa solids)

METHOD

1. Boil together the cream, milk, syrup, butter and sugar until it amalgamates and thickens.
2. Remove from the heat and add the vanilla essence and the chocolate. Stir until the chocolate is fully melted.

GOUGÉRE WITH STRAWBERRIES & CREAM

EQUIPMENT

Baking sheets

INGREDIENTS (SERVES 4)

200ml double cream (whipped)

200g fresh strawberries (hulled and halved)

110g icing sugar

Chocolate sauce / or melted plain chocolate

METHOD

1. Heat the oven to 220°C/gas mark 7.
2. Make the choux pastry as in the previous recipe.
3. Pipe out onto baking sheets in rings about 10cm in diameter.
4. Bake for 20 minutes or until puffed up and golden brown.
5. Pierce the base of each one with the point of a knife and then place back in the oven for 2 minutes to drive out the steam.
6. Allow to cool then cut the rings in half through the circumference.
7. Whip the cream and fill the gougeres with cream and strawberries. Place the other half back on top.
8. Mix the icing sugar with a little hot water to make pouring consistency white icing and drizzle over the gougeres.
9. Zigzag with chocolate/sauce for decoration.

TREACLE TART

EQUIPMENT

20cm diameter x 3.5cm deep tart tin

INGREDIENTS (SERVES 4-6)

Sweet pastry (see page 425)

FOR THE FILLING

280g golden syrup

75g fresh white breadcrumbs

Zest of 1 lemon

METHOD

1. Heat the oven to 180°C/gas mark 4.
2. Line the flan tin with the pastry and part bake blind (see page 424).
3. Warm the golden syrup. Finely grate the zest from the lemon and stir it into the syrup with the breadcrumbs.
4. Pour the filling into the pastry case.
5. Cut some strips of pastry and decorate the top of it if you like that sort of thing then return the tart to the oven for 15-20 minutes.
6. You can add a squeeze of lemon juice to the filling which will balance the intense sweetness of this if you like.

LEMON SOUFFLÉ

Soufflés work better with strong flavours because the amount of egg you have to use dilutes any original flavour so lemon, lime, passion fruit all work well.

Using cornflour gives a lighter texture and a better crust. Also, leaving out any butter in the mixture means you get a more stable egg foam and therefore better rise.

EQUIPMENT

4 medium ramekins

INGREDIENTS (MAKES 4)

15g cornflour

110ml milk

25g butter

35g caster sugar (plus extra for the dishes)

1-2 lemons depending on juiciness

2 eggs

METHOD

1. Heat the oven to 200°C/gas mark 6.
2. Mix the cornflour with a little of the milk.
3. Bring the rest of the milk to the boil and then whisk in the cornflour mixture until it thickens. Transfer to a bowl and cover with cling film.
4. Soften the butter and make sure the ramekins are very cold.
5. Butter the insides of the ramekins, then coat with caster sugar.
6. Grate the zest from the lemon and squeeze the juice. Place these in a food processor with the thickened milk.
7. Separate the eggs and put the yolks in the food processor and the whites in a clean bowl. Whizz up the mixture in the food processor to a smooth custard.
8. Whisk the egg whites with the 35g of sugar until stiff.
9. Fold the two mixtures together carefully and spoon into the ramekins to the top.
10. Place the ramekins into a shallow pan with a little hot water in it.
11. Cook for 20-25 minutes until well risen.
12. Dust with icing sugar and serve immediately.

PASSION FRUIT SOUFFLÉ

EQUIPMENT

4 medium ramekins

INGREDIENTS (MAKES 4)

5-6 passion fruit

Juice of ½ a lemon

15g cornflour

100ml milk

25g butter

2 eggs

35g caster sugar (plus extra for the dishes)

METHOD

1. Halve the passion fruit, scoop out the juice and pips from the centres and place it in a food processor with the lemon juice.
2. Whizz up the mixture and strain to remove the pips. Put a few pips back (for authenticity).
3. Heat the oven to 200°C/gas mark 6.
4. Mix the cornflour with a little of the milk.
5. Bring the rest of the milk to the boil and then whisk in the cornflour mixture until it thickens.
6. Transfer to a bowl and cover with cling film.
7. Soften the butter. Make sure the ramekins are very cold then butter the insides. Coat them with caster sugar.
8. Place the passion fruit and lemon juice in a food processor with the thickened milk.
9. Separate the eggs and put the yolks in the food processor and the whites in a clean glass or ceramic bowl. Whizz up the ingredients in the food processor.
10. Whisk the egg whites with the sugar until stiff.
11. Fold the two mixtures together, carefully, and spoon into the ramekins to the top.
12. Place the ramekins into a shallow pan with a little hot water in it.
13. Cook for 20-25 minutes until well risen.
14. Dust with icing sugar and serve immediately.

QUEEN OF PUDDINGS

One of the best old-fashioned puddings!

INGREDIENTS (SERVES 4)

110g sponge cake or brioche crumbs

50g caster sugar (plus extra for the top of the meringue)

450ml of milk

150ml double cream

3 eggs

15g butter

Jam (of your choice)

175g granulated sugar

METHOD

1. Heat the oven to 180°C/gas mark 4.
2. Mix the crumbs and sugar.
3. Separate the eggs and place the yolks and whites in separate bowls.
4. Place the milk and cream in a saucepan and bring to the boil.
5. Whisk the boiling mixture onto the egg yolks then fold in the crumbs and sugar.
6. Butter a suitable dish and pour the mixture in it.
7. Bake for 30-35 minutes until set.
8. Reduce the oven heat to 110°C/gas mark ¼.
9. Whip the egg whites with the sugar until you have a thick meringue.
10. Spread a little jam over the top of the pudding then pipe the meringue over the top leaving some little gaps.
11. Sprinkle the top with caster sugar and bake for 30 minutes until the meringue is crisp.
12. Spoon a little jam into the gaps you left in the meringue.

SWEET CUSTARD TARTS WITH RHUBARB

EQUIPMENT

Large muffin tin with 6 wells or 6 individual tart tins

INGREDIENTS (MAKES 6)

Sweet pastry (see page 425)

450g rhubarb

50g caster sugar

FOR THE CUSTARD

400ml milk

Vanilla pod or ½ teaspoon vanilla paste

110g caster sugar

2 eggs

20g plain flour

15g custard powder

Nutmeg

METHOD

1. Heat the oven to 180°C/gas mark 4.
2. Line the muffin / tart tins with pastry and bake blind, (see page 424).
3. Cut the rhubarb into 2cm lengths and place it in an oven proof dish (not metal).
4. Sprinkle with the sugar and place in the oven until cooked, about 35–45 minutes.
5. For the custard, place the milk in a saucepan and bring to the boil with the split vanilla pod and 75g of the sugar.
6. Whisk together the eggs and the rest of the sugar.
7. Add the flour and custard powder and whisk thoroughly.
8. When the milk boils, remove the vanilla pod scraping some of the seeds from it back into the milk. Whisk the milk onto the eggs etc.
9. Return to the heat and mix whilst it thickens.
10. Strain, pour into the pastry cases and sprinkle with grated nutmeg.
11. Allow to cool slightly then arrange some rhubarb on the top of each custard tart.
12. Serve warm or at room temperature.

CHOCOLATE TORTE

EQUIPMENT

20cm diameter spring-form or loose-based cake tin

INGREDIENTS (MAKES 4-6)

110g plain chocolate (70% cocoa solids)

110g butter

3 eggs

110g caster sugar

60g plain flour

60g Amaretti biscuits crushed

2 tablespoons Amaretto

TO SERVE

Raspberries

Thick cream

METHOD

1. Line the base of the cake tin with parchment paper.
2. Heat oven to 150°C/gas mark 2.
3. Melt the chocolate then work the butter into it until it is melted and smooth.
4. Using an electric beater and a glass or ceramic bowl whisk the eggs with half the sugar to a light foam.
5. Place half the egg mixture into the chocolate with the rest of the sugar and the (sifted) flour and fold it in.
6. Fold in the rest of the egg mixture, the Amaretti biscuits and the Amaretto.
7. Transfer to the cake tin and bake for 35-40 minutes until cooked.
8. Allow to cool a little then turn out onto a cooling rack. Dust with icing sugar.
9. Serve with raspberries and thick cream.

CHOCOLATE PEAR TART

EQUIPMENT

25cm diameter x 4cm deep tart tin

INGREDIENTS

3 ripe medium size William pears

Caster sugar for sprinkling

FOR THE SWEET CHOCOLATE PASTRY

200g plain flour

85g icing sugar

50g cocoa powder

85g butter

1 egg

1 egg yolk

FOR THE CHOCOLATE FILLING

75g plain chocolate (70% cocoa solids minimum)

75g butter

75g caster sugar

1 egg

25g plain flour

METHOD

1. Heat the oven to 180°C/gas mark 4.
2. For the pastry, mix together the flour, icing sugar and cocoa.
3. Cut the butter into cubes and rub into the dry ingredients until it resembles fine breadcrumbs.
4. Work in the egg and yolk to make a dough.
5. Chill while you make the chocolate cream.
6. Melt the chocolate over hot water.
7. For the chocolate filling beat together the butter and caster sugar until light and fluffy.
8. Work in the egg and the flour and finally fold in the melted chocolate.
9. Line the flan dish with the pastry and part blind bake (see page 424).
10. Fill the pastry case three quarters full with the chocolate filling.
11. Peel, halve and de core the pears.
12. Arrange the six halves of pear, flat-side down, on the chocolate.
13. Sprinkle caster sugar over the pear flesh and bake in the oven for 30-40 minutes until cooked.

BAKEWELL TART

Use any jam of your preference or try a good quality marmalade like Tiptrees for an Orange Bakewell.

The filling for this takes quite a while to cook so the pastry should be cooked through when the frangipane is done. If you are concerned about this you can part blind bake the pastry first (see page 424).

EQUIPMENT

25cm diameter x 4cm deep tart tin

INGREDIENTS (SERVES 6-8)

150g butter

150g icing sugar

40g plain flour

2 eggs

150g ground almonds

A few drops of almond essence (optional)

Sweet pastry (see page 425)

2-3 tablespoons jam

25g flaked almonds

Caster sugar

METHOD

1. Set the oven to 150°C/gas mark 2.
2. To make the frangipane filling, soften the butter and beat it together with the icing sugar.
3. Beat in the flour, eggs, ground almonds and essence if you are using it. Set aside.
4. Line the tart tin with the pastry then spread a layer of the jam (not too thick) over the base. Top with the almond filling taking care to seal in the jam.
5. Scatter with flaked almonds and sprinkle with caster sugar.
6. Bake for 45-55 minutes. Test the middle with a skewer to check it is cooked in the middle.

APPLE CUSTARD WITH CINNAMON TOAST CRUMBLE

EQUIPMENT

6 ramekins

INGREDIENTS (SERVES 6)

3 small Cox apples

1 tablespoon orange juice

50g caster sugar

300ml double cream

4 egg yolks

FOR THE CRUMBLE

25g butter

25g caster sugar

75g brown breadcrumbs

1 rounded teaspoon cinnamon

METHOD

1. Set the oven to 150°C/gas mark 2.
2. Peel, core and slice the apples and place them in a pan with the orange juice and sugar.
3. Cook slowly until the apples are really soft then mash them to a purée with the back of a fork. Set aside.
4. Place the cream into a clean pan and bring to the boil.
5. Place the egg yolks into a basin with the caster sugar and whisk until smooth. When the cream is boiling, pour it onto the egg yolks and sugar.
6. Strain the mixture onto the apple, mix well and then spoon into 6 ramekins.
7. Stand the ramekins in a shallow tray and pour boiling water into the tray to a depth of about 2cm.
8. Cover the whole tray with foil and place in the oven for 20-30 minutes until the custards are set. Cool, then chill in the refrigerator.
9. To make the crumble, melt the butter in a frying pan, add the breadcrumbs and cook over a low heat, turning regularly, to get the breadcrumbs fried and crisp but without getting them too dark.
10. Sprinkle over the caster sugar and cinnamon and continue cooking, and turning, until the sugar caramelizes.
11. Spread them out on a tray to cool down.
12. To serve spread a layer of the crumble on top of each custard just before serving.
13. The crumble will keep fresh for a few days in a sealed container.

BANOFFI PIE

What follows here is a small selection of Banoffi variations including the classic Banoffi Pie. There are now a lot of products on the market of ready-made toffee for the making of this dish. Unfortunately they can be too soft and tend to ooze after cutting one or two slices, so for the real thing you will need to boil cans of condensed milk. The Chocolate Banoffi included here is the exception as it has melted chocolate added to it and therefore sets more firmly.

BOILING THE CANS OF CONDENSED MILK

There are a few points worth bearing in mind when making the toffee. The cans must be boiled unopened. They must always be fully immersed in the water at all times. Only if the water boils dry is there a danger of the cans exploding. It is worth boiling several cans at once to save on power especially as spare cans can be stored like any other can. After a couple of months they will start to form sugar crystals in the toffee creating crunchy bits - known as 'vintage Banoffi'.

The method I use is to put the cans into a casserole so they fit neatly and can be well covered with water. Fill with boiling water and cover with a lid. Put in a low oven at 140°C (less for fan assisted) or gas mark 1 and cook for 3½ hours. Check the water half way through the cooking time.

With this method there is very little likelihood of the pan boiling dry and the temperature is more consistent giving a better result

CLASSIC BANOFFI PIE

EQUIPMENT

25cm diameter x 4cm deep tart tin

INGREDIENTS (SERVES 8)

Sweet pastry (see page 425)

1½ cans of Banoffi toffee (as above)

550g ripe bananas

425ml of double cream

1 teaspoon instant coffee

25g caster sugar

1 teaspoon ground coffee (to decorate)

METHOD

1. Roll out the pastry and line the flan dish. Bake the pastry blind (see page 424). Allow to cool.
2. Spread the toffee over the pastry base.
3. Peel the bananas, split them lengthways and make a layer over the toffee.
4. Whip the cream with the instant coffee and the sugar to 'soft peaks'. Spread over the top of the bananas.
5. Sprinkle lightly with the ground coffee.

APPLOFFI PIE

I find this version very pleasant as the acidity of the apple cuts the richness of the dish and, after all, toffee and apple are natural partners.

EQUIPMENT

25cm diameter x 4cm deep tart tin

INGREDIENTS (SERVES 8)

1 large Bramley apple

2 Cox apples

50ml orange juice

50g light brown sugar (Muscovado)

Sweet pastry (see page 425)

1½ cans of Banoffi toffee

425ml double cream

25g caster sugar

½ teaspoon ground cinnamon

Nutmeg

METHOD

1. Roll out the pastry and line the flan dish. Bake the pastry blind (see page 424). Allow to cool.
2. Peel, quarter, core and slice the apples and cook them slowly in the orange juice and brown sugar. Allow to cool completely.
3. Spread the toffee over the pastry base then make a layer of the apple on top of this.
4. Whip the cream with the caster sugar and the cinnamon to 'soft peaks' and spread over the top of the apple. Grate nutmeg over the top of the cream.

HOT BANOFFI

INGREDIENTS (SERVES 4)

250g ready-made puff pastry

1 can of Banoffi toffee

2 ripe bananas

4 scoops of coffee & rum ice cream (see page 342), or a proprietory ice cream of your choice

Caster sugar

Melted butter

METHOD

1. Heat the oven to 200°C/gas mark 6.
2. Cut the pastry into four pieces and roll each piece to about the thickness of a pound coin. Cut four circles of about 12cm in diameter and place them on a baking sheet.
3. Spoon a disc of the toffee less than 1cm thick into the centre of each pastry round leaving a 2cm wide border.
4. Slice the bananas and arrange on top of the toffee. Brush them with melted butter and sprinkle with caster sugar.
5. Bake in the oven for 10-15 minutes until the sides of the pastry are puffed up and golden. Serve immediately with a scoop of your chosen ice cream on the top.

CHOCOLATE BANOFFI

EQUIPMENT

20cm diameter loose-based tart tin

INGREDIENTS (SERVES 6)

1 can of 'Banoffi' toffee or Dulce du Leche ready-made soft toffee

75g dark chocolate (70% cocoa solids)

4 small bananas

300ml double cream

2 teaspoons soft brown sugar (Muscovado)

1 teaspoon instant coffee powder

1 measure of dark rum

FOR THE BASE

250g digestive biscuits – finely crushed

110g butter – melted

2 tablespoons unsweetened cocoa powder

METHOD

1. To make the base, mix together the biscuit crumbs, cocoa powder and butter. Use this to line the tart tin bottom and sides.
2. To make the filling, melt the chocolate over hot water then work in the toffee until smooth.
3. Pour it into the biscuit base.
4. Peel the bananas, split them lengthways and arrange them over the toffee.
5. Whip the cream with the sugar, coffee and rum until it holds its shape.
6. Spread it over the bananas.
7. Lightly dust with cocoa powder.

APPLE, SULTANA & ORANGE COBBLER

EQUIPMENT

2 litre baking dish

INGREDIENTS (SERVES 6)

2 large Bramley apples

Zest and juice from 2 juicy oranges

75g light brown Muscovado sugar

50g sultanas

200g self-raising flour

110g butter

110g caster sugar

2 eggs

150ml milk

METHOD

1. Heat the oven to 180°C/gas mark 4.
2. Peel, quarter, core and slice the apples and place them in a pan with the orange juice, zest, brown sugar and sultanas. Cook gently until the apple starts to break up and absorb the orange juice. Place this mixture into the bottom of the baking dish.
3. Put the flour into a mixing bowl, cut up the butter and then rub it into the flour until it resembles breadcrumbs.
4. Add the sugar then work in the egg and milk until the mixture is like a thick batter.
5. Spoon it over the top of the apple.
6. Bake in the oven for 35-40 minutes until the top is brown and crusty and cooked through.
7. Serve with cream, custard or ice cream.

TARTE TATIN

A French classic – an upside-down apple tart. It should be simple but it isn't. Making the caramel is the first hurdle. Then choose your favourite eating apple – I prefer Cox's for flavour. The amount of juice in an apple varies and makes a difference to the finished dish. Then choose your pastry. I don't think there is a right or wrong pastry here – a lot of people use puff pastry but it can go soggy in the juice when you turn it. I prefer sweet shortcrust pastry. It takes a few goes to perfect – good luck.

EQUIPMENT

A shallow, ovenproof pie dish or cake tin about 25cm in diameter, preferably non-stick and not with a loose base.

INGREDIENTS (SERVES 4-6)

50g butter

6 Cox's apples

150g caster sugar

250g ready-made puff pastry or sweet pastry (see page 425)

METHOD

1. Preheat the oven to 200°C/gas mark 6.
2. Butter the dish with half the butter.
3. Peel, quarter and core the apples and arrange them in the tin cut side up.
4. Now for the caramel. This is a dangerous operation so take care. Place the sugar in a clean, dry saucepan and place it over a medium heat. After a little while you will notice it going liquid at the edges. Swirl the pan around to move the sugar about but resist the temptation to use a spoon. Keep cooking the sugar until it is an even nut-brown colour. When ready, pour it over the apples as evenly as possible.
5. Dot the rest of the butter on the apples.
6. Roll out the pastry and cut out a circle the same diameter as the tin.
7. Lay it over the top of the apples and tuck the edges down the sides.
8. Transfer the dish to the oven.
9. Cook for 25-30 minutes until the pastry is cooked.
10. Leave to cool for 10 minutes, as the caramel will be very hot.
11. To serve, invert the pie dish onto a plate and cut into portions.
12. Serve with whipped or thick cream.

PEAR 'TARTE TATIN'

As pears tend to hold less water than apples this version can achieve more consistent results.

EQUIPMENT

A shallow, ovenproof pie dish or cake tin about 25cm in diameter, preferably non-stick and not with a loose base.

INGREDIENTS (SERVES 6)

50g butter

4 ripe William pears

150g caster sugar

Juice of a lemon

250g ready-made puff pastry or the sweet pastry (see page 425)

METHOD

1. Set the oven to 200°C/gas mark 6.
2. Butter the cake tin with half the butter.
3. Peel, quarter and core the pears and arrange the quarters, cut side up in the tin.
4. Now for the caramel. This is a dangerous operation so take care. Place the sugar in a clean, dry saucepan and place it over a medium heat. After a little while you will notice it going liquid at the edges. Swirl the pan around to move the sugar about but resist the temptation to use a spoon. Keep cooking the sugar until it is an even nut-brown colour. When ready, pour it over the pears as evenly as possible.
5. Squeeze over a bit of lemon and dot the rest of the butter over the pears.
6. Roll out the pastry and cut out a circle slightly larger than the diameter of the tin.
7. Lay the pastry over the top of the pears tucking the sides well down.
8. Place in the oven and cook for 25-30 minutes.
9. Leave to cool for 10 minutes, as the centre will be very hot.
10. To serve, invert the pie dish onto a plate and cut into portions.
11. Serve with whipped or thick cream.

PECAN PIE

EQUIPMENT

20cm diameter tart tin

INGREDIENTS (SERVES 6)

Sweet pastry (see page 425)

FOR THE FILLING

110g butter

2 tablespoons golden syrup

3 eggs

150g Muscovado sugar

175g condensed milk

1 teaspoon vanilla extract

150g pecan nuts

METHOD

1. Heat the oven to 180°C/gas mark 4.
2. Line the tart tin with the pastry and bake it part blind (see page 424).
3. Reduce the oven temperature to 170°C/gas mark 3.
4. In a pan, melt the butter with the syrup and stir well until they amalgamate.
5. Remove from the heat and allow to cool slightly.
6. Whisk in the eggs, condensed milk, Muscovado sugar and vanilla.
7. Pour the mixture into the pastry case and scatter the pecans over the top.
8. Bake for 35–45 minutes until the filling is just set.

STEAMED GINGER SPONGE PUDDING

EQUIPMENT

6 x 150ml aluminium pudding basins

INGREDIENTS (SERVES 6)

Butter and caster sugar for lining the pudding basins

100ml golden syrup

1 small jar of stem ginger in syrup

175g butter

175g soft brown sugar

175g self-raising flour

1 level teaspoon ground ginger

3 eggs

Bay custard (see next page)

METHOD

1. Set the oven to 150°C/gas mark 2.
2. Butter the insides of the basins and dust with caster sugar.
3. Mix 100ml of the syrup from the jar of ginger with the golden syrup.
4. Pour a little of this syrup into the bottom of each basin.
5. Take 6 pieces of the stem ginger and cut into small dice.
6. Place the butter, sugar, flour and ground ginger into the bowl of a food processor.
7. Process until it looks like crumble, then add the eggs and process again until smooth.
8. Fold in the chopped stem ginger.
9. Spoon or pipe the mixture into the pudding basins about three quarters full.
10. Place the basins in a shallow roasting tray and pour in boiling water to come half way up the basins.
11. Brush a sheet of foil with a little oil and cover the whole thing tucking the edges under the rim of the tray.
12. Cook in the oven for 40–50 minutes until the puddings are risen and firm.
13. To serve, turn each pudding out onto a plate and spoon a little warmed syrup over each one. Serve with bay custard (see next page).

BAY CUSTARD

The flavour of bay goes surprisingly well in sweet dishes.

INGREDIENTS

150ml milk

150ml double cream

3 bay leaves

4 egg yolks

25g caster sugar

METHOD

1. Put the milk and cream into a saucepan.
2. Bruise the bay leaves and add them, then heat the mixture.
3. Remove from the heat and allow it to stand and infuse for about 20 minutes.
4. Whisk the egg yolks with the caster sugar.
5. Bring the milk and cream to the boil and pour it on the egg yolks whilst continuing to whisk.
6. Remove the bay leaves and return the mixture to the saucepan and cook until it thickens, taking care not to let it boil and therefore curdle the custard.
7. Take away from the heat and strain it immediately into a clean jug. Keep warm.

JELLY & ICE CREAM

A grown-up version of the universal child's favourite.

Unlike packet jelly, this easy-to-make version uses the pulp of the raspberries so it is not clear but, the flavour is sensational. Also, you have more control over the amount of sugar that goes into it.

EQUIPMENT

4 tall glasses, sundae dishes or the knicker-bocker-glory variety.

INGREDIENTS (SERVES 4)

450g fresh raspberries

150ml water

50g caster sugar

10g leaf gelatine

A tub of the best vanilla ice cream

METHOD

1. To make the jelly, place 350g of the raspberries into a saucepan with the water and sugar.
2. Soften the gelatine in cold water.
3. Simmer the raspberries for one minute then melt the drained gelatine into them.
4. Whiz up in a blender, sieve the mixture and allow to cool and set.
5. Alternate scooped layers of ice cream and jelly into the glasses.
6. Decorate with the remaining raspberries, wafer biscuits or crushed macaroons, mini umbrellas, flowers, sparklers or whatever takes your fancy.
7. Eat with eyes closed and imagine you're a child again.

SUMMER PUDDING

This recipe uses brioche instead of bread for a lighter result. Also, in the method, the individual puddings do not have a top or bottom, this is because the smaller versions would end up with too much brioche to fruit.

EQUIPMENT

A 900ml pudding basin or 4 medium ramekins.

INGREDIENTS (SERVES 4)

250g raspberries

150g redcurrants

150g blackcurrants

150g caster sugar

Half a brioche loaf

METHOD

1. Remove all stalks from the fruit and pick out any unsound ones.
2. Place all the fruit in a saucepan with the sugar.
3. Place over a medium heat and cook until the sugar dissolves and the fruit begins to collapse (do not overcook).
4. Cut the brioche into slices about 1cm thick and line the bottom and sides of your basin. If using ramekins, just line the sides and not the bottom or top.
5. Spoon the mixture into the basin/ramekins and, if using a basin, make a brioche lid.
6. For the larger pudding place a plate on the top and weight it. (Remember to stand the basin on a tray or plate to catch any juice that runs out.)
7. Chill overnight.
8. Serve cold with clotted or whipped cream.

ALMOND & STRAWBERRY ROULADE

EQUIPMENT

Aluminium baking tray 30 x 20cm and 1cm deep

INGREDIENTS (SERVES 6)

110g flaked almonds

4 eggs

150g caster sugar

40g plain flour

300ml double cream

225g fresh strawberries

METHOD

1. Heat the oven to 180°C/gas mark 4.
2. Toast the almonds in the oven to a golden brown. Allow to cool.
3. Lightly oil the tray and line it with parchment paper then turn the paper over so it is oiled both sides.
4. Grind the almonds in the food processor.
5. Place the eggs and sugar into a glass or ceramic bowl and using an electric whisk beat the mixture to a pale foam (see egg foams on page 420).
6. Fold-in the ground almonds followed by the flour.
7. Spread the mixture out on the tray and bake for 15-20 minutes. Allow to cool.
8. Whip the cream and slice the strawberries - keeping a few back for decoration.
9. When the roulade is cool invert the whole thing (tray and all) onto a clean piece of parchment paper. Remove the tray then carefully peel off the parchment paper.
10. Spread the whipped cream over the roulade leaving a 2½cm gap at either end then scatter over the sliced strawberries.
11. Roll up the roulade starting where there is one of the 2½ cm gaps and using the paper underneath to help you roll it. Finish rolling so it is sitting on the join.
12. Dust with icing sugar and decorate with the rest of the strawberries. Serve in slices.

KEY LIME PIE

Named after the limes that grow in the Florida Keys.

EQUIPMENT

20cm diameter x 4cm deep tart tin

INGREDIENTS (SERVES 6)

250g Hobnob biscuits

100g melted butter

5 juicy limes plus one extra for decoration

397g can of condensed milk

300ml double cream

METHOD

1. Crush the Hobnobs to fine crumbs and mix with the melted butter.
2. Use them to line the tart tin (base and sides) refrigerate to set.
3. Using a zester cut the zest from two of the limes and set aside. If you don't have a zester cut the zest from the limes with a peeler and cut into fine strips.
4. Grate the zest from the other three limes with the fine side of the grater (or a micro plane).
5. Squeeze the juice from the limes.
6. Mix together the condensed milk, cream, grated lime zest and juice until it thickens.
7. Pour into the biscuit case and refrigerate for 2 hours.
8. Toss the strips of lime zest in a little caster sugar and use to decorate the top of the pie. Thin slices of lime can also be used for garnish.

LEMON TART

EQUIPMENT

25cm diameter x 4cm deep tart tin

INGREDIENTS (SERVES 8)

Sweet pastry (see page 425)

FOR THE FILLING

2–3 lemons – depending on size and juiciness

3 eggs

110g caster sugar

300ml double cream

METHOD

1. Heat the oven to 180°C/gas mark 4.
2. Make the pastry, line the tart tin and bake it blind (see page 424).
3. Grate the zest from the lemons very finely and squeeze the juice.
4. Place these in a bowl with the eggs and the sugar. Mix together then slowly add the cream.
5. Reduce the heat of the oven to 150°C/gas mark 2.
6. Pour the lemon cream into the pastry case and carefully transfer to the oven. Bake until the filling is set – about 20–30 minutes. Serve warm or cool. This is best eaten the same day it is cooked. Fresh raspberries make a pleasant and colourful accompaniment.

ORANGE CRÉME CARAMEL

Crème caramel is lighter and just as delicious as crème brûleé. This method allows for extra caramel sauce to be served with the dish and the addition of fresh orange gives it a lift.

EQUIPMENT

6 dariole moulds

INGREDIENTS (SERVES 6)

3 oranges

150g granulated sugar

300ml full cream milk

200ml single cream

3 large eggs

50g caster sugar

METHOD

1. Heat the oven to 150°C/gas mark 2.
2. Take the zest from one orange with a potato peeler and cut into fine strips.
3. Grate the zest from one of the other oranges as finely as possible.
4. Remove the peel and pith from these two oranges with a knife and fillet them (i.e. – cut into segments).
5. Squeeze the juice from orange number three. Measure the orange juice and make up to 100ml if necessary with water.
6. Have ready your 6 dariole moulds. Now to make the caramel, take care as this gets very hot. Place the granulated sugar into a small saucepan and place it over a low heat. The sugar will slowly melt (do not attempt to stir it, just shake the pan to move it about). It will slowly darken to a pale gold or light brown. The darker it gets the more flavour it has but don't let it burn. When it has reached the right colour, pour a small amount into each dariole mould to coat the bottom.
7. When this is done, put the strips of orange zest into the remaining caramel and stir with a fork. Remember the caramel carries on cooking even when away from the heat so you have to work fast.
8. When the zest is well coated add the 100ml of orange juice. This will now stop the caramel cooking. Any hard lumps of caramel will melt into the liquid in time so just set the saucepan aside.
9. Place the milk and cream in another saucepan with the grated zest and bring to the boil.
10. Beat the eggs and caster sugar in a separate bowl.
11. When the milk and cream mixture is boiling, pour it onto the eggs continuing to beat.
12. Strain the mixture and pour it into the 6 dariole moulds. Stand the moulds into a deep pan and pour boiling water around them.

13. Cover with a sheet of tin foil and cook in the oven for 20–30 minutes until the custards are just set. Take care, overcooking will result in the eggs scrambling.
14. Remove from the oven, allow to cool, then refrigerate overnight. (Leaving the custards overnight allows the moisture from the custard to melt the little bit of caramel at the bottom of the mould.)
15. To serve, carefully run a knife around the mould and turn out onto the serving plate. Decorate around the custard with orange segments and finish by pouring the extra caramel with the zest strips over the custards. Decorate with shards of cracknel (see below).

CRACKNEL DECORATION

Make the caramel in the same way as described in the previous recipe except when you reach the right colour pour it out onto parchment paper or silicone matting and spread it as thinly as possible with a palette knife. Allow to cool and go crisp then break into pieces and store in an air tight jar. Put it on a high shelf (children love it!).

PEAR & MINCEMEAT TART

EQUIPMENT

25cm diameter x 4cm deep tart tin

INGREDIENTS (SERVES 6-8)

Sweet pastry (see page 425)

250g jar of good quality mincemeat

3 ripe pears (preferably Williams)

25g ground almonds

25g Muscovado sugar

METHOD

1. Heat the oven to 180°C/gas mark 4.
2. Roll out the pastry, line the tart tin and bake part blind (see page 424).
3. Spread the mincemeat into the pastry case.
4. Peel, quarter and core the pears and arrange them on top of the mincemeat in a fan pattern.
5. Mix the ground almonds and Muscovado sugar together and sprinkle over the pears/mincemeat.
6. Bake for 25-30 minutes.
7. Serve warm with thick cream.

CHOCOLATE SOUFFLÉ PUDDING

The problem with most chocolate soufflés is that they never taste chocolatey enough. This isn't a true soufflé but it's very chocolatey. It is also very quick and easy to make. If that was not enough it has a third plus – if allowed to cool it will sink as soufflés will - but, served like this, with a dollop of clotted cream, it is the most delicious chocolate pudding.

EQUIPMENT

6 large ramekins or individual pots

INGREDIENTS (SERVES 6)

Butter and sugar for lining the ramekins/pots

225g chocolate

100g butter

3 eggs

25g caster sugar

METHOD

1. Heat the oven to 180°C/gas mark 4.
2. Butter and sugar the ramekins or pots.
3. Melt the chocolate then whisk in the butter until the mixture is smooth.
4. Using an electric beater and a glass or ceramic bowl whisk the eggs and sugar to a pale, light foam.
5. Fold it into the chocolate mix.
6. Pour into the dishes to just three quarters full.
7. Bake for approximately 20-25 minutes until well risen.
8. Either serve immediately or allow to cool when the puddings will collapse - either way they are delicious.
9. Can be served with clotted cream.
10. They can also be microwaved successfully for serving later although they won't rise again!

COCONUT PANNA COTTA WITH WINTER FRUIT SALAD

EQUIPMENT

8 dariole moulds or ramekins

INGREDIENTS (SERVES 8)

10g leaf gelatine

400ml can of full-fat coconut milk

100g caster sugar

500g plain yoghurt

FOR THE SALAD

One small pineapple

2 oranges

150g white seedless grapes

1 tablespoon golden caster sugar

Juice of one lime

Seeds from 2 cardamom pods, crushed

1 pomegranate

METHOD

1. Soften the gelatine leaves in cold water.
2. Heat the coconut milk with the sugar until the sugar dissolves. Remove from the heat.
3. Drain the gelatine and add to the hot coconut milk. Stir until dissolved.
4. Strain and add the yoghurt. Pour the mixture into the dariole moulds or ramekins.
5. Refrigerate overnight before turning out.
6. Prepare the pineapple and cut into cubes. Peel and fillet the orange.
7. Halve the grapes and mix together the prepared fruit with the sugar, lime juice and the cardamom.
8. Spoon the seeds of the pomegranate into the salad.
9. To serve, place the panna cotta in the centre of the plate and spoon the salad around it.

AUTHENTIC BAKED CHEESECAKE

Cheesecakes made with cream cheese and set with gelatine, usually with some sort of fruit in it or on it, are now the accepted form of cheesecake but it is a modern concept if a little dated. From Eastern Europe, to Yorkshire and in the Jewish communities of New York the baked cheesecake was the norm for several hundred years.
This recipe is a classic.

EQUIPMENT

20cm diameter x 4cm deep cake tin

INGREDIENTS (SERVES 6)
FOR THE BASE

25g butter

25g brioche or cake crumbs

FOR THE FILLING

700g cream cheese

225g caster sugar

2 eggs

50g plain flour

350ml whipping cream

Vanilla essence and grated nutmeg

75g raisins

METHOD

1. Heat the oven to 180°C/gas mark 4.
2. Butter the cake tin generously then coat with the brioche crumbs.
3. Beat together the cream cheese, sugar, eggs, flour, cream and flavourings.
4. Stir in the raisins and pour the mixture into the cake tin taking care not to disturb the crumbs.
5. Bake for 45-55 minutes lowering the heat if it colours before the time is up.
6. Allow to cool then refrigerate.

PANETTONE BREAD & BUTTER PUDDING

A useful way of using the panettone that nobody eats at Christmas.

EQUIPMENT

1 litre shallow baking dish

INGREDIENTS (SERVES 6)

50g butter

8 slices of panettone

300ml milk

150ml single cream

2 eggs

100g caster sugar

METHOD

1. Heat the oven to 170° C/gas mark 3.
2. Butter the baking dish with half the butter.
3. Butter the slices of panettone thinly with the rest of the butter.
4. Layer the slices of panettone in the dish.
5. Place the milk and cream in a saucepan and bring to the boil.
6. Whisk the eggs and 50g of the sugar together.
7. Pour the boiling milk and cream over the egg/sugar mixture whilst stirring.
8. Strain and pour the resulting mixture over the panettone.
9. Allow the liquid to soak into the panettone for about 20 minutes.
10. Sprinkle the remaining 50g of sugar over the top of the pudding and bake for 30–40 minutes.
11. Serve warm.

PLUM 'TATIN' WITH ALMOND PASTRY

EQUIPMENT

20cm diameter sponge cake tin (not loose based)

INGREDIENTS (SERVES 4)

200g plain flour

50g ground almonds

50g icing sugar

150g butter plus extra for greasing the cake tin

1 egg

2-3 drops of almond essence

400g smallish plums

75g granulated sugar

METHOD

1. Heat the oven to 180°C/gas mark 4.
2. Place the flour, almonds and icing sugar into a bowl and rub in the butter until it is like crumble.
3. Add the egg and the almond essence and mix to a dough. Chill for 30 minutes.
4. Grease the cake tin with butter.
5. Halve the plums, remove the stones, and place them cut side down tightly in the cake tin.
6. Now for the caramel. This is a dangerous operation so take care. Place the sugar in a clean, dry saucepan and place it over a medium heat. After a little while you will notice it going liquid at the edges. Swirl the pan around to move the sugar about but resist the temptation to use a spoon. Keep cooking the sugar until it is an even nut-brown colour.
7. When ready, pour it over the plums as evenly as possible. (Alternatively, you can just sprinkle the sugar over the plums without caramelising it or replace the sugar with the same amount of honey.)
8. Using half the pastry (the rest will freeze well) roll out to the size of the cake tin keeping it reasonably thick.
9. Place the pastry over the plums tucking the edges well down the sides. Place the tin on a tray and bake for 25-30 minutes.
10. Invert onto a plate (take care as the juices are very hot) and serve immediately.

ETON MESS

This looks great served in nice glasses or sundae dishes but don't worry about the presentation too much or you will have Eton Tidy!

INGREDIENTS (SERVES 4)

300ml double cream

450g strawberries

1 tablespoon icing sugar

8 meringues (see page 389)

Borage flowers (optional)

METHOD

1. Whip the cream until it just holds its shape.
2. Hull the strawberries and cut any large ones into halves or quarters.
3. Take half the strawberries and mash them with the back of a fork with the icing sugar. Set aside.
4. Take four of the meringues and crush them into a bowl.
5. Add the whole strawberries and double cream and mix gently.
6. Add the crushed strawberries last.
7. Pile the mix into your dishes and decorate with more strawberries and/or borage flowers.

HOT STRAWBERRY CROISSANTS WITH VANILLA ICE CREAM & HOT CHOCOLATE SAUCE

INGREDIENTS

Allow one regular croissant per person or 2 mini croissants

Strawberries

Vanilla ice cream

Caster sugar

Chocolate sauce (see page 421)

METHOD

1. Split the croissants across the middle and halve the strawberries.
2. Put a layer of strawberries on the lower half of the croissant.
3. Sprinkle with some caster sugar and put the other half on top.
4. Bake in a hot oven until piping hot.
5. To serve: take a curl of vanilla ice cream and slide it into the split with the strawberries and drizzle with chocolate sauce.

STRAWBERRY VACHERIN

An impressive dessert for a special occasion.

INGREDIENTS (SERVES 8-10)

12 egg whites

700g granulated sugar

600ml double cream

450g fresh strawberries

Caster sugar for sprinkling

Raspberry Coulis (optional, see page 421)

Mint or verbena leaves (optional)

METHOD

1. Heat the oven to 110°C/gas mark ¼.
2. Take two baking sheets and line them with parchment paper.
3. Draw three circles on them: one 25cm, one 20cm, and the third 15cm (diameter).
4. Lightly oil the paper then scatter some caster sugar over it.
5. Using an electric beater and a glass or ceramic bowl whisk the egg whites and sugar until stiff (meringue).
6. Pipe the meringue to make three discs in your drawn circles.
7. Use any meringue that is over to make separate rosettes for decoration.
8. Sprinkle some more caster sugar over the meringue.
9. Dry the meringue discs in the oven for 2½-3 hours until they are crisp and firm. Cool and carefully peel off the parchment paper.
10. Whip the cream to soft peaks.
11. Hull the strawberries and cut the large ones in half.
12. Assemble the vacherin by layering up the discs of meringue (starting with the larger one as a base) with the strawberries and whipped cream.
13. Decorate with the extra rosettes of meringue and some mint or lemon verbena leaves.
14. A little raspberry coulis can be drizzled over the top prior to serving.

BLACKCURRANT MOUSSE

INGREDIENTS (SERVES 4-6)

15g leaf gelatine

450g blackcurrants

110g caster sugar

300ml double cream

4 egg whites

Blackcurrant leaves (optional)

METHOD

1. Soften the gelatine leaves in cold water.
2. Place the blackcurrants in a saucepan with the sugar and a tablespoon of water.
3. Cook gently until all the fruit is soft.
4. Whizz it in a food processor or liquidizer, then sieve it to remove the pips etc.
5. While the resulting purée is still warm melt the drained gelatine into it.
6. Allow to get cold but not enough for the gelatine to start setting. Ideally it should be on the point of starting to gel.
7. Whip the cream and in a separate bowl whip the egg whites.
8. Fold the cream (leave some aside for decoration) into the blackcurrant mixture followed by the egg whites.
9. Spoon into tall glasses or into a mould.
10. If you intend to use a mould and then turn out the mousse for serving, use a little extra gelatine.
11. The finished mousse can be decorated with whipped cream and blackcurrant leaves.

APPLE & BLACKBERRY CRUMBLE TART

EQUIPMENT

25cm diameter x 4cm deep tart tin

INGREDIENTS (SERVES 6-8)

Sweet pastry recipe (see page 425)

FOR THE FILLING

2 Bramley apples

3 Cox apples

150ml orange juice

50g light Muscovado sugar

175g wild blackberries

FOR THE TOPPING

110g flour

110g light Muscovado sugar

110g ground almonds

50g butter

METHOD

1. Heat the oven to 180°C/gas mark 4.
2. Line the tart tin with the pastry and bake it part blind (see page 424).
3. Peel, quarter, core and slice all the apples and place in a pan with the orange juice and sugar.
4. Cook until the Bramley apple disintegrates and absorbs the orange juice. This should give you a firm apple mixture, part purée with chunks in it.
5. Remove from the heat and stir in the blackberries.
6. For the topping mix together the flour, sugar and almonds then rub in the butter until fully blended.
7. To finish the dish, spoon the fruit into the pastry case, sprinkle over a layer of the crumble mix and place into the oven (180°C/gas mark 4) for 35–45 minutes until the crumble is golden.

CHOCOLATE & RASPBERRY ROULADE

EQUIPMENT

Aluminium baking tray 30 x 20cm and 1cm deep

INGREDIENTS (SERVES 6)

75g good quality plain chocolate (70% cocoa solids)

2 eggs

75g caster sugar

150ml double cream

110g fresh raspberries

1 measure of brandy or liqueur (optional)

METHOD

1. Heat the oven to 190°C/gas mark 5.
2. Lightly oil the tray, line it with parchment paper then turn the paper over so it is oiled on both sides and press it well into the corners.
3. Melt the chocolate.
4. Using an electric beater and a glass or ceramic bowl whisk the eggs and sugar together until pale, frothy and holding its shape (see egg foams on page 420).
5. Fold the melted chocolate into the egg/sugar mixture and pour onto the tray. Spread out evenly and then bake it in the oven for 8-10 minutes. Allow to cool.
6. Whip the cream.
7. Invert the roulade, tray and all, onto a clean piece of parchment paper.
8. Remove the tray and then carefully peel away the lining paper.
9. Spread the cream onto the chocolate base, up to the sides but leaving a 3cm strip top and bottom.
10. Arrange the raspberries on the cream and sprinkle over the liqueur if you are using it. Carefully roll up the roulade towards you using the paper to facilitate easy rolling.
11. End with the join underneath the roll and shape to a cylinder with your hands.
12. The outside will crack slightly but this is normal.
13. Dust with icing sugar and serve in thick slices.

STRAWBERRY SHORTCAKE

INGREDIENTS (SERVES 4)

50g icing sugar

150g plain flour

100g butter

1 egg yolk

300ml double cream

225g fresh, even sized strawberries

Raspberry coulis (see page 421)

METHOD

1. Heat the oven to 200°C/gas mark 6.
2. Mix the icing sugar with the flour and sieve if necessary.
3. Rub the butter into the flour/icing sugar until it is like fine breadcrumbs.
4. Add the egg yolk, then work the mixture into a dough.
5. Chill the dough if it is too soft, then roll out to a thickness of about 2mm and cut out circles with a pastry cutter of about 8-9cm diameter. Make 12 biscuits.
6. Place on a baking sheet and cook for about 8 minutes until baked and showing a golden colour at the edges. Cool on a wire rack.
7. Whip the cream and halve the strawberries.
8. To assemble, place a shortcake in the centre of each plate anchored with a dab of cream, spread a little cream on the biscuit, followed by a layer of halved strawberries and levelled with a little more cream.
9. Put another biscuit on top of this and repeat the process, finishing with a third biscuit. Dust the top with icing sugar and decorate with a perfect strawberry.
10. Pour some raspberry sauce around the plate, drizzle some cream in it and drag the point of a knife through it to make a pattern.
11. For a lighter version of this dessert use tuile biscuits (see page 386) of the same size and shape.

APPLE / PEAR FRANGIPANE

These can also be made as individual tarts in the mini tart tins – no need to bake the pastry blind for these.

EQUIPMENT

25cm diameter x 4cm deep tart tin

INGREDIENTS (SERVES 6-8)

Sweet pastry (see page 425)

3 ripe William pears or 3 Cox's apples

FOR THE FRANGIPANE

110g butter

110g icing sugar

1 teaspoon flour

2 eggs

110g ground almonds

Melted butter for brushing

Caster sugar for sprinkling

METHOD

1. Pre heat the oven to 180°C/gas mark 4.
2. Make the pastry, line the tart tin and part blind bake it, (see page 424).
3. Reduce oven to 150°C/gas mark 2.
4. Beat the butter and sugar together until it is light and fluffy then add the flour, eggs and ground almonds. Alternatively combine the ingredients in the food processor. Set aside. When the tart case has cooled spread the frangipane into the pastry case so it comes half way up the sides.
5. Peel, halve and core the pears or apples and arrange onto the frangipane flat side down. They can be sliced through or left as halves.
6. Brush lightly with melted butter and sprinkle with caster sugar.
7. Bake for 30–40 minutes until golden. Serve warm or at room temperature.

GYPSY TART WITH CARAMELISED APPLE

EQUIPMENT

25cm diameter x 4cm deep tart tin

INGREDIENTS (SERVES 6-8)

Sweet pastry (see page 425)

FOR THE FILLING

400g can of evaporated milk

350g dark brown Muscovado sugar

1 egg

FOR THE CARAMELISED APPLE

3 Russet or Cox's apples

3 tablespoons caster sugar

METHOD

1. Heat the oven to 180°C/gas mark 4.
2. Line the tart tin with the pastry and part blind bake it (see page 424).
3. Reduce the oven temperature to 170°C/gas mark 3.
4. Stir the sugar into the milk until it is dissolved then beat in the egg.
5. Pour the mixture into the pastry case and bake in the oven for 20-30 minutes until the filling is set. Allow to cool.
6. Peel, quarter and core the apples and chop into neat dice.
7. Place the sugar in a shallow pan over a medium heat.
8. Shake the pan occasionally while the sugar melts (do not stir with an implement).
9. After the sugar melts it will start to brown.
10. When it has reached the colour of caramel put in the apple (take care at this point as the sugar is very hot).
11. Now stir the apple around in the caramel until all of the apple is coated. If the caramel goes firm, like toffee, add a few drops of water.
12. To serve, slice the tart into portions and spoon some apple over each one.

PASSION FRUIT MOUSSE WITH TROPICAL FRUITS

Some red fruits such as raspberries or strawberries make a nice contrast though they are not tropical. You may also find different unusual fruits depending on the time of year and where you shop. It is worth experimenting to find the ones you really like.

EQUIPMENT

1½ litre jelly mould or basin

INGREDIENTS (SERVES 8)
FOR THE MOUSSE

15g leaf gelatine

12 passion fruit

Orange juice

4 eggs

225g caster sugar

600ml double cream

FOR THE TROPICAL FRUITS

1 small pineapple

1 mango

1 papaya

4 kiwi fruit

4 passion fruit

Juice of an orange

Caster sugar

METHOD

1. Soften the gelatine leaves in cold water.
2. Halve the passion fruit and scoop out the contents. Whizz in a food processor then sieve the contents to remove the bulk of the pips.
3. Make the juice up to 600ml with the orange juice.
4. Separate the eggs, place half the sugar with the yolks and beat together.
5. Bring the passion fruit juice to the boil and whisk it onto the egg yolks.
6. Return the mixture to the pan and cook until you have a thick custard. Do not boil. Remove from the heat, drain the gelatine well and stir it into the warm custard until it is dissolved. Strain and set aside to cool.
7. Whip the cream until it just holds its shape.
8. Using an electric beater and a glass or ceramic bowl whisk the egg whites and remaining caster sugar to form soft peaks.
9. When the passion fruit custard starts to gel (it must be cold), fold in the whipped cream followed by the egg whites.
10. Pour the mousse into the mould and refrigerate, preferably overnight.
11. Peel, quarter, core and chop the pineapple.
12. Peel and prepare the mango and papaya.
13. Peel the kiwi and cut them into eights. Put all the chopped fruit into a bowl, halve the passion fruit and scoop the contents into the bowl. Pour over the orange juice and sweeten to taste.
14. To serve the dish, turn the set mousse out onto the centre of a large plate or platter and spoon the fruit around it.

PEAR, HONEY & WALNUT TART

EQUIPMENT

25cm diameter x 4cm deep tart tin

INGREDIENTS (SERVES 6-8)

Sweet pastry (see page 425)

150g walnuts

75g caster sugar

50g butter

75g honey

50ml double cream

2 large egg yolks

4-5 ripe pears

Whipped cream for serving

METHOD

1. Heat the oven to 180°C/gas mark 4.
2. Make the pastry, line the tart tin and part blind bake it (see page 424).
3. Meanwhile, crush the walnuts and mix them with the sugar.
4. Melt the butter with the honey and cream until just warm.
5. Whisk the egg yolks until smooth then stir in the honey etc.
6. Peel and halve the pears then remove the core with a teaspoon. Make a scant layer of the honey mixture on the pastry base then arrange the pears, flat-side down on top of this.
7. Stir the nuts and sugar into the remaining honey mixture and spoon it over the pears, filling the gaps between the pears.
8. Place the tart back in the oven and bake for 30-40 minutes.
9. Serve warm with whipped cream.

CARAMELISED PEACHES FLAMED IN BRANDY WITH VANILLA ICE CREAM

This dish comes with a health and safety warning – first hot sugar and secondly flaming brandy – please take care!

INGREDIENTS (SERVES 4)

4 ripe peaches

1 vanilla pod

110g granulated sugar

1 double measure of brandy

4 scoops of good quality vanilla ice cream

METHOD

1. Cut the peaches into quarters and remove the stone.
2. Snip the vanilla pod into 1cm pieces.
3. Place the sugar in a shallow pan and place over a low heat until it melts.
4. Continue cooking until the sugar turns a light caramel colour.
5. Carefully put in the peach quarters and the vanilla pieces.
6. Shake the pan to coat the peaches in caramel, place a lid on it and continue to cook until the peaches are hot and have released some juices into the pan.
7. Put the brandy in and ignite it.
8. Serve immediately into deep bowls and top with a scoop of vanilla ice cream.

REGENCY RECIPES

I was asked to cook for the television programme Regency House Party, a sort of Big Brother in corsets. To make sure the food was authentic and there were no anachronisms I was advised by the brilliant food historian, Ivan Day. We delved through many of his books and resurrected some strange and wonderful dishes. The following four desserts were the ones that came out tops.

NESSELRODE PUDDING

The king of old-fashioned desserts.

INGREDIENTS (SERVES 6-8)

50g candied peel

30g glacé cherries (natural colour) cut in quarters

30g Maraschino cherries – cut in quarters

50g currants

50g sultanas

110ml Madeira

1 tablespoon Maraschino liquid from the cherry jar

8g gelatine

5 egg yolks

124g caster sugar

500ml milk

125g tinned chestnut purée (unsweetened)

500ml whipping cream

Marron glacé, extra whipped cream and tuile (see page 386) or Amaretti biscuits to decorate.

METHOD

1. Marinate all the fruit, including the cherries and peel, in the Madeira and Maraschino juice overnight.
2. Soak the gelatine leaves in cold water.
3. Whisk together the egg yolks and sugar.
4. Bring the milk to the boil and whisk it onto the egg yolks and sugar.
5. Return the mixture to the pan and cook until it thickens. Do not allow it to boil or it will curdle.
6. Stir in the drained gelatine and allow it to melt into the custard. Strain the mixture through a fine sieve. Mix the chestnut purée into the custard followed by the fruit and alcohol. Chill well.
7. Whip the cream until it is just holding its shape and fold it into the custard. Turn the mixture into a decorative mould and freeze.
8. To serve, turn out and decorate with whipped cream, marron glacé and tuile or Amaretti biscuits.

BAY BLANCMANGE WITH PEARS IN BURGUNDY

This recipe for blancmange comes from Mrs Beeton's book although not flavoured with bay – that came from another book. Blancmange is probably not the most appetizing or fashionable sounding dessert but the recipe is very close to the one I use for panna cotta so, if you think anyone might turn their nose up at blancmange, tell them it's panna cotta.

EQUIPMENT

6 x 150ml aluminium or plastic pudding basins

INGREDIENTS (SERVES 6)

375ml single cream

6 bay leaves plus 1 for decoration

10g leaf gelatine

110g caster sugar

500g plain yoghurt

FOR THE PEARS

4 ripe dessert pears (Williams or Roche are good for this dish)

Half a bottle of red wine

50g caster sugar

1 stick of cinnamon

2 cloves

2 strips of lemon zest

Nutmeg

Cochineal (optional)

FOR DECORATION

Viennese or Tuile biscuits (see page 386)

METHOD

1. Bring the cream to the boil with the bay leaves in then take off the heat and leave to infuse.
2. Soften the gelatine leaves in cold water.
3. Stir the softened drained gelatine and the sugar into the hot cream and keep stirring to make sure it has all dissolved.
4. Strain the mixture then whisk in the cold yoghurt.
5. Pour into individual dishes and refrigerate until set.
6. Peel the pears, leaving them whole and with the stalks still on. Place them in a saucepan and pour in the red wine.
7. Use more wine or a little water to make sure the pears are covered.
8. Add the rest of the ingredients and place over the heat.
9. Bring to the boil and then simmer until the pears are soft which won't take long if the pears were ripe. Allow to cool in the red wine syrup.
10. To serve, briefly warm the outside of the blancmange moulds and turn out onto individual plates. Lift the pears from the wine and dab dry with kitchen towel. Cut the base flat so that each pear will stand upright. Decorate with Viennese or Tuile biscuits and a fresh bay leaf.

QUAKING PUDDING

We assumed the 'quaking' was another way of saying wobbly.

EQUIPMENT

6 x 150ml aluminium pudding basins

INGREDIENTS (SERVES 8-10)

300ml milk

300ml double cream

The grated rind of a lemon

Nutmeg, cinnamon and mace

110g fresh white breadcrumbs

225g ground almonds

175g caster sugar

A pinch of salt

1 teaspoon baking powder

4 eggs

Butter for greasing

FOR THE SWEET WINE SAUCE

175ml white wine

25g caster sugar

25g sultanas

25g mixed candied peel (optional)

50ml double cream

25g unsalted butter

FOR THE SWEET TOASTED ALMONDS

50g flaked almonds

25g icing sugar

METHOD

1. Heat the oven to 170°C/gas mark 3.
2. Bring the milk and cream to the boil with the grated lemon rind and a pinch of each of the spices.
3. In a bowl, mix together the breadcrumbs, ground almonds, caster sugar, baking powder and salt.
4. Make a well in the centre and break in the eggs.
5. Start mixing the eggs with the dry ingredients and then add the milk/cream mixture a little at a time until it is all mixed in.
6. Butter pudding basins and pour in the mixture to about three quarters full. Bake in the oven for 35-45 minutes until set.
7. To make the sauce, simmer the wine in a saucepan with the sugar, sultanas and mixed peel.
8. When the raisins have become plump add the cream and then whisk in the butter to thicken it.
9. To toast the almonds, heat the grill and spread the almonds onto a tray.
10. Sprinkle them with the icing sugar using a sieve (not all 25g).
11. Place the tray under the grill and watch the progress like a hawk. As the almonds brown take the tray out from under the grill, turn them over and sprinkle over a bit more icing sugar. Place under the grill again until they are all nicely toasted and caramelized.
12. To serve the puddings turn them out onto plates, spoon over the sauce and decorate with the toasted almonds.

WHIM WHAM

The name, like 'trifle', is based on whimsy. There are no quantities here – use what is available or can be bought ready-made. Use up that strange liqueur you bought on holiday several years ago and is still in the back of the cupboard!

Recipes for some of the things on the list are in miscellaneous (page 399).

EQUIPMENT

6 sundae dishes or tall glasses (anything frivolous or fanciful)

INGREDIENTS (SERVES 6 - POSSIBLY)

Sponge cake – any you have or use sponge fingers

Raspberry coulis (see page 421)

Dried cherries soaked in brandy

Amaretti biscuits

Sherry or Marsala

Caramel sauce

Custard

Praline

Whipped cream

Rolled almond tuile biscuits (see page 386)

METHOD

1. Cut the sponge into dice and soak well in the sherry (have some yourself as well).
2. Layer the ingredients in the glass in no particular order (on a whim). Try those cherries! Put a few crushed Amaretti biscuits in now and again.
3. Have another drink - well it is Christmas, isn't it?
4. Make sure you end up with a layer of custard then the whipped cream and a bit of crunchy praline on the top.
5. Where were we - oh yes, now decorate with an almond biscuit.
6. Eat – wham!

CAKES

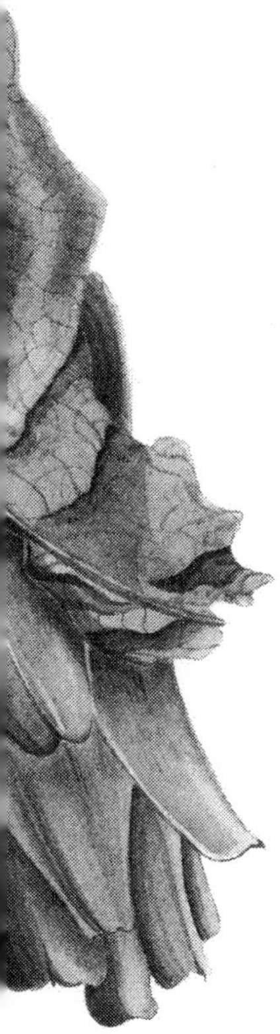

INDIVIDUAL STRAWBERRY & PASSION FRUIT GÂTEAUX

EQUIPMENT

6 mini sponge cake tins (9cm diameter)

INGREDIENTS (MAKES 6)

3 eggs

75g caster sugar

75g plain flour

Butter and caster sugar – for lining the cake tins

1 tablespoon strawberry jam

300ml double cream

225g small strawberries

3 passion fruit

110g icing sugar

METHOD

1. Heat the oven to 190°C/gas mark 5.
2. Prepare 6 mini sponge tins by rubbing the insides with butter and coating with caster sugar.
3. Whisk the eggs and caster sugar together to a ribbon stage (i.e. really thick and aerated, see egg foams on page 420).
4. Sieve the flour and fold it into the egg/sugar mix.
5. Pour into the sponge tins and bake for 15-20 minutes until cooked.
6. Turn out onto a wire rack and cool.
7. Whip the cream.
8. Split the sponges and sandwich the two halves back together with some jam, cream and thinly sliced strawberries. Put the rest of the cream in a piping bag with a star nozzle.
9. Cut two passion fruit in half and scoop out the seeds into a food processor.
10. Whizz them up and sieve to remove the seeds.
11. Make an icing by mixing enough passion fruit juice with the icing sugar to a consistency that is just runny.
12. Spoon it over the sponges, then put a rosette of cream on the top of each one.
13. Decorate with halved strawberries and with the final passion fruit, spoon a little pulp on the top of each one.

DATE, WALNUT & BANANA LOAF

EQUIPMENT

1lt loaf tin

INGREDIENTS

110ml sunflower oil

175g light Muscovado sugar

150g self-raising white or wholemeal flour

1 banana

2 eggs

½ teaspoon baking powder

75g chopped dates

50g walnuts

Pinch of salt

METHOD

1. Heat the oven to 150°C/gas mark 2.
2. Oil the loaf tin and line it with a strip of parchment paper.
3. Place all the ingredients except the dates and walnuts into the bowl of a food processor and process until smooth.
4. If you do not have a food processor mash the banana with a fork and beat all the ingredients, except the dates and walnuts, until smooth.
5. Stir the dates and walnuts into the mixture and place it into the prepared tin.
6. Bake for 50 minutes – 1 hour or until the top of the loaf is firm to the touch. Allow to cool a little then turn it out onto a cooling rack.

BUTTERSCOTCH APPLE UPSIDE-DOWN CAKE

EQUIPMENT

20cm diameter x 7cm deep cake tin that is watertight (i.e. not spring form or loose based).

INGREDIENTS

175g golden syrup

50g butter

2 medium size Bramley cooking apples*

FOR THE CAKE

175g butter

175g soft brown sugar

3 eggs

175g self-raising flour

Extra butter for greasing the tin

* For a banana version substitute the apple with 4-5 bananas.

METHOD

1. Lightly butter the sides of the cake tin. Heat the oven to 170°C/gas mark 3.
2. Place the syrup into a pan and bring to the boil.
3. Remove from the heat and whisk in the 50g of butter a bit at a time.
4. When you have a thick smooth sauce, pour it into the cake tin.
5. Peel the apples, cut them into quarters and remove the core.
6. Cut into thick slices and layer them on top of the butterscotch sauce.
7. Beat together the butter and brown sugar until light and fluffy.
8. Add the eggs, one at a time, and then the flour. Mix well for a good texture.
9. Spread the mixture over the apple slices right to the edges of the tin. Place the tin on a tray (the butterscotch may bubble over a bit).
10. Bake in the oven for 45 – 55 minutes until cooked.

BANOFFI CAKE

EQUIPMENT

3 x 20cm sponge cake tins

INGREDIENTS (MAKES 6)
FOR THE SPONGE

175g self-raising flour

175g light brown sugar

1½ teaspoons baking powder

175ml sunflower oil

50ml milk

3 eggs

TO ASSEMBLE

1 can of Banoffi toffee – the ready-made is fine for this.

4 ripe bananas

500g Mascarpone

50g caster sugar

1 tablespoon of Camp coffee or a teaspoon of instant dissolved in a tablespoon of boiling water

1 teaspoon of ground coffee

METHOD

1. Heat the oven to 150°C/gas mark 2.
2. Line the bottom of each cake tin with a disc of baking parchment lightly oiled.
3. Mix together the dry ingredients, then beat in the oil, milk and eggs.
4. Divide the mixture between the 3 cake tins. (It may seem a scant quantity when doing this but we are aiming for thin layers and the mixture does rise).
5. Bake for 20-25 minutes.
6. Turn them out and cool them on a wire rack.
7. There are three layers of cake so there will be two layers of filling.
8. Spread the bottom layer of sponge with the toffee and then make a layer of thinly sliced banana (best cut on the slant).
9. Spread a layer of toffee on the next sponge and place it over the banana layer, toffee-side down.
10. Repeat with another layer of toffee and bananas before placing the final sponge on top.
11. Beat the coffee and sugar into the Mascarpone and spread it around the outside and top of the cake.
12. Sprinkle with the ground coffee sparingly.

APPLE GINGERBREAD WITH CINNAMON ICING

EQUIPMENT

20 x 20cm (5cm deep) baking tin

INGREDIENTS

110g golden syrup

75g butter

75g soft brown sugar

175g self-raising flour

1 teaspoon ground ginger

½ teaspoon ground cloves

1 egg

125g Bramley apple (total weight peeled, cored and diced)

FOR THE ICING

175g icing sugar

1 level teaspoon ground cinnamon

1-2 tablespoons boiling water

METHOD

1. Heat the oven to 150°C/gas mark 2.
2. Put the golden syrup in a pan with the butter and the sugar.
3. Bring to the boil whilst whisking and then leave to cool.
4. Sift the flour into a basin with the ginger and cloves.
5. Make a well in the centre and put in the egg, along with the sugar and butter mixture.
6. When it is all well mixed, fold in the apple and turn it into a well-greased rectangular tin and bake for 50-60 minutes.
7. When cooked allow it to stand before removing from the tin.
8. Sieve the icing sugar and add the cinnamon. Add enough water to make a thick icing and spread it over the cooled gingerbread. Allow to set.

BLUEBERRY CAKE WITH LIMONCELLO ICING

Limoncello is a wonderful lemon liqueur from southern Italy and like all great liqueurs is fantastic in cooking as well as drinking.

EQUIPMENT

20cm diameter spring-form cake tin

INGREDIENTS

225g butter

225g caster sugar

225g self-raising flour

4 eggs

200g fresh blueberries

Extra butter for greasing the cake tin

FOR THE ICING

110g butter – softened

225g icing sugar

3 tablespoons of Limoncello

METHOD

1. Heat the oven to 170°C/gas mark 3.
2. Lightly butter the cake tin and place a round sheet of baking parchment in the bottom.
3. Cream the butter and sugar together until light and fluffy.
4. Sieve the flour. Add the eggs one at a time with a spoonful of the flour.
5. Add the rest of the flour and mix together thoroughly.
6. Finally stir in the blueberries and spoon the mixture into the cake tin.
7. Place in the oven for 35-45 minutes or until the centre feels firm and springy to the touch. Allow to cool.
8. To make the icing, beat together the butter and icing sugar, then work in the Limoncello.
9. When the cake is cool spread the icing over the top of the cake whilst still in the tin.
10. For an extra hit of Limoncello drizzle some over the cake before icing it.

STICKY TOFFEE CAKE WITH FUDGE ICING

The great thing about this cake is that it can be served cold for tea but if a portion is warmed briefly in a microwave the icing becomes a delicious fudge sauce – serve with ice cream.

EQUIPMENT

20cm diameter spring-form cake tin

INGREDIENTS

175g stoned dates - chopped

300ml water

50g butter

225g self-raising flour

175g light Muscovado sugar

1 egg

1 teaspoon bicarbonate of soda

FOR THE FUDGE ICING

75g light brown Muscovado sugar

50g butter

50ml double cream

METHOD

1. Heat the oven to 180°C/gas mark 4.
2. Lightly butter the cake tin and place a round sheet of baking parchment in the bottom.
3. Place the dates, water and butter in a saucepan and simmer gently until the dates start to break up. Whizz to a purée with a blender. Allow to cool.
4. Mix together the flour, sugar and bicarbonate of soda in a mixing bowl and make a well in the centre and put in the egg.
5. Start mixing whilst adding the date purée slowly.
6. When everything is thoroughly mixed, transfer the mixture to the cake tin.
7. Bake for 35-45 minutes until cooked through.
8. To make the fudge icing, place the sugar, butter and cream into a saucepan and simmer together until it is like a thick sauce. Allow to cool until it is just setting then spread it on top of the cake.

VARIATION

Can also be made with a layer of ripe, prepared pears in the bottom of the tin.

SUMMER PIMMS CAKE

The whole of summer summed up in a cake. To be eaten with a glass of Pimm's, of course.

EQUIPMENT

3 x 20cm sponge cake tins

INGREDIENTS
FOR THE GENOESE SPONGE

5 eggs

150g caster sugar

150g plain flour

FOR THE NEXT STAGE

100ml Pimm's No1

450ml double cream

225g fresh strawberries

225g fresh raspberries

TO COMPLETE THE CAKE

150ml double cream

250g fruit – choose from strawberries, raspberries, kiwi fruit, blueberries, redcurrants

¼ cucumber peeled and cut into cubes

Sprigs of mint and edible flowers

Tuile biscuits (optional, see page 386)

METHOD

1. Heat the oven to 180°C/gas mark 4.
2. Line the base of the cake tins with a disc of baking parchment and oil the sides lightly.
3. Whisk the eggs and sugar together until they make a pale, light foam (see egg foams on page 420).
4. Sieve the flour and fold it into the egg foam.
5. Divide the mixture into the prepared cake tins and bake for 15-20 minutes until the centre when touched feels springy.
6. Allow to cool then turn out onto a wire rack until completely cold.
7. Place one of the sponges on to your chosen dish or platter.
8. Sprinkle all 3 sponges with the Pimm's.
9. Whip the cream until it is just holding its shape.
10. Hull and slice the strawberries.
11. Spread the bottom layer of the cake with cream and place a layer of strawberries and raspberries on top of it.
12. Spread a little more cream over the top so the surface is flat.
13. Place the next disc of sponge on top of that and repeat the process with the cream and fruit.
14. Place the final disc on top.
15. Spread the remaining cream in a thin layer around the sides and on top of the cake.
16. Whip the 150ml of cream and decorate the top with the cream (piped in rosettes), fruit, cucumber, mint, flowers and tuile biscuits.
17. Serve at a boozy afternoon tea with jugs of iced Pimm's. Don't drive home!

CHOCOLATE BROWNIE

EQUIPMENT

20 x 30cm (2cm deep) rectangular baking tin

INGREDIENTS

275g quality plain chocolate (70% cocoa solids)

275g butter

375g Muscovado or light brown sugar

90g self-raising wholemeal flour

90g self-raising white flour

5 eggs

110g walnuts

METHOD

1. Set oven to 180°C/gas mark 4.
2. Line the base of the tin with baking parchment.
3. Melt the chocolate and work in the butter until it is smooth.
4. Break up the walnuts a little and then add these with the rest of the ingredients and mix thoroughly.
5. Transfer to the tin and bake 35-45 minutes.
6. When cool cut into squares.

BATTENBURG

One of those cakes that needs to be re-discovered. Perfect sponge, jam and marzipan - what more could you ask.

EQUIPMENT

A loaf tin 26cm long and 7 x 6cm (height and width) with a capacity of 1.2lt, lined with parchment paper. (Approximate measurements).

INGREDIENTS (MAKES 2 CAKES)

2 quantities of the following sponge mixture; one per loaf tin.

175g butter

175g caster sugar

175g self-raising flour

3 eggs

Pink colouring for the second batch

FOR THE MARZIPAN

150g ground almonds

150g icing sugar

1 teaspoon lemon juice

1 teaspoon sherry

A few drops of almond essence

1 small egg white

TO ASSEMBLE THE CAKE

1 jar of seedless raspberry jam

METHOD

1. Heat the oven to 170°C/gas mark 3.
2. For the first batch, beat the butter and caster sugar together until light and fluffy.
3. Sift the flour well. Add the eggs one at a time with a spoonful of the flour.
4. Finally add the flour and combine thoroughly.
5. Transfer to the laof tin and bake for 25-35 minutes until risen and cooked.
6. Allow to cool then remove from the loaf tin.
7. Make the second batch adding pink colouring to the desired effect.
8. To make the marzipan, combine the almonds and sugar in a bowl. Add the lemon juice, sherry and almond essence.
9. Beat the egg white to break it up and use enough to combine the mixture to a paste.
10. Wrap it in cling film and refrigerate overnight. This makes it less sticky and easier to work with.
11. Trim the cakes so all the sides are square and cut each one into 4 long bars. Assemble 4 bars together alternating the pink and plain colours using the jam to make them stick.
12. Divide the marzipan in two then roll one half with enough width to accommodate the cake and about the thickness of a pound coin. Spread one side of the assembled cake with jam and place it across the marzipan at the end nearest you. Trim the end of the marzipan where the cake sits and also trim each end to fit the cake. Spread the other 3 sides of the cake with jam and roll it forwards wrapping it in the marzipan. When it is completely encased, trim the last edge of the marzipan.
    It is now ready to slice.

BEST EVER CHOCOLATE CAKE

EQUIPMENT

2 round sponge cake tins 20cm in diameter - buttered

INGREDIENTS

150g plain flour

25g cocoa powder (unsweetened)

2 teaspoons baking powder

100ml boiling water

50g plain chocolate (70% cocoa solids)

110g butter

150g Muscovado sugar

2 eggs

75g ground almonds

150g condensed milk

FOR THE CHOCOLATE FROSTING

225g plain chocolate (70% cocoa solids)

300ml soured cream

METHOD

1. Set oven 180°C/gas mark 4.
2. Sift together the flour, cocoa and baking powder.
3. Pour the boiling water onto the chocolate and stir until it melts.
4. Beat together the butter and sugar until light and fluffy.
5. Work in the eggs, one at a time, with a spoonful of flour with each one.
6. Work in the chocolate, almonds and condensed milk with the rest of the flour and mix until smooth.
7. Divide between the two cake tins.
8. Bake in the oven for 25–35 minutes until the centre is springy to the touch.
9. Allow to cool for 10 minutes before turning out onto a wire rack.
10. To make the frosting, melt the chocolate until it is smooth and there are no lumps in it.
11. Pour in the cream in one go and stir until smooth and glossy. It should now be the right consistency to use, if not, let it cool further until it is.
12. Sandwich the two halves of the cake with half the frosting and spread the remaining half on the top. If you want to do the sides as well you may need a bit more. Alternatively, you can sandwich your 2 cakes together with some jam and cream and then you will have enough chocolate to do the sides and the top.

BANANA CUP CAKES WITH PEANUT BUTTER ICING

EQUIPMENT

16 cup-cake cases and a 16-hole muffin tray

INGREDIENTS (MAKES ABOUT 16)

2 small ripe bananas

225g plain flour

½ teaspoon bicarbonate of soda

2½ teaspoons baking powder

110g butter

110g golden caster sugar

2 eggs

1 teaspoon vanilla extract

FOR THE ICING

110g unsalted butter

150g icing sugar

225g crunchy peanut butter

TO DECORATE

Chopped roasted peanuts

Chocolate flake

METHOD

1. Heat the oven to 180°C/gas mark 4.
2. Mash the bananas well.
3. Sift the flour with the bicarbonate of soda and the baking powder.
4. Beat the butter with the sugar until light and fluffy.
5. Add the eggs, one at a time, with a spoonful of the flour.
6. Finally work in the rest of the flour, the vanilla and the mashed banana – mix well.
7. Pipe into the cup-cake cases about three quarters full and bake for 20-25 minutes. Allow to cool.
8. To make the icing, beat together the butter and icing sugar until light and fluffy, then work in the peanut butter.
9. Using a star nozzle pipe the icing onto the cooled cup cakes.
10. Decorate with chopped roasted peanuts and crumbled chocolate flake.

CHOCOLATE CHESTNUT GÂTEAU

EQUIPMENT

2 x 20cm sponge cake tins

INGREDIENTS
FOR THE SPONGE

150g self-raising flour

25g cocoa powder (unsweetened)

175g light brown sugar

1½ teaspoons baking powder

175ml sunflower oil

50ml milk

3 eggs

TO SANDWICH THE SPONGE

50g sweetened chestnut purée

150ml double cream (whipped)

TO FINISH AND DECORATE

225g plain chocolate (70% cocoa solids)

300ml double cream

1 tablespoon brandy

8-10 whole marron glacé (crystallized chestnuts)

METHOD

1. Heat the oven to 150°C/gas mark 2.
2. Line the tins with a disc of baking parchment.
3. Sift the flour and the cocoa powder together then mix in the sugar and baking powder.
4. Make a well in the centre, add the oil, milk and eggs and beat to a smooth batter.
5. Divide the mixture between the two cake tins.
6. Bake for 25-35 minutes. When cooled slightly turn them out onto a wire rack.
7. Sandwich the 2 cakes together with the chestnut purée and whipped cream.
8. To make the chocolate covering, melt the chocolate until it is smooth and there are no lumps in it.
9. Tip in the cream and brandy and stir until smooth and glossy. It should now be of a spreading consistency but if it is still a little soft wait for it to cool further.
10. Spread the chocolate over the top of the cake and around the sides.
11. Put any chocolate frosting you have over in a piping bag with a star nozzle. Decorate the cake with rosettes of chocolate and the marron glace.

LEMON POLENTA CAKE WITH ROASTED PLUMS

EQUIPMENT

A spring-form cake tin 25cm in diameter lined with parchment paper

INGREDIENTS

225g butter

225g caster sugar

225g ground almonds

3 eggs

110g polenta flour

1 teaspoon baking powder

Zest of 2 lemons

Juice of ½ a lemon

1 teaspoon vanilla essence

15–18 Victoria plums

110g caster sugar

Thick cream to serve

METHOD

1. Heat the oven to 170°C/gas mark 3.
2. Beat together the softened butter, caster sugar (225g) and ground almonds until light and fluffy.
3. Then beat in the eggs and polenta flour, baking powder, lemon and vanilla. Turn the mixture into the cake tin and bake for 45 minutes or until springy to the touch. Allow to cool.
4. Increase the oven heat to 230°C/gas mark 8.
5. Halve and stone the plums and place them in an ovenproof dish.
6. Sprinkle with caster sugar and cook in the oven until they are just collapsing (about 10-15 minutes).
7. Decorate the top of the cake with the plums and serve with thick cream.

ICE CREAM

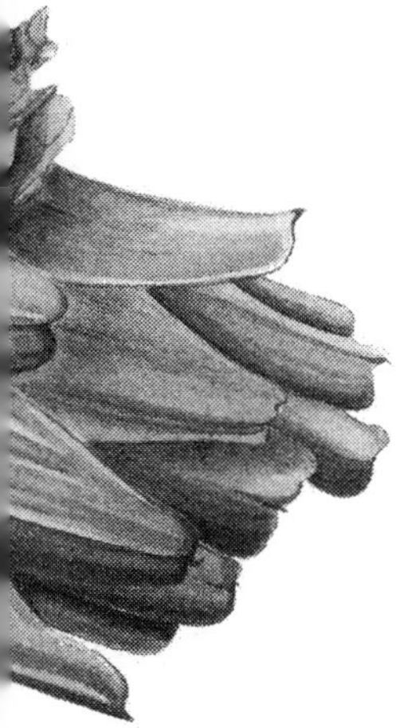

ICE CREAM, SORBET & FROZEN DESSERTS

A proper ice cream machine with its own freezing unit is ideal for making ice cream and sorbet. Unfortunately, they are expensive and not worthwhile unless you are going to use it a lot. The cheaper versions where you freeze the bowl are not always that efficient unless you can put the whole unit in the freezer as it is going round.

However, there are ways around this without a machine and without having to keep taking the mixture out of the freezer to stir it every half hour. It is called 'semi- freddo' and is actually a frozen mousse. As one of the things that keeps ice cream soft is the air that gets incorporated, by whipping the cream and the eggs and sugar first it does not require churning. Recipes marked thus* use this method.

Also, please be aware that this method uses raw egg and it is advisable to use eggs that are salmonella free (i.e. eggs that are stamped).

In hot weather, chill all your ingredients first.

*COFFEE & RUM ICE CREAM

INGREDIENTS

2 eggs

50g caster sugar

300ml double cream

2 teaspoons instant coffee dissolved in a few drops of warm water

One double measure of rum

METHOD

1. Using an electric beater and a glass or ceramic bowl whisk the eggs and sugar until thick and pale.
2. In another bowl, whip the double cream until it holds its shape.
3. Add the coffee and rum to the cream then fold in the egg/sugar mixture.
4. Transfer to a plastic container and freeze.

*WHITE CHOCOLATE ICE CREAM

INGREDIENTS

225g white chocolate

300ml double cream

4 egg whites

1 tablespoon of caster sugar

METHOD

1. Melt the chocolate over hot water.
2. Remove from the heat and stir in the double cream.
3. Whisk the egg whites and sugar until stiff.
4. Fold into the chocolate, place in a suitable container and freeze.

CARAMEL ICE CREAM

INGREDIENTS (SERVES 6)

225g granulated sugar

600ml double cream

6 egg yolks

50g caster sugar

300ml full-cream milk

METHOD

1. To make the caramel put the granulated sugar in a heavy-based pan over a low heat.
2. Keep shaking the pan as the sugar melts (do not stir).
3. Cook the sugar to a rich caramel colour and, when the desired colour is reached, pour in the cream. (Take great care as it may well spit and bubble.)
4. Some of the sugar will harden but just leave it off the heat and eventually it will dissolve into the cream.
5. Place the egg yolks and caster sugar into a bowl and whisk together to amalgamate them.
6. Add the milk to the caramel/cream mixture and bring to the boil.
7. When it is boiling pour it onto the egg and sugar mixture.
8. Return the mixture to the pan and cook gently until it thickens (i.e. coats the back of a spoon).
9. Strain into a clean container and cool.
10. Refrigerate overnight and the next day churn it in the ice-cream maker.

*CARAMEL ICE CREAM

INGREDIENTS (SERVES 6)

Caramel sauce (see page 423) cooled

2 eggs

50g caster sugar

300ml double cream

METHOD

1. Using an electric beater and a glass or ceramic bowl whisk the eggs and sugar until thick and pale.
2. In a separate bowl, whip the cream until it is just holding its shape.
3. Fold the 2 amounts together whilst drizzling in the caramel sauce.
4. Transfer to a container and freeze.

BROWN BREAD ICE CREAM

As with all ice creams that have crunchy bits in them (Praline Ice Cream as well) they need to be eaten within a couple of days because the crunchy effect will start to soften.

INGREDIENTS
FOR THE BREADCRUMBS

25g butter

75g fresh brown breadcrumbs

25g caster sugar

FOR THE ICE CREAM

1 vanilla pod or 1 teaspoon of vanilla paste (this also contains the seeds, unlike vanilla essence)

250ml full cream milk

3 egg yolks

75g caster sugar

300ml double cream

METHOD

1. Melt the butter in a frying pan, add the breadcrumbs and cook over a low heat, slowly, to get the breadcrumbs fried and crisp but without getting them too dark (you will need to stir them frequently).
2. Sprinkle over the caster sugar and continue cooking until the sugar caramelizes.
3. Spread them out on a tray to cool down.
4. Add the vanilla paste, or split the vanilla pod if you are using it, scrape out the seeds and put it all (pod and seeds) into the milk in a saucepan.
5. Place egg yolks and sugar in a bowl and mix to amalgamate.
6. Bring the milk to the boil and then whisk it onto the yolks and sugar.
7. Remove the vanilla pod. Put the mixture back into the saucepan and place it back over the heat.
8. Cook carefully until the mixture thickens (it must not boil) and will coat the back of a spoon. Remove from the heat and immediately strain it into a clean container. Stir in the double cream.
9. Allow to cool, leave overnight in the refrigerator.
10. Churn the mixture in an ice-cream maker and add the caramelized breadcrumbs towards the end of the process.

ROAST NECTARINES WITH GERANIUM ICE CREAM

INGREDIENTS (SERVES 6)

6 ripe nectarines

Caster sugar

Geranium flowers for garnish

FOR THE ICE CREAM

50g geranium leaves (Attar of rose variety)

500ml full-cream milk

600ml double cream

8 egg yolks

175g caster sugar

METHOD

1. To make the ice cream, chop the geranium leaves, place in a saucepan with the milk and cream and bring to the boil.
2. Remove from the heat and leave to infuse for about 20 minutes. Strain to remove the geranuim leaves.
3. Whisk together the egg yolks and caster sugar.
4. Bring the cream/milk to the boil again and whisk it into the egg mixture.
5. Return it to the saucepan and cook until it thickens, taking care it does not boil.
6. Strain through a fine sieve. Chill the mixture before churning in the ice-cream maker.
7. Heat the oven to 230°C/gas mark 8.
8. Quarter the nectarines and remove the stone.
9. Place the quarters on a baking tray and sprinkle with the caster sugar.
10. Bake in the oven until they are hot and starting to singe.
11. Serve immediately in bowls with scoops of the ice cream and garnished with geranium flowers.

CHAR-GRILLED PINEAPPLE WITH ELDERFLOWER ICE CREAM

Dessert for a summer's day barbecue.

INGREDIENTS

1 whole pineapple

Pineapple sage leaves to garnish (optional). This is a herb that looks like sage but smells of pineapple – not easy to find unless you grow your own.

FOR THE ICE CREAM

2-3 heads of elder flowers

425ml of full-cream milk

600ml of double cream

6 egg yolks

175g caster sugar

METHOD

1. Pick over the elder flowers to remove any insects. (Unfortunately washing them removes the pollen and therefore some of the flavour.)
2. Put the elder flowers in a pan and pour over the milk and cream (you will now see any bugs you missed and be able to pick them out).
3. Bring this to the boil and then allow it to stand for 45 minutes.
4. Whisk together the egg yolks and sugar.
5. Bring the milk and cream to the boil again then strain it onto the egg-yolk mixture whilst whisking.
6. Return to the pan and heat until it thickens (do not allow the mixture to boil as it will curdle).
7. Remove from the heat and strain again.
8. Cool, then chill well before churning in an ice-cream machine.
9. Peel the pineapple and cut into thick slices. Remove the centre core with a small cutter.
10. Make sure the bars of the barbecue are as clean as possible and place the slices of pineapple on the grill.
11. Allow the pineapple slices to brown slightly then serve them hot and juicy with a scoop of elderflower ice cream garnished with the leaves of pineapple sage.

YELLOW GRAPEFRUIT SORBET WITH PINK GRAPEFRUIT SEGMENTS

Simplicity itself!

INGREDIENTS

225g granulated sugar

600ml freshly-squeezed yellow grapefruit juice (strained)

TO SERVE

Pink grapefruit segments

Mint leaves

METHOD

1. Stir the sugar into the grapefruit juice until it dissolves then churn in an ice-cream machine.
2. Serve spooned into chilled glasses decorated with the pink segments and mint leaves.

ROAST STRAWBERRY & BASIL ICE CREAM

INGREDIENTS

700g fresh strawberries

500ml full-cream milk

600ml double cream

250g caster sugar

8 egg yolks

1 small bunch of fresh basil

Juice of a lemon

METHOD

1. Heat the oven to 150°C/gas mark 2.
2. Hull and halve the strawberries and place cut side up in a shallow oven dish.
3. Sprinkle with 50g of the sugar and place in the oven for 30 minutes.
4. Place the cream and milk in a saucepan and place over the heat.
5. Beat the egg yolks with the sugar.
6. When the cream/milk boils pour it onto the egg yolks whilst whisking.
7. Return the mixture to the saucepan and heat carefully, stirring all the time until the mixture thickens. (Do not boil).
8. When it is ready pour it into a clean bowl through a sieve.
9. Place the strawberries in a food processor with the basil and lemon juice and process. Combine with the custard.
10. Chill completely before putting through an ice cream machine.

*PRALINE & RAISIN ICE CREAM

INGREDIENTS

2 eggs

50g caster sugar

300ml double cream

1 tablespoon praline (see page 422)

1 tablespoon boozy soaked raisins (see page 423)

METHOD

1. Using an electric beater and a glass or ceramic bowl whisk the eggs and sugar until thick and pale.
2. In a separate bowl whip the cream until it is just holding its shape.
3. Fold the two amounts together with the praline and raisins.
4. Transfer to a container and freeze.
5. Eat within a few days or the praline loses its crunch.

BREADS BUNS PASTRIES

BREAD

There is a lot of mystique, old wives' tales, wrong information and myths about making bread. Bread is easy and, if you understand the simple chemistry of it, there is no mystique. This is a straightforward method. It is by no means the only method but it is quick and easy. Kneading your bread dough stretches and strengthens the gluten in it. Don't wear yourself out doing it – if you are using a high-gluten flour, only a minimum of kneading is required. Knocking on the bottom of your cooked loaf will only tell you that there is nobody in - it won't tell you whether it is cooked or not – old wives' tale. Rolls, flat breads and small baguettes will be cooked when nicely brown, everything else has to be timed.

YEAST

Yeast is a living organism and, although it behaves like a bacterium, it is in fact a type of fungi. Most recipes recommend the use of dried yeast. Fresh is better and easier to get hold of than you might think. Supermarkets that bake bread on the premises will usually sell you some but you have to ask for it at the bakery counter. Morrisons have it on the shelf by the butter. Kept in a sealed container, in the refrigerator, it will keep for up to a fortnight. Fresh yeast works more quickly and vigorously than dried. Use dried yeast for emergencies or if you can't get fresh. As a living organism it requires moisture, warmth and food (sugar and starch) to work. When the yeast starts working in the bread dough it produces carbon dioxide that gives the bubbles in the dough and eventually the loaf. Try to keep your dough at a constant temperature, between 40° and 45°C (just warm to the touch). Make sure your water and flour are about this temperature before starting.

FLOUR

There are a lot of different flours available for bread making and they will usually have the word 'strong' or 'very strong' on the packet. This means it is made from hard wheat which is high in gluten – proper bread flour. White flour has had all of the bran and the germ removed. Brown flour contains 85% of the whole wheat and has had some of the bran and germ removed. Wholemeal flour contains all of it. Some flours come with various additions including other grains, malted flakes and a variety of seeds but, generally speaking, white flour is the lightest and wholemeal, although better for you, can be a bit on the heavy side – try mixing different types of flour for something that suits you.

BREAD MAKING TIPS

Use honey to get your yeast going rather than sugar (although any sugar will do) as it seems to get it started more quickly.

A recipe is a guide line, the amount of water may vary a little as the absorbency of different flours may vary also.

It is much easier to add more flour to a wet dough than it is to add more water to a dry dough so err on the side of wet.

You can't time proving the bread as it all hinges on the temperature of the dough and surrounding area – you have to use your judgement.

Warming the flour speeds up the proving process – use either a microwave (30 seconds is about right) or put it in a dry saucepan over a heat source – stir with your hand until the right temperature is reached then transfer it to the bowl.

At the first stage of mixing up your dough, i.e. when you put the liquid into the flour, use a table knife to mix; it is an ideal tool and saves you getting sticky dough up to your elbows.

If you are baking your loaf in a tin be sure to remove it from the tin soon after it comes out of the oven otherwise the steam will condense around the loaf making it wet.

The minimum for the first proving is when the dough has doubled in size. It doesn't matter too much if this goes over but on the second prove it is crucial because if it over proves it may collapse or start to hang over the edges of your loaf tin.

And remember – nobody knows all there is about making bread – and nobody ever will.

A CLASSIC WHITE LOAF

EQUIPMENT

1.5 litre loaf tin

INGREDIENTS

20g fresh yeast

240ml warm water

1 teaspoon runny honey

400g strong or extra strong white bread flour

1 teaspoon salt

2 tablespoons of oil – sunflower or olive

METHOD

1. Heat the oven to 220°C/gas mark 7.
2. Crumble the yeast into the warm water and add the honey.
3. Warm the flour with the salt, add the oil and when the yeast mixture is fizzing add this also.
4. Mix with a table knife until you have a rough dough then place it on the work top lightly dusted with flour and knead until the dough is smooth.
5. Put it back in the bowl, cover with a cloth, and put it in a warm place.
6. Oil your loaf tin.
7. When the dough has doubled in size remove from the bowl again and knead briefly.
8. Shape to a loaf and drop it into the loaf tin.
9. Put it in a warm place and prove again until it is doubled in size.
10. Bake the loaf for 15 minutes at the higher temperature then drop the temperature down to 150°C/gas mark 2 for a further 45 minutes.
11. Remove from the tin once it has cooled slightly.

A GOOD WHOLEMEAL LOAF

Wholemeal bread is good for you but can be a bit on the heavy side. Using a proportion of a lighter flour (i.e. white or Granary) you still get the goodness but in a lighter loaf. In fact, there are so many interesting flours on the market for bread making it is quite good to experiment with different mixtures to create something that is tailor-made to your taste.

EQUIPMENT

1.5 litre loaf tin

INGREDIENTS

300g wholemeal bread flour

200g white or Granary type

300ml of warm water

25g fresh yeast

1 teaspoon runny honey

2 tablespoons of oil (sunflower or olive)

1 teaspoon salt

METHOD

1. Heat the oven to 220°C/gas mark 7.
2. Crumble the yeast into the warm water and add the honey.
3. Warm the flour with the salt, add the oil and when the yeast mixture is fizzing add this also.
4. Mix with a table knife until you have a rough dough then place it on the work top lightly dusted with flour and knead until the dough is smooth.
5. Put it back in the bowl, cover with a cloth, and put it in a warm place.
6. Oil your loaf tin.
7. When the dough has doubled in size remove from the bowl again and knead briefly.
8. Shape to a loaf and drop it into the loaf tin.
9. Put it in a warm place and prove again until it is doubled in size.
10. Bake the loaf for 15 minutes at the higher temperature then drop the temperature down to 150°C/gas mark 2 for a further 45 minutes.
11. Remove from the tin once it has cooled slightly.

FOCACCIA BREAD

INGREDIENTS

500g strong, white bread flour

25g fresh yeast

300ml warm water

1 teaspoon runny honey

2 tablespoons olive oil

2 sprigs rosemary

2 cloves of garlic

Ground black pepper

1 teaspoon salt

Extra olive oil

METHOD

1. Heat the oven to 200°C/gas mark 6.
2. Dissolve the yeast in the warm water and add the honey.
3. Wait for the mixture to fizz while you chop the garlic and the rosemary.
4. Warm the flour then make a well in the centre and add the oil, rosemary, garlic, salt and pepper.
5. Add the yeast mix to the flour and mix to a dough. Put in a warm place to prove.
6. When it has doubled in size, remove it from the bowl and knead briefly.
7. Oil a baking sheet, roll out the dough to a rough circle and place it on the baking sheet.
8. Drizzle with some more olive oil and place somewhere warm to prove. When it is doubled in size, make dimples in the surface with your (floured) finger tips before placing in the oven. Cook for 25–30 minutes.

SUN-DRIED TOMATO BREAD

INGREDIENTS

250g white bread flour

15g fresh yeast

1 teaspoon runny honey

150ml warm water

½ teaspoon salt

4 sun dried tomatoes (the ones in oil) - chopped

1 teaspoon sun dried tomato paste

1 tablespoon of oil from the jar of tomatoes

METHOD

1. Heat the oven to 220°C/gas mark 7.
2. Dissolve the yeast and honey in the warm water.
3. Warm the flour. Add the salt, oil, tomatoes and tomato paste.
4. Make a well in the centre.
5. When the water/yeast mixture is fizzing, mix it into the flour to form a dough.
6. Knead until smooth and elastic.
7. Cover with a cloth and put in a warm place.
8. Allow to prove until double in size, then knead and shape into 2 baguette shapes. Place on an oiled baking sheet.
9. Spray with a little water and allow to prove again.
10. When they have doubled in size bake for 25-35 minutes.

SODA BREAD

Soda bread uses bicarbonate of soda rather than yeast to raise the bread – so, in effect, it is similar to making a cake. Baking powder is a mixture of bicarbonate of soda and tartaric acid, as bicarbonate of soda needs an acid to make it react (it produces carbon dioxide as yeast does). In this recipe, the lactic acid in the buttermilk is the acid that reacts with the soda – it also produces the pleasant sour flavour. Porridge oats help the loaf retain its moisture and the black treacle gives the bread a good dark colour. The sweetness from the treacle and honey helps hide the slight bitterness of the bicarb.

Soda bread is naturally a bit heavier than yeast-risen bread.

INGREDIENTS

150g strong wholemeal flour

100g strong white or granary bread flour

50g porridge oats

1 level teaspoon bicarbonate of soda

1 level teaspoon salt

1 teaspoon runny honey

1 teaspoon black treacle

225ml buttermilk

METHOD

1. Heat the oven to 200°C/gas mark 6.
2. Place both flours, oats, salt and soda into a bowl with the honey and treacle.
3. Stir in the buttermilk and mix to form a dough.
4. Knead until well mixed.
5. Shape into a round, place on a greased baking sheet and cut a cross in the top.
6. Flick or spray a little water over the loaf and tray.
7. Cover with a large cake tin and bake for 30 minutes.
8. Remove the cover and bake for a further 10 minutes to colour the crust.

SAGE & ONION BREAD

The onions can make this bread dough a little wet so be prepared to judge the consistency of your dough.

INGREDIENTS

1 large onion

Salt and ground black pepper

3 tablespoons olive oil

8 sage leaves

250g white bread flour

½ teaspoon salt

15g fresh yeast

150ml warm water

1 teaspoon runny honey

METHOD

1. Slice the onion and fry in 1 tablespoon of the oil, with the seasoning, until soft and a bit caramelized.
2. Cut the sage into thin strips and stir into the onions. Set aside.
3. Heat the oven to 200°C/gas mark 6.
4. Dissolve the yeast in the warm water and add the honey. Wait for the mixture to fizz.
5. Warm the flour and add the salt and the other 2 tablespoons of oil to it.
6. Add the yeast mix and the onion and sage to the flour and mix with a table knife until it forms a dough.
7. Add a little more water if it is too dry or some flour if it is too wet.
8. Turn it out on to your work surface and knead until it is smooth.
9. Put in a warm place to prove.
10. When it has doubled in bulk remove from the bowl and knead again.
11. Cut the dough in half and shape each half into a baguette. Place on an oiled baking sheet.
12. Spray with water, prove until doubled in size and bake for 25–30 minutes.

OLIVE FLAT BREAD

INGREDIENTS

250g white bread flour

15g fresh yeast

½ teaspoon sugar

150ml warm water

½ teaspoon salt

2 tablespoons olive oil

15 black olives (chopped)

1 teaspoon olive tapenade

METHOD

1. Heat the oven to 220°C/gas mark 7.
2. Dissolve the yeast and sugar in the warm water.
3. Warm the flour. Add the salt, oil, olives and tapenade to the flour and make a well in the centre.
4. When the water/yeast mixture is fizzing, mix it into the flour to form a dough.
5. Knead until smooth and elastic.
6. Cover with a cloth and put in a warm place.
7. Allow to prove until double in size, then knead and shape into 2 flat loaves. Place on an oiled baking sheet.
8. Spray with a little water and allow to prove again.
9. When they have doubled in bulk bake for 20–25 minutes

SEEDED FLAT BREAD

INGREDIENTS

250g strong white bread flour

15g fresh yeast

150ml warm water

1 teaspoon honey

½ teaspoon salt

2 tablespoons olive oil

2 teaspoons mixed seeds (choose from sesame, poppy, sunflower, pumpkin, linseed and black onion seeds)

Extra olive oil

Course sea salt

METHOD

1. Heat the oven to 220°C/gas mark 7.
2. Dissolve the yeast in the warm water and add the honey.
3. Warm the flour then add the oil and salt.
4. When the yeast mixture is fizzing, add it to the flour and mix to a dough.
5. Leave to prove until it is doubled in bulk.
6. Knock back the dough and knead until smooth.
7. Roll out with a rolling pin to a rough circle and place on an oiled baking sheet.
8. Spray with water and scatter liberally with the seeds and a little sea salt – press them into the dough. Prove again until doubled in size.
9. Bake for 20-25 minutes.

GRANARY WALNUT BREAD

EQUIPMENT

800ml loaf tin

INGREDIENTS

250g Granary flour

15g fresh yeast

1 teaspoon runny honey

150ml warm water

½ teaspoon salt

1 tablespoon of walnut oil

50g chopped walnuts

METHOD

1. Heat the oven to 220°C/gas mark 7.
2. Dissolve the yeast and honey in the warm water.
3. Warm the flour, then add the salt, oil and walnuts.
4. When the yeast/water mix is fizzing, stir it into the flour to form a dough.
5. Knead until smooth and elastic.
6. Cover with a cloth and put in a warm place until doubled in size.
7. Oil the loaf tin. Knead briefly and then shape into a loaf and place in the tin.
8. Prove until doubled in bulk and then bake for 35-40 minutes.
9. Cool slightly and remove from the loaf tin.

LEOPARD BREAD

I know this is normally called tiger bread but to me the distinctive crust has more of a spotty look than a striped one.

INGREDIENTS

250g strong white bread flour

15g fresh yeast

1 teaspoon runny honey

150ml warm water

½ teaspoon salt

1 tablespoon sunflower oil

A handful of coarse polenta

FOR THE TOPPING

5g fresh yeast

110ml warm water

110g semolina or ground rice

1 tablespoon sunflower oil

15g caster sugar

METHOD

1. Heat the oven to 220°C/gas mark 7.
2. Dissolve the yeast in the warm water with the honey.
3. Warm the flour then add the salt and oil.
4. When the yeast water is fizzing, put it into the bowl with the flour and mix to a dough.
5. Knead briefly and put in a warm place to prove.
6. To make the topping, dissolve the yeast in the warm water then add the other ingredients.
7. Mix until smooth then leave in a warm place.
8. When your dough has doubled in size turn it out onto the work surface and knock it back.
9. Knead briefly then form it into two batons (baguettes).
10. Oil a tray and scatter some course polenta across the surface.
11. Lay the batons on this and put in a warm place to prove.
12. When it has doubled in size, stir the topping and carefully spoon some on top of each baton. You may not need it all!
13. Place in the hot oven and bake for 25-30 minutes or until the crust is crisp and golden.
14. The topping mixture running down the sides makes the bread more liable to stick to the tray. As a precaution you can line the tray with baking parchment or a silicon mat to prevent this.

PESTO BREAD

You can use pesto from a jar but it won't taste as good as this.

INGREDIENTS

250g strong white bread flour

12g fresh yeast

150ml warm water

½ teaspoon salt

1 teaspoon runny honey

FOR THE PESTO*

1 bunch basil (10g)

2 cloves of garlic

50g freshly grated Parmesan

50g pine kernels

Black pepper

2-3 tablespoons olive oil

*Use just half of this for the recipe, the rest can be used for something else or frozen.

METHOD

1. Heat the oven to 220°C/gas mark 7.
2. To make the pesto, place the basil, garlic, Parmesan, pine kernels and pepper into the food processor and run it to make a paste.
3. Pour the oil in through the funnel, slowly, to incorporate it.
4. Dissolve the yeast in the warm water and mix in the honey.
5. Warm the flour then add the salt and pesto to the flour.
6. When the yeast is fizzing add this to the flour and mix to a dough.
7. Turn it out onto a lightly-floured work top and knead until smooth.
8. Place it back in the bowl and cover with a cloth.
9. When it has doubled in size, turn out, knead again and shape it into two loaf shapes (baguettes). Place on an oiled baking sheet.
10. Prove until doubled in size then bake for 25–35 minutes.

PIZZA

The dough is identical to the white bread recipe at the beginning of this section and pizza is so much better made with fresh dough.

INGREDIENTS (MAKES 2)

250g strong white bread flour

15g fresh yeast

150ml warm water

1 teaspoon runny honey

½ teaspoon salt

1 tablespoon olive oil

FOR THE TOPPING

10 cherry or Pomodoro tomatoes

Olive oil

Salt and ground black pepper

2 tablespoons sun-dried tomato purée

16 slices of Milano salami

1-2 courgettes sliced thinly longways

150g grated mozzarella cheese

50g shaved or grated Parmesan

24 stoned olives – green, black or a mix

METHOD

1. Heat the oven to 230°C/gas mark 8.
2. Dissolve the yeast in the warm water with the honey.
3. Warm the flour then add the salt and oil.
4. When the yeast water is fizzing put it into the bowl with the flour and mix to a dough.
5. Knead briefly and put in a warm place to prove.
6. Halve the cherry tomatoes and toss them in a little oil and seasoning.
7. Re-knead the dough and cut it into two pieces.
8. Increase the oven temperature to its highest setting.
9. Roll each piece out to a rough circle and place it on an oiled tray or suitable baking appliance.
10. Spread each round with the tomato purée followed by the mozzarella cheese.
11. Arrange the other ingredients on top of this then finally sprinkle over the Parmesan.
12. Bake until, hot, bubbling and crisp at the edges.

PEANUT & SESAME BREAD

INGREDIENTS

250g strong white bread flour

15g fresh yeast

1 teaspoon runny honey

150ml warm water

1 level teaspoon salt

1 tablespoon crunchy peanut butter

1 tablespoon sesame seeds

Egg wash (see page 426)

METHOD

1. Heat the oven to 220°C/gas mark 7.
2. Dissolve the yeast and honey in the warm water.
3. Warm the flour then add the salt, and peanut butter.
4. When the yeast mixture is fizzing, mix it into the flour to form a dough.
5. Knead until smooth and elastic. Cover with a cloth and put in a warm place.
6. Allow to prove until double in size, then remove from the bowl, knead and shape into two batons (baguettes).
7. Brush with egg wash and scatter with sesame seeds.
8. Allow to prove again until doubled in size.
9. Bake for 25-35 minutes.

CHORIZO & THYME FOUGASSE

I have heard the origin of this word for a flat Provençal loaf with holes is anything from a roof tile to a land mine. My vote goes for 'fern' but who knows?

INGREDIENTS

250g strong white bread flour

15g fresh yeast

1 teaspoon runny honey

150ml warm water

75g chorizo sausage

1 tablespoon chopped fresh thyme

1 level teaspoon salt and ground black pepper

2 tablespoons olive oil

Coarse sea salt – for the top

METHOD

1. Heat the oven to 220°C/gas mark 7.
2. Dissolve the yeast and honey in the warm water.
3. Warm the flour. Chop the chorizo into small pieces, chop the thyme and add them to the flour with the salt, pepper and oil.
4. When the yeast water is fizzing, add it to the flour and mix with a knife to a soft dough.
5. Knead until smooth, place it back in the bowl, cover with a cloth and put in a warm place to prove.
6. When the dough has doubled in size, remove it from the bowl and knead again.
7. Roll the dough out flat and place it on an oiled baking sheet.
8. Slash the dough with a sharp knife to make the distinctive 'fougasse' pattern. The fougasse pattern is a leaf shape. Once you have your flat oval of dough on the tray make a cut down the centre right the way through the dough but do not cut to the outer edge. Then make 3 cuts at an angle either side of the first cut. Do not join the cuts up. Stretch the dough outwards to open up the cuts so they don't close as the bread proves. The cuts mean you get more crust.
9. Spray with a little water and prove in a warm place.
10. When it has doubled in size (i.e. depth) put it in the oven.
11. Cook for 15-20 minutes until golden brown.

CRUMPETS

EQUIPMENT

A heavy flat-based frying pan and crumpet rings.

INGREDIENTS (MAKES 6)

225g plain flour

½ teaspoon salt

175ml milk

175ml water

15g fresh yeast

1 teaspoon caster sugar

½ teaspoon baking powder

Sunflower oil for frying

METHOD

1. Mix the milk and water and warm to just above blood heat. Dissolve the yeast into it with the sugar.
2. Warm the flour and add the salt to it.
3. When the yeast mix is fizzing, work it into the flour to make a smooth batter.
4. Allow to stand for 15-30 minutes while it bubbles.
5. Beat the baking powder into the batter thoroughly.
6. Prepare the pan by heating it with the oiled crumpet rings in it. Get it hot but then turn the heat down.
7. Oil the pan then pour about 2-3 tablespoons of the batter into each ring.
8. Allow to cook for 6-8 minutes making sure the batter is no longer runny then turn the crumpet and rings over and cook for a further 2-3 minutes.
9. Place on a warm, dry cloth as they come out of the pan.
10. Eat whilst still warm with lots of butter.

BRIOCHE

INGREDIENTS

20g fresh yeast

3 tablespoons warm milk

25g caster sugar

75g softened butter

225g strong white bread flour

½ teaspoon salt

1 egg

Egg wash (see page 426)

METHOD

1. Heat the oven to 180°C/gas mark 4.
2. Dissolve the yeast into the milk with a pinch of the sugar.
3. Rub the butter into the flour. Add the salt and sugar.
4. Make a well in the centre of the flour.
5. Place the egg into the well with the yeast mixture and mix to a dough with a table knife.
6. Knead the dough until smooth and elastic then put it in a warm place to prove.
7. When it has doubled in size remove it from the bowl and knead briefly.
8. Shape into loaves or rolls or even a plait.
9. Brush with egg wash.
10. Prove until doubled in size again.
11. Bake for 30-35 minutes until golden brown.

TEA CAKES

INGREDIENTS (MAKES 6)

325g strong white bread flour

150ml milk

1 level teaspoon salt

20g yeast

50g soft brown sugar

75g mixed fruit with peel

1 egg

50g butter

Honey for brushing

METHOD

1. Heat the oven to 200°C/gas mark 6.
2. Warm the milk and dissolve the yeast in it with a pinch of the sugar.
3. Warm the flour. Melt the butter and put this in the flour with the rest of the sugar, salt, fruit and egg.
4. Mix together with a table knife adding the yeast/milk mixture as you go.
5. When it has formed a dough, put it in a warm place to prove.
6. When it has doubled in size, knead the dough on a floured surface until smooth.
7. Divide into 6 pieces, make them into rounds and flatten slightly.
8. Place them on an oiled baking sheet and prove to double their size.
9. Bake for 15-20 minutes.
10. Brush with honey while still warm to produce a sticky crust.

LARDY CAKE

EQUIPMENT

Square tin 20 x 20cm

INGREDIENTS

280g white bread flour

20g fresh yeast

160ml warm water

50g caster sugar

½ teaspoon salt

25g lard

FOR THE FILLING

75g lard plus extra for greasing the tin and brushing the top of the lardy cake

75g soft light brown sugar

75g mixed fruit with peel

½ teaspoon allspice

Caster sugar to sprinkle over the top

METHOD

1. Heat the oven to 180°C/gas mark 4.
2. Rub a little lard around the tin.
3. Dissolve the yeast into the warm water with half a teaspoon of the sugar.
4. Warm the flour. Rub the 25g of lard into the flour and add the salt and the rest of the sugar.
5. When the yeast is fizzing, tip the mixture into the flour and mix to a dough.
6. Lightly knead on a floured work top until smooth.
7. Place it somewhere warm until doubled in size.
8. Remove from the bowl and re-knead briefly.
9. Roll it out to a rectangle 1cm thick.
10. Dot one half of the rectangle with half the lard, sprinkle with half the fruit, half the sugar and half the spice.
11. Fold the other half of the dough over the fruit etc. and roll again to the original size.
12. Repeat the process then roll out the dough to the size of the tin. Put the dough in the tin.
13. Brush the top with a little melted lard, scatter with caster sugar and place it somewhere warm to prove until doubled in size.
14. Score the top with a criss-cross pattern and place in the oven to bake for 30-40 minutes until golden.
15. Turn out onto a wire rack.

FRUIT LOAF

EQUIPMENT

1.25 litre loaf tin

INGREDIENTS

325g strong white bread flour

50g butter

150ml water

25g fresh yeast

35g light brown sugar

Pinch of salt

1 level teaspoon allspice

75g mixed fruit with peel

1 egg

Extra butter for greasing the loaf tin

METHOD

1. Heat the oven to 180°C/gas mark 4.
2. Melt the butter.
3. Warm the water and dissolve the yeast in it with a pinch of the sugar.
4. Warm the flour. Put the melted butter in with the flour along with the rest of the sugar, salt, allspice, fruit and egg.
5. Add the yeast/water and mix to a dough with a table knife. Knead briefly until smooth then put it in a warm place to prove.
6. When it has doubled in size remove it from the bowl, re-knead briefly and shape it to fit the loaf tin.
7. Butter the loaf tin, place the dough in the tin and put it in a warm place to prove again.
8. When it has doubled in bulk, place in the oven for 45–50 minutes.
9. Reduce the oven temperature if the crust starts to look too dark before the cooking time is reached.
10. Brushing with honey produces a sticky crust.

STOLLEN

INGREDIENTS

50g sultanas

25g currants

25g chopped mixed peel

2 tablespoons rum

60ml warm milk

20g fresh yeast

25g caster sugar – plus extra for the top

250g strong white flour

25g whole blanched almonds

¼ teaspoon ground cardamom

½ teaspoon ground cinnamon

25g melted butter- plus extra for the tray and brushing the top of the loaf

1 egg

1 level teaspoon salt

FOR THE ALMOND FILLING

110g ground almonds

110g icing sugar

2 teaspoons lemon juice

1 small egg white

A few drops of almond essence

METHOD

1. Soak all the dried fruit including the mixed peel in the rum first (overnight if possible).
2. To make the almond filling, place the ground almonds in a bowl with the icing sugar.
3. Add the lemon juice, egg white and almond essence and work to a paste.
4. Wrap in cling film and allow to rest.
5. Heat the oven to 180°C/gas mark 4.
6. Warm the milk and crumble the yeast into it with a pinch of the sugar.
7. Warm the flour and then place the almonds, spices and fruit into it.
8. Make a well in the centre and place into it the butter, milk / yeast, the egg and salt. All the dough ingredients should now be in the bowl.
9. Mix to a smooth dough with a table knife.
10. When mixed, sprinkle some flour on the work surface and knead lightly to get the dough smooth.
11. Place it back in the bowl cover with a cloth and place it in a warm place to prove.
12. When doubled in size turn it out onto the work surface again, knead lightly and roll out the dough to an oval.
13. Roll the almond filling into a sausage shape the length of the widest part of the oval. You may not need all the almond filling.
14. Fold the dough over the almond filling.
15. Place the whole thing on a buttered baking sheet and brush with melted butter then scatter caster sugar over it. Place in a warm place to prove.
16. When the stollen has doubled in size place it in the oven and bake for 25–35 minutes. Drop the oven temperature if at any time it is getting too dark.

CROISSANT DOUGH

Making croissants is a very precise and exacting process. Do not worry if your first attempt is not perfect they will still be delicious even if they don't look ideal. Each time you make them they will get better and better.

INGREDIENTS

500g strong bread flour

1 teaspoon salt

25g fresh yeast

270ml warm water (40°C)

75g caster sugar

250g softened butter at room temperature

METHOD

1. Place the flour into a bowl with the salt.
2. Crumble the yeast into the warm water and place in it a teaspoonful of the caster sugar.
3. Put the rest of the sugar in with the flour.
4. When the yeast is fizzing, pour it into the bowl with the flour etc. and mix to a dough with a table knife.
5. Remove the dough from the bowl and knead it until smooth.
6. Place the dough back in the bowl, cover with a cloth and leave in a warm place to prove.
7. When it has doubled in size, remove it from the bowl once again, and knead briefly.
8. Roll it out with a rolling pin to an approximate square roughly 28x28cm.
9. Form the butter (which, ideally, should be the same consistency as the dough) into a block the same thickness as the dough and roughly half the size and place it diagonally on the square of dough.
10. Roll out the 4 corners of the dough slightly thinner and then fold these corners over the butter until it is completely encased in the dough.
11. Roll the completed square out into a rectangle (28x38cm) about 1cm thick and fold into three.
12. Wrap the croissant dough in cling film and place it in the refrigerator.
13. You will now need to repeat the process of rolling out and folding 2 more times leaving it to rest in the refrigerator for 30 minutes between each rolling.
14. The dough is now ready to use when these stages are completed.

CROISSANTS

INGREDIENTS (MAKES 16)

Croissant dough

Egg wash (see page 426)

METHOD

1. Heat the oven to 220°C/gas mark 7.
2. Cut the dough in half and roll each half out to a 25 x 38cm rectangle. Cut each rectangle into 8 long thin triangles. Roll up from the flat edge to the point of the triangle and curl the ends in to get the typical shape.
3. Place them on a baking sheet, brush with egg wash and allow to prove until doubled in size.
4. Bake for 15–20 minutes until golden and well risen.

ALMOND CROISSANTS

INGREDIENTS (MAKES 16)

Croissant dough

Flaked almonds

Icing sugar for dusting

FOR THE MARZIPAN

110g ground almonds

110g icing sugar

A squeeze of lemon juice

1 teaspoon dry sherry (optional)

1 small egg white

A few drops of almond essence

METHOD

1. Amalgamate all the ingredients for the marzipan to a paste.
2. Heat the oven to 220°C/gas mark 7.
3. Create the croissants in the same way as above but including a piece of marzipan the size of a quail's egg before rolling up the triangle.
4. Brush with egg wash and scatter with the flaked almonds.
5. Bake in the same way and then dust with icing sugar when removed from the oven.

PAIN AU CHOCOLATE

INGREDIENTS (MAKES 16)

Croissant dough

300g dark chocolate (70% cocoa solids)

METHOD

1. Cut the dough in half and roll each half out to a 25 x 38cm rectangle. Cut each rectangle into 8 long thin rectangles, placing a piece of dark chocolate (about 25g) on the dough before rolling up.
2. Prove and bake in the same way as for croissants.

DANISH PASTRIES

These danish pastry recipes all use the croissant dough on page 374 and some will require the crème patissiére below.

CRÈME PATISSIÉRE

INGREDIENTS

50g caster sugar

20g plain flour

3 egg yolks

250ml milk

½ teaspoon vanilla paste

METHOD

1. Beat together the sugar, flour and egg yolks.
2. Bring the milk to the boil and pour it over the flour/egg mixture whilst whisking.
3. Return the mixture to the saucepan and bring to the boil stirring all the time.
4. Add the vanilla paste.
5. Pour the resulting custard through a sieve into a suitable receptacle.
6. Dust the surface with a little icing sugar to prevent a skin forming then cover with cling film and allow to cool.

CUSTARD & APPLE DANISH

INGREDIENTS (MAKES 8)

½ quantity croissant dough

1-2 Cox's eating apple

Crème patissiére

Melted butter

Caster sugar (for sprinkling)

Egg wash (see page 426)

METHOD

1. Roll the dough out to about ½ a centimetre and cut into squares approximately 10cm square.
2. Place a teaspoonful of crème patissiére into the centre of each one.
3. Peel, quarter, core and slice the apple.
4. Place 3 slices diagonally across the pastry on top of the custard.
5. Brush the apple lightly with the butter and sprinkle with caster sugar.
6. Fold the 4 corners of pastry up and over the apple.
7. Brush with egg wash – prove and bake as in the previous recipes.

PAIN AU RAISIN

INGREDIENTS (MAKES 8)

½ quantity croissant dough

110g of raisins soaked overnight (or possibly longer) in rum

½ quantity crème patissiére

FOR THE APRICOT JAM GLAZE

½ jar apricot jam

A little water

METHOD

1. Roll out the dough to a rectangle 25 x 38cm.
2. Spread with the crème patissiére and scatter over the raisins.
3. Roll the dough up into a cylinder and cut it into slices.
4. Grease a baking tray and lay the buns on it leaving enough space for them to expand. Leave in a warm place until proved.
5. Bake for 20–25 minutes.
6. Warm the apricot jam and thin it with a little water.
7. Brush the apricot glaze over the pastries when they are still warm.

TOFFEE PECAN DANISH

INGREDIENTS (MAKES 8)

½ quantity croissant dough

½ can of Dulce du Leche (or Nestlé's soft toffee)

Pecan nuts

Demerara sugar

Egg wash (see page 426)

METHOD

1. Roll out the croissant dough to about ½ a centimetre and cut into rectangles approximately 10 x 15cm.
2. Cut through with a lattice cutter on 2 sides leaving the middle uncut.
3. Spread the middle with the toffee and sprinkle with pecan nuts.
4. Fold the two sides over to meet in the middle.
5. Brush with egg wash and sprinkle with Demerara sugar.
6. Prove and bake for 20-25 minutes until golden brown.

APRICOT JAM GLAZE

Sieve half a jar of apricot jam and thin it with a little water. Use for glazing Danish pastries.

DOUGHNUTS

INGREDIENTS (SERVES 6)

250g strong white flour

1 level teaspoon salt

20g butter

125ml milk

20g fresh yeast

1 teaspoon caster sugar plus extra for dredging

1 egg

Raspberry jam

Sunflower oil for deep frying

METHOD

1. Warm the flour with the salt and make a well in the centre.
2. Melt the butter and allow it to cool.
3. Warm the milk and dissolve the yeast in it with a teaspoon of the sugar.
4. Place the butter and egg into the flour then add the yeast mix.
5. Mix with a table knife to form a dough.
6. Knead until smooth then cover with a cloth and allow to prove until doubled in size.
7. Knead again then cut it into 6 pieces and roll into balls.
8. Place on a floured tray and put somewhere warm until they are doubled in size.
9. Heat the deep fryer filled with clean sunflower oil to 190C.
10. Lower the doughnuts gently into the oil and cook until golden brown all over turning them over if necessary.
11. Remove and place on kitchen paper and allow to cool.
12. Sieve the raspberry jam if it has pips in it and put some in a piping bag with a fine-pointed nozzle.
13. Make an incision with a knife into each doughnut and pipe some jam generously into each one.
14. Dredge with caster sugar.

BISCUITS & PETIT FOURS

SABLÉ BISCUITS

INGREDIENTS (MAKES 10-12)

125g plain flour

50g icing sugar

100g butter

2 egg yolks

METHOD

1. Heat the oven to 170°C/gas mark 3.
2. Sift the flour and icing sugar into a bowl.
3. Chop the butter into cubes and rub it in to the flour/icing sugar.
4. Make a well in the centre and place the egg yolks in it.
5. Mix it into a smooth dough with your fingertips.
6. Wrap in cling film and place in the refrigerator for 30 minutes.
7. Roll out the dough to a thickness of about 2-3mm and cut out circles with a cutter of about 9cm in diameter.
8. Line a baking sheet with baking parchment or a silicone mat and bake for 6-8 minutes until pale blonde.
9. Transfer to a wire rack to cool.

BISCOTTI

INGREDIENTS (MAKES 24)

50g butter

175g self-raising flour

110g caster sugar

2 teaspoons baking powder

1 teaspoon ground coriander

Finely grated rind of 1 lemon

50g polenta (maize meal)

50g unblanched almonds

50g pistachios

1 egg

2 teaspoons brandy, Grand Marnier or Amaretto

METHOD

1. Heat the oven to 150°C/gas mark 2.
2. Lightly grease a baking sheet and line it with baking parchment.
3. Rub the butter into the flour until it resembles crumble.
4. Add the sugar, baking powder, coriander, lemon rind, polenta, and nuts. Mix well.
5. Make a well in the centre and put in the egg and liqueur.
6. Mix the ingredients together with a table knife until it forms a dough.
7. Shape into two sausage shapes and place on the baking sheet leaving some distance between the two.
8. Bake for 30 minutes until expanded and firm (they will spread width-ways).
9. Allow to cool then cut into one centimetre slices. (You will need a thin, sharp serrated knife).
10. Place the slices back on to the tray and cook for a further 10 minutes until crisp.
11. Treat yourself to some Vin Santo for dipping!

FLORENTINES

EQUIPMENT

Small non-stick jam tart tins

INGREDIENTS (MAKES APPROXIMATELY 35)

50g butter

150g flaked almonds

40g plain flour

90g granulated sugar

120ml double cream

30ml runny honey

115g dried fruit with peel
(You can experiment with different combinations of fruit and peel and include things such as glacé cherries and crystallised ginger).

50g plain chocolate (70% cocoa solids)

METHOD

1. Heat the oven to 170°C/gas mark 3.
2. Melt the butter. Mix all ingredients together.
3. Place a teaspoon of the mixture into each well of the tins and flatten down with the back of a spoon. It may take a bit of experimentation to get the exact amount right. Bake for 15-20 minutes.
4. Remove from the oven – allow to cool.
5. Remove from the tin and place on a cooling rack.
6. Melt the chocolate and coat the flat side of the florentines.
7. Chill to set the chocolate.

VIENNESE BISCUITS

EQUIPMENT

A 1cm wide star nozzle

INGREDIENTS (MAKES 8-10)

110g plain flour

110g butter - softened

25g caster sugar

½ teaspoon vanilla paste

METHOD

1. Heat the oven to 180°C/gas mark 4.
2. Line a baking sheet with baking parchment or a silicone mat.
3. Beat all the ingredients together into a paste and pipe into biscuits about 4cm across onto the baking sheet.
4. Bake in the oven until golden, about 15–20 minutes.
5. Cool on a wire rack.

CEREAL BARS

EQUIPMENT

A 20 x 30cm rectangular tin lined with a sheet of baking parchment lightly oiled

INGREDIENTS (MAKES 20)

200g porridge oats

50g sunflower seeds

50g flaked almonds

40g pecan nuts

40g pumpkin seeds

60g light brown sugar

15g rye flakes (optional)

90g maple syrup or honey

60g sunflower oil

50g golden syrup

METHOD

1. Heat the oven to 150°C/gas mark 2.
2. Place the oats, almonds, pecan nuts, pumpkin seeds, sugar and rye flakes into a bowl.
3. Put in the maple syrup/honey, oil and golden syrup and mix well.
4. Place the mixture in the tin, press it down flat and bake for 30-40 minutes. Cut into bars when cool.

TUILE BISCUITS

Very useful for decorating cakes and desserts.

EQUIPMENT

Small flexible palette knife

INGREDIENTS (10-12)

50g butter

50g caster sugar

35g plain flour

1 egg white

Flaked almonds

Extra caster sugar for sprinkling

METHOD

1. Heat the oven to 220°C/gas mark 7.
2. Place the butter, caster sugar and flour into a bowl and rub the butter in until you get a breadcrumb-like consistency. This can also be done in a food processor, as can the step below.
3. Add the egg white and beat with a wooden spoon until it forms a paste.
4. Spread the mixture into circles of about 9-10cm diameter and the thickness of a 10 pence piece onto baking parchment. Place the parchment on a flat baking tray.
5. Sprinkle with flaked almonds and then caster sugar.
6. Bake for 4-5 minutes until the biscuits are golden.
7. Remove from the oven and mould to shapes whilst still hot. They can be draped over a rolling pin or rolled into cigar shapes or cornets. They can also be draped over a suitable receptacle (i.e. a small glass) to make cup shapes for serving ice cream and other desserts.
8. They will become crisp when cool and should then be stored in an air tight container.

THE PERFECT COOKIE RECIPE

INGREDIENTS (MAKES 24)

150g butter

150g medium brown (Muscovado) sugar

100g self-raising flour

50g plain flour

1 teaspoon vanilla paste

75g porridge oats

1 egg

*This is the basic cookie recipe. To this you can add other ingredients of your choice. Here are some ideas that work well (total amount recommended 100g - 150g):

Various nuts (or a tablespoon crunchy peanut butter)

Dried fruits – either mixed fruits, dates, figs or apricots

Chopped chocolate – white, dark or milk

Seeds – pumpkin or sunflower

Crystallized ginger or pineapple

Desiccated coconut

METHOD

1. Heat the oven to 170°C/gas mark 3.
2. Beat the butter and sugar together.
3. Add the flours, vanilla and oats and any other ingredients of your choice.*
4. Add the egg and mix to a dough.
5. Lay out a piece of baking parchment 30cm wide and place the mixture across it in a rough cylinder. Roll the paper around it and roll gently to a perfect cylinder.
6. Chill until very firm. Unwrap the dough and cut it into rounds about 1cm thick.
7. Bake in the oven for 15–20 minutes until lightly coloured. Transfer to a cooling rack.
8. The rolled cylinder can also be kept in the freezer for impromptu cookie requirements.

SHORTBREAD

INGREDIENTS (MAKES 8-10)

175g plain flour

75g caster sugar

75g fine semolina

175g butter

METHOD

1. Heat the oven to 150°C/gas mark 2.
2. Mix the flour, sugar and semolina together in a bowl.
3. Chop the butter and then rub it into the mixture.
4. Keep mixing with your hands until it forms a dough.
5. Refrigerate for half an hour then roll the dough out to a thickness 1-1½cm.
6. Cut out biscuit shapes or create a large circle to cut into wedges when cooked. You can also cook it in a rectangle so it can be cut into fingers.
7. Place the shortbread on a baking sheet, prick with a fork and sprinkle with caster sugar.
8. Bake in the oven for one hour. Cut the shortbread into the shapes you require while it is still warm then allow to cool. Can be presented in tins, boxes or even 'Parfait' jars.

MERINGUES

I learned this recipe from a Swiss pastry chef many years ago. It cuts out a lot of the fuss such as whipping the egg whites first and adding the sugar gradually. It also uses granulated sugar which seems odd but it works every time. But you do need an electric whisk – and free standing, rather than hand held, is better (see egg foams on page 420).

INGREDIENTS

50g granulated sugar to every egg white*

Caster sugar

*One egg white makes about 2 medium meringues.

METHOD

1. Heat the oven to 110°C/gas mark ¼.
2. Place the egg whites and granulated sugar into a non plastic bowl and using an electric mixer, beat until the meringue is stiff and holds its shape.
3. Line a baking sheet with lightly oiled parchment (baking) paper and sprinkle it with caster sugar. Spoon or pipe your meringues onto it and sprinkle them with caster sugar.
4. Bake for 2 hours.
5. The meringues should have a crisp outer shell with a soft interior. Stored for any length of time they will dry out completely in a dry atmosphere or go soft in a closed container. So, eat them soon!

PETITS FOURS

This section is unclassifiable as it can mean any small biscuit, cake or sweet. They are traditionally served with coffee at the end of a meal but equally useful as gifts presented in a fancy box. Petit four translates as 'small oven' but why it is used to describe these sweets is a mystery that can only be guessed at.

MINISTRY CRUMB FUDGE

This was originally a recipe from a government pamphlet from WW2 which used breadcrumbs and margarine. Slightly updated here as we don't have rationing any more – but what a lovely name.

INGREDIENTS

110g golden syrup

110g butter

110g Muscovado sugar

25g cocoa powder

175g digestive biscuits

METHOD

1. Boil together the syrup, butter and sugar and whisk together to get them well mixed.
2. Crush the biscuits quite fine and sift the cocoa over them in a bowl.
3. Pour over the butter/syrup mixture and mix well.
4. Spoon into a shallow tray to a thickness of about 1½cm.
5. When cold cut into squares.

MARZIPAN BATTENBURGS

INGREDIENTS (MAKES 2 CAKES)

250g ground almonds

250g icing sugar

2 teaspoons lemon juice

2 teaspoons sherry or rum

A few drops of almond essence

2 small egg whites

Green & pink food colouring

METHOD

1. Combine the almonds and sugar in a bowl. Add the lemon juice and the rum or sherry.
2. Beat the egg whites to break them up a bit and use enough to combine the mixture to a paste. Wrap in cling film and refrigerate overnight.
3. Divide the mixture into 3. Colour one third pink, one third green and leave the final third plain. Shape into rectangular blocks.
4. Cut the pink and green into bars about 1½cm square and place 4 together in alternating colours.
5. Roll out the plain almond paste to the thickness of a pound coin and wrap around the 4 bars. Trim and cut into slices.

STUFFED MEDJOOL DATES

INGREDIENTS

Medjool dates

Marzipan from the previous recipe (uncoloured)

METHOD

1. Cut a slit in the dates and remove the stone.
2. Shape a piece of plain almond paste to roughly the shape of the stone but a bit bigger.
3. Stuff the date, closing the slit but allowing the stuffing to be visible.
4. Decorate with a toasted almond.

MINI CHRISTMAS PUDDINGS

EQUIPMENT

Paper sweet cases

INGREDIENTS (MAKES 10-12)

125g finely chopped dried figs

50g ground almonds

50g plain chocolate (grated)

2 teaspoons rum

1 teaspoon lemon juice

1 egg white

Glacé cherries

Angelica

METHOD

1. Place the figs, ground almonds and chocolate into a bowl and then add the rum and lemon juice.
2. Bind to a paste using the egg white.
3. Form into walnut-sized pieces and flatten the bottom so they are stable.
4. Make a little white icing to spoon over the tops and decorate with pieces of glacé cherry and angelica.
5. Place them in the paper cases.

MINI BAKEWELLS

EQUIPMENT

Mini muffin tins that come with a wooden plunger for lining with pastry. These are available from good cook shops.

INGREDIENTS (MAKES 24)

Sweet pastry (see page 425)

1 tablespoon of your favourite jam, marmalade or even mincemeat (for Christmas).

FOR THE ALMOND CREAM

125g butter

125g ground almonds

125g icing sugar

25g plain flour

2 eggs

METHOD

1. Heat the oven to 180°C/gas mark 4.
2. Make the pastry in the usual way and refrigerate for half an hour.
3. For the almond cream, place the flour, icing sugar and ground almonds in the bowl of the food processor with the cold butter cut into cubes.
4. Process until the mixture looks like bread crumbs, then add the eggs.
5. Process again until it becomes a smooth cream.
6. Line the tart cases with the sweet pastry using the wooden plunger, then put a small amount of the jam, marmalade or mincemeat in the bottom.
7. Pipe some almond cream to cover the jam and fill the tarts.
8. Bake in the oven for 20-30 minutes until cooked.
9. Dust with icing sugar when cool.

CHOCOLATE DIPPED CHERRY MARZIPANS

INGREDIENTS (MAKES 18)

150g ground almonds

150g icing sugar

1 teaspoon lemon juice

1 teaspoon cherry brandy

A few drops of red food colouring

A few drops of almond essence

1 small egg white

10 green pistachios

50g dark chocolate (70% cocoa solids)

METHOD

1. Combine the almonds and sugar in a bowl.
2. Add the lemon juice and the cherry brandy.
3. Beat the egg white to break it up and use enough to combine the mixture to a paste.
4. Colour with the red colouring taking care to keep it subtle.
5. Melt the chocolate over hot water.
6. Roll pieces of marzipan between your palms to resemble cherries.
7. Using a cocktail stick, dip each one in chocolate to half its depth, and transfer to a non-stick surface.
8. Chill to set the chocolate while you cut the pistachios lengthways to resemble stalks.
9. Place a pistachio stalk into each marzipan cherry.

CHOCOLATE RUM TRUFFLES

INGREDIENTS (MAKES 36)

225g plain chocolate (70% cocoa solids)

50g butter

75g icing sugar

4 egg yolks

1 tablespoon of rum

Cocoa powder or chocolate vermicelli

METHOD

1. Melt the chocolate over hot water.
2. Remove from the heat source then work in the butter followed by the icing sugar, egg yolks and rum.
3. Allow to cool to a temperature where it can be easily handled.
4. Spoon or mould into shapes and dust with cocoa powder or roll in chocolate vermicelli.
5. Refrigerate before serving.

CHOCOLATE CUPS FILLED WITH CHERRIES & WHITE CHOCOLATE GANACHE

EQUIPMENT

A flexible silicone mould for making individual chocolates.

INGREDIENTS (MAKES 12)

50g dried cherries

50ml port and a splash of brandy

110g dark chocolate (70% cocoa solids)

110g white chocolate

50ml double cream

METHOD

1. First you will need to put the cherries in a jam jar and cover them with the port and brandy. Leave them overnight or, better still, a couple of days.
2. Melt the dark chocolate and line the muffin cups. The best way to do this is to pour the melted chocolate into the mould, swirl it around so it covers all the surface then turn it over onto a cooling rack and let the excess chocolate drip out onto a tray underneath.
3. Allow the chocolate to set firm.
4. Drain the cherries and put 1 or 2 into each chocolate cup depending on their size.
5. Melt the white chocolate and then stir in the cream until thoroughly mixed. Spoon or pipe this white chocolate ganache onto the cherries leaving a scant gap at the top.
6. Chill until the chocolate ganache is firm.
7. Retrieve the chocolate that has dripped out of the moulds, re-melt it and use it to close the top of the cups.
8. Refrigerate until perfectly set then pop them out of the moulds.

CANDIED GRAPEFRUIT PEEL

INGREDIENTS

4 pink grapefruit

900g granulated sugar

600ml water

METHOD

1. Cut the grapefruits in half and squeeze the juice. (Strain the juice and refrigerate. Buy a bottle of Campari if you don't already have one and drink it as 1-part Campari to 2-parts juice, on some ice.) This is nothing to do with the recipe but it's a delicious aperitif.
2. Scrape out any fibrous bits from the grapefruit 'shells' and cut each half in half again.
3. Now cut into thin wedges from the centre to the outside.
4. Put the sugar and water into a saucepan and bring slowly to the boil.
5. When the sugar has dissolved add the grapefruit strips and simmer until they are tender (about 30 minutes).
6. Place the grapefruit and syrup in a plastic tub and when cold, refrigerate.
7. Leave for 2 weeks then drain and place the pieces on a wire rack in a warm dry place. Leave overnight then coat in caster sugar.
8. Can also be done with orange skins but the grapefruit has a pleasant bitterness that balances the sweetness. Keep the syrup to make some more or use it for making sorbet.

MISCELLANEOUS

MAYONNAISE

It is possible to add more (or less) of the flavouring ingredients to get a taste that suits your palate. Use for prawn cocktail sauce, dill and mustard sauce, tartare sauce, aioli and for coronation chicken.

INGREDIENTS

1 egg yolk

1 teaspoon Dijon mustard

1 teaspoon white wine vinegar

Salt and ground black pepper

Sugar / honey

300ml sunflower oil

Lemon juice

METHOD

1. Make sure all ingredients are at room temperature.
2. Mix together egg yolk, mustard, vinegar and salt, into a bowl with half a tablespoon of warm water. Whisk well.
3. Slowly pour the oil into this mixture adding it slowly in a thin stream.
4. Add a little more water if, at any point it looks like it is getting too thick.
5. Correct the seasoning and adjust the flavour balance by adding either lemon or sugar / honey if necessary.
6. Using a stick blender or food processor for this operation will reduce your chances of it curdling to virtually nil.

SALAD DRESSING (VINAIGRETTE)

Use for salads, grilled meats and fish and as a base for some salsas.

INGREDIENTS

1 teaspoon Dijon mustard

½ teaspoon honey

1 dessertspoon white wine vinegar

200ml olive oil or 50/50 olive and sunflower oil

1 dessertspoon water

METHOD

1. Place all the ingredients, except the oil, into a glass bowl.
2. Whisk them together until thoroughly mixed.
3. Pour the oil onto the ingredients in a thin stream whisking continuously.
4. With careful mixing you can create a dressing that stays emulsified but this is not necessarily important.

QUINCE CHEESE

Quince cheese, quince paste or even membrillo (nothing to do with scouring pads) was the forerunner of fruit pastilles and marmalade. Unlike things such as lemon curd there are no animal products in quince cheese, the term merely pertains to the texture of the finished product. Quince is very high in pectin, which makes for a very firm result - hence 'cheese'. Fabulous with cold meats, pâté and strong cheeses. Can also be made with cranberries or damsons.

INGREDIENTS

1.5kg quinces

Water to cover

Granulated sugar

METHOD

1. Wash the quinces and cut them up small - there is no need to peel or core them.
2. Cover with water and bring to the boil. Reduce the heat and simmer until all the fruit is very soft.
3. Purée the mixture in a blender then pass it through a sieve. (This is hard work but worth it). For each 100g of purée weigh out 100g of sugar and place both in a pan together. Over a low heat stir until the sugar is dissolved then cook gently until the mixture is really thick.
4. Pour or spoon into warm, wide-necked, sterilized jars.

MARROW CHUTNEY

This is a wartime recipe my mother handed down to me. It's great with cheese on toast.

It can also be made with pumpkin, in which case there is no need for the overnight salting, just add 2 teaspoons of salt (instead of the 175g!) to the recipe.

INGREDIENTS (MAKES 6 JARS)

2.7kg prepared marrow (i.e. – peeled and de-seeded)

175g salt

235g onion

600ml white wine or cider vinegar

1 level tablespoon turmeric

4 level tablespoons curry powder

3 level tablespoons mustard powder

675g granulated sugar

METHOD

1. Cut the marrow into 1½cm cubes, place in a dish and sprinkle over the salt.
2. Leave overnight for the salt to draw a lot of the moisture out of the marrow.
3. Rinse the marrow well and then drain well.
4. Chop the onion and put it in a saucepan large enough to take all the ingredients.
5. Add the vinegar, spices and sugar then bring to the boil and simmer for 10 minutes.
6. Add the marrow, stir well and simmer for about an hour until the marrow is tender and the chutney is of a thick consistency.
7. Spoon into hot jars and seal in the usual way.

GREEN SALSA

Great served with grilled meat or fish. You can replace the basil with mint for a salsa to go with roast lamb.

INGREDIENTS

1–2 cloves of garlic

A large bunch of flat leaf parsley

A bunch of basil

2 tablespoons capers (rinsed)

1 tablespoon Dijon mustard

A few drops of white wine vinegar

50ml olive oil

METHOD

1. Place all the ingredients, except the oil, into a food processor.
2. Run the machine, stopping occasionally to press the ingredients down from the sides.
3. Finally add the olive oil slowly as the machine runs. Store in a refrigerator.

SWEET CHILLI JAM

INGREDIENTS

8 red peppers

10 red chillies

25g root ginger

8 cloves of garlic

400g can of tomatoes

500g golden caster sugar

250ml red wine vinegar

Salt

2 teaspoons ground coriander seed

2 teaspoons smoked paprika

METHOD

1. Remove the stalk, core and seed from the peppers and chop them roughly.
2. Remove the stalk and core from the chillies and chop them. Peel the ginger and garlic.
3. Tip the peppers, chillies (with seeds), ginger and garlic into a food processor, then whizz until very finely chopped.
4. Place the mixture into a heavy-based pan with the tomatoes, sugar and vinegar, salt and spices.
5. Bring to the boil then turn down the heat and simmer for about an hour, stirring occasionally.
6. Keep cooking until the mixture is thick and jam-like in consistency.
7. Heat treat your jars and fill them while the mixture is still hot.
8. Sterilize the lids and tighten them onto the jars.
9. The jam will mature with keeping but can be eaten straight away. Refrigerate after opening.

CORIANDER RELISH

Can be used as an accompaniment to curries or as a dip for samosas and fish cakes

INGREDIENTS

75g fresh coriander (leaves and fine stems)

½ a hot green chilli

2 teaspoons ground cumin

Juice of 1-2 limes

Salt and ground black pepper

1 teaspoon Dijon mustard

2-3 tablespoons sesame oil

METHOD

1. Put all the ingredients into the food processor, except the oil, and process until it produces a smooth purée. It may be necessary to push the ingredients down from the sides periodically.
2. Finally, drizzle in the oil.

PRESERVING, SMOKING AND CURING

ON SALTING AND SMOKING

If early man had had fridges we may not have discovered this way of treating foods as it was originally used as a method of preservation. Salting draws moisture out of the foods which aids the process of drying – yet another way of preserving. I would imagine that smoking was discovered by accident. Probably sticking stuff up a chimney to aid the drying process when it was raining outdoors. What is interesting is that one of the chemicals imparted by the smoke is formaldehyde, another preservative. When cod was plentiful, nearly every coastal community had a culture of making salt-cod. All we need to know is that today it makes for some very interesting and tasty dishes that we might not otherwise have had.

You can buy home smoking devices from specialist shops (mainly fishing tackle shops) or online. These are usually for hot-smoking, cold-smoking requires slightly more complicated apparatus. Cold-smoking (not covered here) typically gives us smoked salmon, kippers and bacon which are smoked but still in a raw state.

Sawdust is usually supplied with the smoker or at least some to start you off. It is also available online. Resinous woods like pine are not good for smoking. Most that are sold for this purpose are hard woods such as oak, beech and apple wood. You can also add extra flavours of your own like whole spices (star anise, cinnamon, cloves etc), twigs from woody herbs like rosemary and bay; even Lapsang Souchong or Earl Grey tea leaves.

THE CURING MIX

INGREDIENTS

110g coarse sea salt

110g granulated sugar

1 teaspoon black peppercorns

1 piece star anise

1 teaspoon coriander seeds

METHOD

1. Coarsely crush the spices then mix all the ingredients together.
2. Store in a sealed jar ready for use.

SMOKED MACKEREL OR TROUT FILLETS

Oily fish works better for smoking than non-oily. These will keep for up to a week in the fridge.

EQUIPMENT

Smoker

Sawdust (see intro)

INGREDIENTS

4 mackerel/trout fillets

2 tablespoons of the curing mix

METHOD

1. Using a flat dish or plastic container (not metal) that will take the fish fillets in one layer, sprinkle one tablespoon of the curing mix evenly over the bottom.
2. Place the mackerel fillets skin-side down onto the cure.
3. Sprinkle the other tablespoon of the mix evenly over the fish. Leave for two hours in the refrigerator.
4. Set up the smoker so it is hot and making plenty of smoke.
5. Rinse the cure-mix from the fish and pat it dry with kitchen paper.
6. Place the mackerel fillets skin-side down on the rack in your smoker.
7. Replace the lid and smoke for about 30 minutes.

SMOKE-ROAST PORK OR CHICKEN FILLET

EQUIPMENT

Smoker

Sawdust (see intro)

INGREDIENTS

1 whole pork fillet or 2 boneless breasts of chicken

4 tablespoons of the curing mix

METHOD

1. Sprinkle 2 tablespoons of the dry-cure in the bottom of a plastic, glass or ceramic container (not metal). Place the meat on this and sprinkle some more cure over the top.
2. Rub the cure well into the meat. Leave for 4-6 hours turning the meat over occasionally.
3. Set up the smoker so it is hot and making plenty of smoke.
4. Rinse the cure mix from the meat and pat it dry with kitchen paper.
5. Place it on the rack in your smoker. Replace the lid and smoke for about 35-45 minutes. (This may take longer depending on the size of the pieces).
6. Check that the meat is cooked. Eat hot or cold.

PRESERVED LEMONS

This is a typical Moroccan condiment used in tagines and couscous. You can buy it in some specialist shops and delicatessens but it usually comprises whole small lemons in a saline solution. This home-made version is better, easy to make, keeps well and has many uses. The juice in the jar becomes like a salty, lemony syrup which is great brushed on fish and chicken prior to grilling.

EQUIPMENT

1 wide necked jam jar

INGREDIENTS

4 unwaxed lemons

Up to 2 tablespoons coarse sea salt

METHOD

1. Top and tail 3 lemons and cut in half lengthways.
2. Cut into slices about 3mm thick. Remove all pips.
3. Fill the jar alternating a layer of lemon slices with sea salt.
4. Squeeze the final lemon and top up the jar with juice.
5. Place the lid on and leave at room temperature until the lemon slices start to go opaque. Refrigerate ready for use.

SPICED PLUMS

INGREDIENTS

900g dark red plums

450g granulated sugar

600ml white wine vinegar

Cinnamon stick, cloves, juniper, mace, peppercorns

METHOD

1. Cut the plums in half and remove the stone. Cut them in half again.
2. Place the sugar and vinegar in a saucepan with the spices and place over a low heat until the sugar dissolves.
3. Bring to the boil and put in the plums. Bring back to the boil.
4. If the plums are ripe and soft there is no need to cook them further. Pack into warmed jars and heat seal.
5. Serve with cheese or pâté or cold meats.

ORIGINAL MINCE PIE

This was a popular dish in Tudor times and is the forerunner of the mince pie we know and love today. It is typical of their taste for meat with fruit and mixing sweet and savoury flavours.

EQUIPMENT

A 20cm diameter tart tin or 4 individual tart tins.

INGREDIENTS

1 onion

1 small clove garlic

25g butter

1 eating apple

350g minced lamb or beef

50g grated suet

Salt

A small bunch of chopped mixed herbs (thyme, sage, basil)

A teaspoon of the Aromatic spice mix (see page 411)

50g raisins

50g currants

A small glass of white wine or sherry

1 teaspoon of sugar

Short pastry (see page 424)

Egg wash (see page 426)

METHOD

1. Heat the oven to 180°C/gas mark 4.
2. Chop the onion and garlic very fine and fry them in the butter until they start to colour.
3. Peel, core and chop the apple and fry with the onion. Set aside.
4. Place the minced meat and grated suet into a bowl.
5. Chop the herbs and add these with the aromatic spice, salt, fruit, sugar and the onion/apple mixture.
6. Moisten with the sherry or wine and mix well.
7. Roll out the pastry and line the tin(s).
8. Place in the meat mixture and then cover with a pastry lid.
9. Decorate the top with any pastry trimmings, if desired, and brush with egg wash.
10. Bake in the oven for 45 minutes to one hour.
11. Turn down the heat once the pastry is nicely browned.
12. Serve hot or cold.

MARMALADE WITH STAR ANISE

This is an interesting twist on straight marmalade but only if you like the flavour of aniseed. I think it works brilliantly with the bitterness of the oranges - that subtle burst of aniseed as you come across a piece of it in the marmalade. If you are not sure, this is still a great recipe for marmalade so just leave it out.

EQUIPMENT

6-8 medium size jam jars with lids

INGREDIENTS (TOTAL VOLUME SHOULD BE ABOUT 1.8 LITRES)

1kg Seville oranges

2 lemons

500g soft brown sugar

500g preserving sugar

1.4 litres water

6 pieces of star anise lightly crushed

METHOD

1. Wash the fruit, cut them in half and squeeze the juice.
2. Put the pips into a muslin bag.
3. Cut the orange peel into thin strips and place it in the preserving pan with the orange and lemon juice, the water and the bag of pips. Discard the lemon skin.
4. Simmer for about two hours until the orange peel is really soft and the liquid well reduced.
5. Warm the sugar on a tray in a low oven.
6. Squeeze the muslin bag and remove it. Then add the crushed star anise.
7. Add the warmed sugar and bring to the boil.
8. Boil rapidly until setting point is reached.
9. Place the jars in a low oven to sterilise them and avoid them cracking when you put in the hot marmalade.
10. Pour boiling water over the lids to sterilise them.
11. Pot the marmalade and seal with the lids while still hot.

FRESH TOMATO KETCHUP

INGREDIENTS

500g of the best ripest tomatoes you can get hold of

2 tablespoons olive oil

Salt and freshly ground black pepper

METHOD

1. Cut the tomatoes up (any old how will do).
2. Put the oil in a shallow pan and add the tomatoes and season.
3. Stew the tomatoes in the oil allowing the moisture to evaporate until the mixture thickens. (Some tomatoes will need more cooking if the water content of the tomatoes is high).
4. Whizz the resulting mixture in a food processor or with a stick blender and then sieve it to remove the pips and skin. Check the seasoning and transfer to a suitable container.
5. Keep refrigerated as this has no preserving agents in it like vinegar or sugar but should keep for at least a fortnight if kept cold.
6. Serve with chips, scrambled eggs or sausages, also great in bacon sandwiches.

OVEN-DRIED CHERRY TOMATOES

Useful if you have a glut of these tomatoes. Use for sandwiches, pasta dishes, cheese on toast, sauces, canapés etc.

INGREDIENTS

500g cherry or Pomodoro plum tomatoes

Olive oil

Salt and ground black pepper

Caster sugar

METHOD

1. Set the oven to 100°C/gas mark ¼.
2. Cut the tomatoes in half across the middle.
3. Oil a tray and place the tomatoes cut side up on the tray.
4. Sprinkle with salt, pepper and sugar and drizzle with a little more olive oil.
5. Place them in the oven for 1½-2 hours.
6. Pack all the tomatoes into sterilized jars, press down gently and pour in enough olive oil to cover.
7. Use within one week or heat treat the jar in the usual way to keep them longer.

HERB JELLY

EQUIPMENT

Jelly bag

INGREDIENTS

1350g Bramley apples or a mixture of cooking and eating apples or even sour crab apples

150ml white wine vinegar

Granulated sugar - see method

750ml water

Herb of your choice, mint, sage and rosemary work well but you can also use tarragon and thyme.

METHOD

1. Wash the fruit and cut it up coarsely without peeling or coring.
2. Place it in a saucepan with the water and vinegar.
3. Cook until the fruit is soft and pulpy stirring regularly to help break up the fruit. Transfer to a jelly bag and allow the juice to strain through overnight.
4. Warm your jars and lids in a low oven to make sure they are dry, sterile and will not break when the hot jelly goes into them.
5. Measure the quantity of juice that you have, and to each pint measure out 450g of sugar.
6. Place these in a clean pan and bring slowly to the boil. Turn the heat down to a simmer and cook until it starts to gel. It will be necessary to skim the top occasionally to remove impurities.
7. Chop the herb you have chosen and add when the jelly has reached setting point.
8. Pour the jelly into the jars and immediately seal with a lid. Label and store.

A NOTE ON SPICES

Unless you are using spices every day the contents of those little jars and tubs that sit in a drawer or line a shelf in your kitchen have probably lost all their flavour.

One solution is to get a little electric coffee grinder, buy your spices whole and grind them as you need them. In the whole state they will retain their flavour for longer and you can toast them in a dry frying pan just prior to use for an even better flavour.

Remember also that only chilli and ginger are hot meaning you can be more generous with spices such as cumin, coriander and cardamom for increased flavour without the dish being overly hot.

AROMATIC SPICE MIX

This was originally created to overcome a problem – that juniper will go mouldy, quite quickly, once it has been ground. The other spices not only help prevent this but they are also chosen because they can add an intriguing flavour without shouting too loudly.

If you put cumin into any spice mix it always tastes of curry, whereas coriander has a sweet citrussy flavour that is mild and aromatic, juniper has that pleasant whiff of gin (strictly speaking gin has that pleasant whiff of juniper), and nutmeg has a flavour that most people have only ever encountered on a custard tart so they find it difficult to name when it is in something savoury.

Try this in casseroles and pies and pâtés or even in something such as steak and kidney pudding; it will not taste out of place and will add interest to your cooking.

INGREDIENTS

1 tablespoon whole juniper berries

1 tablespoon whole coriander seeds

1 tablespoon whole black peppercorns

1 nutmeg (or use the ends you keep putting back in the jar after grating)

METHOD

1. Grind all the ingredients in an electric grinder and keep in a closed jam jar.

A ROAST DINNER

Is there really any need for a recipe for roast dinner? I suppose not but it is one of those meals that we take very seriously in this country and it is important that every element is right. A lot of it is down to individual taste but in my time teaching I have often been asked the secret to good gravy or Yorkshire pudding or even roast potatoes.

THE BEST ROAST POTATOES

It is more to do with the type of potato than it is the cooking. King Edward is my favourite as they are really floury and soak up the dripping well. Second choice would be Maris Piper or Desiree Reds. Par boil the potatoes in plenty of salted water and drain well. (Let them steam for a bit so they get quite dry).

Take care with King Edwards as they can start to break up in the par-boiling process but the outside of the potato needs to be cooked a bit to get really crispy.

Melt the dripping or oil in the roasting tray (you may have some dripping from the cooking of the meat or you can use olive oil or bought duck or goose fat).

Put the potatoes in and get them sizzling on the hob. Season with salt and black pepper and tuck some bay leaves or sprigs of rosemary amongst them. Roast until crisp and golden, turning them over occasionally.

BREAD SAUCE

INGREDIENTS

1 onion

50g butter

425ml full-cream milk

2 bay leaves

6 cloves

6 peppercorns

75g stale white crustless bread

2 tablespoons double cream

METHOD

1. Chop the onion very fine and stew it in the butter until soft.
2. Pour in the milk and add the bay leaves, cloves and peppercorns and bring to the boil. Allow to cool and stand for 30 minutes.
3. Remove the bay, cloves and peppercorns. Make the bread into crumbs and sprinkle into the milk, add the cream and bring to the boil. Add salt if necessary and for a really smooth sauce put it through a food processor.

STUFFING

Stuffing is a very British culinary item. Our foreign neighbours don't understand the concept of it like we do. The French call it 'farce' but to us it is much more serious than that. A roast dinner of chicken, duck or pork is not complete without it.

INGREDIENTS

1 large onion

110g celery

1 tablespoon dripping

110g smoked streaky bacon

A small bunch of fresh herbs, choose from sage, rosemary, thyme, marjoram

10 dried (no need to soak) apricots

75g peeled chestnuts

110g fresh wholemeal bread crumbs

Salt and ground black pepper

METHOD

1. Chop the onion and the celery and fry them in the dripping until they start to colour.
2. Chop the bacon and the herbs, add to the pan and fry until the bacon is cooked.
3. Remove it from the heat. Chop the apricots and add to the mixture with the chestnuts and bread crumbs.
4. Season with the pepper and salt.
5. If it is too crumbly add a few drops of water.
6. An egg can be added to make a more 'set' stuffing. Bake in a dish.
7. Other ingredients you can add to stuffing: chorizo or kabanos sausage (chopped small), black pudding, chopped apple, prunes, chicken livers, sausage meat, walnuts, mushrooms, lemon and orange zest, dried cherries, dried cranberries, hazelnuts.

APPLE SAUCE FOR PORK & DUCK

INGREDIENTS

1 Bramley apple

2 eating apples

150ml orange juice

25g Muscovado sugar

METHOD

1. Peel, quarter and core the apples.
2. Slice them and put them in a saucepan with the orange juice and sugar.
3. Simmer gently until the Bramley apple starts to turn to pulp.
4. The eating apples don't pulp like the Bramley, giving a chunkier texture. You may want to break the eating apple pieces up a bit.

YORKSHIRE PUDDING

INGREDIENTS (SERVES 4)

75g plain flour

1 egg

75ml milk

50ml water

Salt

METHOD

1. Place the flour in a bowl and make a well in the centre.
2. Place the egg in the well with a little of the milk and the salt.
3. Beat to a smooth paste with a whisk (an electric device helps).
4. Add the rest of the milk and when the mixture is smooth allow it to stand for at least 30 minutes.
5. Presumably your oven will be on for cooking the meat but it needs to be at 200°C/gas mark 6.
6. Take a tin of about 20cm in diameter or a tin that makes 4 individual ones.
7. Place some dripping from the meat into it and get it hot in the oven.
8. Pour in the batter and cook for 20–30 minutes until risen around the edges. It should be golden brown around the edges and soft and yellow in the middle.

GRAVY

Good gravy won't rescue disastrous meat but bad gravy can spoil good meat. Things like gravy granules will give you a brown, salty sauce but with little else for flavour.

The tastiest thing to put in gravy is what is in the bottom of your roasting tray, i.e. all the juices that have come from the meat, some of which will have concentrated into solids.

So, when you take the meat out of the oven, remove it from the roasting tin to another receptacle and put it somewhere warm to rest, (it needs to relax anyway).

Tip the excess fat from the roasting tray leaving a spoonful behind.

Put the tray on a low heat on the hob and sprinkle in a heaped teaspoon of plain flour.

Stir this into the fat in the tin and, after it has sizzled a bit, put in a glass of red or white wine.

Stir it well making sure you incorporate all those tasty deposits.

Make up the liquid with some stock to the desired consistency (if you use a cube, make it fairly weak otherwise it will overpower the natural flavours).

Season with salt and pepper and, if you want it a little darker, add some soy sauce.

After the meat has rested you may well find it has leached some natural juices – add these to your gravy.

Strain into a jug for use.

BUBBLE & SQUEAK

This is usually made with leftovers – I often make extra just so I can make bubble and squeak the following day. It needs no recipe really just take the cold mash and cabbage (about two thirds potato to one third cabbage is about right). If you have any other cold vegetables such as carrots, sprouts or onion you can incorporate these. Season well with plenty of black pepper and mix with a fork. Shape into cakes and fry in dripping or oil until golden and crispy on both sides.

Serve with sausages, cold ham or as part of a cooked breakfast.

We know it as Bubble and Squeak but it is called 'Colcannon' in Ireland.

'Champ' or 'Stelk' are both mash with chives added.

'Skirlie Mirlie' is a mixture of half mashed potato and half mashed turnips.

'Poten Ben Fedi' (Welsh, since you asked) is a potato cake with chopped meat in it.

Then there are all the variations of potato cakes in some form or another: Hash browns, Latkes, Rosti etc.

BOXTY WITH SPICED LAMB BURGERS

Boxty is an Irish potato scone sometimes called 'Farls"

INGREDIENTS
FOR THE BOXTY

50g butter

110g plain flour

225g mashed potato

½ teaspoon baking powder

Salt and ground black pepper

1½ tablespoons milk

FOR THE SPICED LAMB BURGERS

225g minced lamb

2 tablespoons chopped mint, parsley and marjoram

Salt and pepper

½ teaspoon ground cumin

½ teaspoon ground cinnamon

½ teaspoon ground ginger

1 small onion, grated or finely chopped

1 clove of garlic - mashed

METHOD
FOR THE BOXTY

1. Heat the oven to 180°C/gas mark 4.
2. Rub the butter into the flour.
3. Add the mash, baking powder and seasoning.
4. Mix to a dough with the milk.
5. Roll out to a circle about 1½cm thick.
6. Place on a baking sheet and cut into 4.
7. Bake for about 20-25 minutes.
8. Cool on a rack.

FOR THE LAMB BURGERS

1. Place the meat in a bowl and mix well with all the other ingredients.
2. Divide into 4 and flatten each one out to burger shape about the same size as the boxty.
3. Shallow fry them slowly until crisp on the outside and cooked through in the centre.
4. Split the boxty and place a lamb burger in each one.

In my research I found this quaint rhyme:

Boxty in the pot

Boxty in the pan

If you can't make boxty

You'll never get a man

COLCANNON WITH BLACK PUDDING & APPLE

INGREDIENTS (SERVES 2 FOR A LUNCH OR SUPPER DISH)

50g smoked streaky bacon

350g mashed potato

225g cooked cabbage

Pepper and nutmeg

1 Cox or similar eating apple

4 slices of good quality black pudding

METHOD

1. Chop the bacon up fine and fry it. Reserve any of the fat you have over.
2. Mix the potato with the chopped cabbage and the bacon and season it well with the pepper and the nutmeg.
3. Shape into four cakes.
4. Peel, quarter and core the apple and cut each quarter into three slices.
5. Fry it in some hot oil until browned. Set aside.
6. Fry the colcannon cakes and black pudding on both sides until golden.
7. Serve the pudding on top of the potato cakes and top with the apple slices.
8. Serve with fried eggs for a stunning breakfast.

PEMMICAN

One of the stranger jobs I was asked to do was to make pemmican for a programme reconstructing the Scott/Amundsen race for the South Pole. Pemmican is an iron ration originally invented by the Cree tribe of Native Americans and kilo for kilo is one of the highest calorie foods there is. They needed enough for the 2 teams for several weeks.

INGREDIENTS (SERVES 2 TEAMS OF POLAR EXPLORERS FOR SEVERAL WEEKS)

165kg biltong (dried beef)

280kg beef dripping

40kg oatmeal

10kg chick pea flour

125kg dried mixed fruit

METHOD

1. Shred the biltong.
2. Melt the dripping.
3. Mix together all the ingredients and spoon into the ice-cream containers.
4. Book a ticket to the South Pole.

CUSTARD

INGREDIENTS

500ml full cream milk

110ml double cream

Half a teaspoon of good quality vanilla essence or the paste as this has the seeds in.

6 egg yolks

110g caster sugar

METHOD

1. Place the milk, cream and vanilla in a saucepan and bring to the boil.
2. Meanwhile whisk the egg yolks and sugar together until smooth.
3. Pour the boiling milk/cream onto the egg/sugar mixture whilst continuing to whisk.
4. Put the mixture back into the saucepan and back over the heat.
5. Now the difficult bit: cook stirring continuously until the custard thickens DO NOT BOIL.
6. Have ready a sieve sitting over a clean bowl.
7. As soon as the custard is ready, pour it through the sieve into the bowl.
8. Sieving it will remove any bits of cooked egg.
9. If it looks like it might have curdled a bit you can usually save the day by giving it a blast in a liquidizer or blender.
10. Serve warm.

GENOESE AND OTHER EGG FOAMS

There at several instances in this book that require you to make an egg foam - Genoese sponge, meringues, soufflés and some ice creams. A hand held electric whisk is fine, a standing electric food mixer is better. Trying to get a result beating by hand is well nigh impossible unless you have tireless muscles.

It is also important that all utensils are free from grease. Glass or ceramic bowls are necessary as plastic will always hold a trace of grease no matter how well washed they are.

The foam you make needs to be thick, pale and firm described in some recipes as being able to see the 'trail of the whisk'

For Genoese sponge and the roulades on pages 300 and 313 it is particularly important as this is the only raising agent.

RASPBERRY COULIS

INGREDIENTS

110g raspberries (fresh or frozen)

25g caster sugar

METHOD

1. Place the raspberries in a saucepan with the sugar and a tablespoon of water.
2. Cook slowly until the raspberries are breaking up.
3. Blitz with a stick blender or liquidizer and then sieve the mixture to remove the pips.
4. Add more sugar if required and add water if it is too thick.

CHOCOLATE FUDGE SAUCE

Universally brilliant chocolate stuff. Use it hot for sauce, cool for cake frosting and éclair topping and fridge cold for chocolate spread.

INGREDIENTS

150ml single cream

75ml full cream milk

75ml golden syrup

25g butter

150g caster sugar

Vanilla essence

110g plain chocolate (70% cocoa solids minimum)

METHOD

1. Boil together the cream, milk, syrup, butter and sugar until it amalgamates and thickens.
2. Remove from the heat and add the vanilla essence and the chocolate. Stir until the chocolate is fully melted.

PRALINE

INGREDIENTS

110g hazelnuts

110g almonds

450g granulated sugar

METHOD

1. Heat the oven to 150°C/gas mark 2.
2. Place the nuts on a tray and roast in the oven to a light golden brown.
3. Line a tray with baking parchment or a silicone mat and place the roasted nuts on it.
4. Heat the sugar slowly in a saucepan until it starts to melt.
5. Continue the cooking process and it will start to colour – do not stir, just shake the pan to move it around a bit.
6. When the sugar has reached a nutty-brown colour pour it over the nuts. Take care this mixture is extremely hot!
7. Allow to cool and solidify.
8. Break the mixture up and place it in a bowl. Using the end of a rolling pin break it up some more.
9. Keep crushing it until you have a granular mixture or you can use a food processor.
10. Store in an airtight jar. Use for ice cream and sprinkling on desserts – trifle etc.

BUTTERSCOTCH SAUCE

INGREDIENTS

300g golden syrup

50g light Muscovado sugar

75ml double cream

50g salted butter

METHOD

1. Boil the golden syrup with the sugar until it is dissolved.
2. Pour in the cream and bring to the boil again.
3. Add the butter a little at a time whilst whisking.
4. Allow to cool. Serve warm

CARAMEL SAUCE

INGREDIENTS

225g granulated sugar

110ml water

110ml double cream

METHOD

1. Place the sugar in a saucepan and heat slowly without stirring (shake the pan a bit to move it around). It will melt then start to colour.
2. Keep cooking until caramel stage is reached – a light brown colour. Pour in the water followed by the cream (with care, it may splutter).
3. Simmer until the sauce is smooth. Serve warm.
4. If the sauce is to be served cold – thin with water when cold to the desired consistency.

MARINATED FRUITS

Lots of delicious things can be made by soaking dried fruits in a bit of booze, whether it is sultanas or raisins for cakes, or bread and butter pudding, prunes for prune tart, dried cherries for chocolate mousse or trifle. Not only does it give the fruit a wonderful flavour it softens it too.

It doesn't have to be pure spirit, although you can if you want, but it needs to be a high alcohol percentage otherwise you risk the stuff starting to ferment and the last thing you want in your kitchen is exploding jars of fruit.

Use a bit of wine, port and any liqueurs that need using up then put a slug of vodka or brandy in it to raise the alcohol content.

HERE ARE A FEW TO TRY

Dried pears: white wine, fruit liqueur or vodka

Dried cherries: red wine, port or brandy

Dried apricots: Amaretto, white wine or brandy

Prunes: sweet sherry or brandy

Raisins or sultanas: dark rum or white wine

Dried peaches: rosé wine or gin

BAKING BLIND

It is necessary sometimes to give the pastry a head start on the filling or in some cases you may want a cooked pastry case for a cold, uncooked filling.

Heat the oven to 180°C/gas mark 4.

Once you have lined your tin or flan case with the pastry line it with some baking parchment cut to size and then fill the case with ceramic baking beans.*

Bake in the oven for 20-25 minutes. This should now be fine for recipes where part blind baking is required. For a complete bake remove the paper and the beans and put it back in the oven for a further 10-15 minutes.

To bake pastry blind in muffin tins (large or small) choose a paper cake case of a suitable size and push it into the lined pastry well. No baking beans are required for this.

Keep back some of your raw pastry to mend any cracks or holes that may appear.

*If you do not have ceramic baking beans (they can be purchased from good cook shops) you can also use dry haricot beans although they tend to smell of burning with continuous use – not a good smell to be coming out of your kitchen. I have also heard of people using coppers from their change jar (they conduct the heat well and are perfectly hygienic as the heat kills any germs), or selected pebbles from the beach which I am obliged to tell you is illegal – so don't let anyone see you.

RICH SHORTCRUST PASTRY

INGREDIENTS

175g plain flour

100g butter

1 egg

METHOD

1. Rub the butter into the flour until it resembles crumble.
2. Add the egg and work the mixture to a paste.
3. You can also use a food processor – process the butter and flour before adding the egg.
4. Pastry doesn't keep well in the refrigerator but freezes very well – remember to label it sweet or short.

SWEET PASTRY

INGREDIENTS

200g plain flour

110g butter

50g icing sugar

1 egg

METHOD

1. Sift the flour and icing sugar together and rub the butter into it until it resembles crumble.
2. Work in the egg to form a paste and refrigerate for 20-30 minutes.

ROUGH PUFF PASTRY

INGREDIENTS

200g butter

250g plain flour

125ml ice-cold water

METHOD

1. Chop the butter into cubes and place it in a bowl with the flour.
2. Break up the butter a little with your fingers as you would for rubbing in.
3. Add the water and form the mixture into a dough. Do not overwork. (It will look like a very untidy mass at this point.)
4. Wrap in cling film and refrigerate for 20 minutes.
5. Roll the pastry into a rectangle about 30x15cm and fold it into three.
6. Turn the block a one quarter turn, roll out again to the same sized rectangle and fold in three again.
7. Wrap the block in cling film and refrigerate for 30 minutes.
8. After this time repeat the process of rolling and folding as before.
9. Refrigerate for at least 30 minutes before using.

CREAM SAUCE

INGREDIENTS

1 small onion

600ml milk

5 cloves

1 bay leaf

35g butter

25g plain flour

Salt and ground black pepper

1 teaspoon Dijon mustard

50ml double cream

METHOD

1. Chop the onion and simmer in the milk with the cloves and bay leaf.
2. In another pan melt the butter and stir in the flour.
3. Cook for a few moments before adding the milk slowly.
4. Mix to a smooth sauce (it will thicken as it boils).
5. Season with the salt, pepper and mustard.
6. Finally add the cream and strain.

CLARIFIED BUTTER

Clarified butter can reach a higher temperature without burning so it is ideal for shallow frying when a recipe requires butter rather than oil.

Melt the butter slowly in a saucepan then transfer it to a glass (Pyrex) jug. Remove any scum from the top. You will also see that the butter has separated into the yellow fat at the top and a white sediment underneath. Using a ladle carefully decant the yellow oil into a separate vessel and use as required. Discard the sediment.

EGG WASH

A lot of recipes in this book require the use of an egg wash - mostly to add a glaze to pastry. I have found the best egg wash requires just the yolk. It gives a rich yellow colour and a burnished shine to the finished pastry. Getting rid of the white of the egg also stops the mixture from being 'gloopy'. However it does require being thinned very slightly with a few drop of water to get the right consistency. Unfortunately it doesn't keep very well so if you are only making a small quantity of something a little milk will do the job almost as well.

INDEX

Notes

Notes

Notes

Notes

Notes

Printed in Poland
by Amazon Fulfillment
Poland Sp. z o.o., Wrocław

64846638R00251